The
Christian Renaissance

WITH INTERPRETATIONS OF
DANTE, SHAKESPEARE AND GOETHE
AND NEW DISCUSSIONS OF
OSCAR WILDE
AND THE GOSPEL OF THOMAS

BY

G. Wilson Knight

The Norton Library
W · W · NORTON & COMPANY · INC ·
NEW YORK

W. W. Norton & Company, Inc. is also the publisher of
The Norton Anthology of English Literature, edited by M. H.
Abrams, Robert M. Adams, David Daiches, E. Talbot Donaldson,
George H. Ford, Samuel Holt Monk, and Hallett Smith; *The American
Tradition in Literature,* edited by Sculley Bradley, Richmond
Croom Beatty, and E. Hudson Long; *World Masterpieces,* edited
by Maynard Mack, Kenneth Douglas, Howard E. Hugo, Bernard
M. W. Knox, John C. McGalliard, P. M. Pasinetti, and René Wellek;
and the paperbound Norton Critical Editions—authoritative texts,
together with the leading critical interpretations, of *Gulliver's
Travels, Adventures of Huckleberry Finn, Henry IV, Part 1,* and
other major works of literature.

FOR
OLIVER CAMPION

CONTENTS

PREFACE

IT is nearly thirty years since I composed the material here presented in revised and abbreviated form. The old text had a number of errors, which have been corrected. It also had many serious weaknesses of style, particularly in the philosophical arguments: too often an unnecessary accumulation of repetitive but inexact sentences was made to do duty for the more precise and inclusive single statements with which they have now been replaced; though the more imaginative and rhetorical passages, being in a manner I could not recapture, remain undoctored. The footnotes are new, and where it seems important to remember it, they are dated. For the rest, revision has been almost entirely confined to rejection, clarification and compression; where any minor insertions have been made they will be found to do no more than clarify what was already implicit. The text must still be read as a document of its time tidied as it should have been tidied at first. A copy of the corrected original is lodged in the City Library at Birmingham.

This new version has nevertheless its weaknesses. My reliance on translations of the Bible, Dante and Goethe may still be involving me in inaccuracies, though I have done some careful checking at the main danger-points, either with other translations or with the original Greek and Italian. For the Bible I use, in my main text, with the kind permission of Messrs. Hodder and Stoughton, James Moffatt's translation, which has a force and vitality that have from the start enlivened my understanding. I have used Cary's Dante and, with gratitude for the permission of Messrs. J. M. Dent & Sons, A. G. Latham's translation of Goethe's *Faust* (see p. 105 below). Thanks are due to Messrs. Collins for allowing me to quote from W. R. Schoedel's translation of the Gospel of Thomas. I have borrowed a few phrases from

W. H. Hamilton's Penguin translation of Plato's *Symposium*. References to Shakespeare and other English poets apply, with a few exceptions, to the Oxford editions.

On its first appearance this book had a generous reception in theological circles. The small edition sold about equally in Great Britain, Canada and the United States of America; and though it has been for many years out of print, it seems to have been exerting a steady, if quiet, influence. I still find the general argument satisfactory, but later researches having brought to my knowledge some limitations in its approach, I have filled the space saved in revision by adding an 'epilogue' which goes some way towards remedying the deficiency.

I would record my gratitude to Mr Melville Chaning-Pearce for introducing me to the work of Jacob Boëhme; and to Mr John Silkin and Dr Saros Cowasjee for help with the checking of references.

G. W. K.

Leeds, January 1961

The publication of my work on British Drama *The Golden Labyrinth*, referred to in my Epilogue, has been temporarily delayed. It should appear soon.

April 1961

Thou hast conquered, O pale Galilean; the
   world has grown grey from thy breath;
We have drunken of things Lethean, and
   fed on the fulness of death.

   A. C. Swinburne, *Hymn to Proserpine*

'Tis life, whereof our nerves are scant,
Oh life, not death, for which we pant;
More life, and fuller, that I want.

   Alfred Lord Tennyson, *The Two Voices*

I am come that they might have life, and that they
   might have it more abundantly.

   The Gospel According to St John, X. x.

Introduction

I

THE PROPHETIC IMAGINATION

THIS book extends my work beyond Shakespearian interpretation to other great poets and the New Testament. A fresh reading of the New Testament and Christianity emerges, as well as a new view of poetry. It has been evident that my interpretations of Shakespeare must eventually be related to Christianity. Shakespeare and the other poets inspected in the following pages cannot henceforward be kept without the pale of our religious consciousness: they are the prophets of the modern world. A deep understanding reveals the New Testament to be the most consummate vision of any, but unless we first focus the imaginative richness of poetry we shall scarcely be able to receive the yet greater richness of revelation. In that they aim to reveal the relation of poetry to Christianity and to expose certain riches in both that are generally neglected, the following chapters themselves lay claim to prophetic validity; and I know that to prophesy a Christian and poetic renaissance in the near future is an ambitious action. But such is the direction I take and such the position to which I arrive.

It is unfortunately inevitable that any new approach to things which are old should result in misunderstanding and misrepresentation; and since this book follows logically from my works on Shakespeare, I devote its preliminary chapters to the theory implicit in my imaginative interpretations. A method that has produced misunderstanding when applied to Shakespeare is scarcely likely to meet a more universal sympathy when applied to the New Testament. But I do not refer only to adverse criticism. It sometimes happens that a generous attempt to meet my point of view only the more clearly reveals a wide divergency in standpoint; for I am not offering yet another variation of critical 'belles-lettres' as is usually supposed: I work rather at a new science of poetic interpretation.

We are today lost in a pseudo-intellectualism which, by claiming a final authority and logical clarity that it in no sense possesses, has made chaos in the world of thought. The criticisms levelled at my Shakespearian interpretations may be regarded as typical of a wider context, and my references here to my own work are introduced to illuminate this general situation. A usual complaint asserts that I do not consider Shakespeare in relation to his time or to his personal intentions. Why should I? It is poetry, not history or biography, that I wish to interpret, and with the greater writers we instinctively make what minor historical allowances may be necessary. Moreover, the critics who say this invariably try to judge my book on its merits; they make no allowances for the strange time in which we live, nor for my own more personal experiences; and they are right not to do so. Similarly, I regard any great work that has survived the centuries as independent of its generation: it is precisely this independence that is the condition of literary greatness, since we habitually and naturally consider as less significant those works which the race is content to forget. But it is not really the Elizabethan Shakespeare at all to which my critics would recall me; it is they who lack the power to see imaginative work objectively. Victorian criticism tended to make Shakespeare a nineteenth-century novelist and that was followed by the modern attempt to see him as a twentieth-century dramatist. He is like neither; he is much nearer to the Elizabethans. I find 'symbolic' qualities in Shakespeare and am told that that is unreasonable. But what of the medieval Miracle and Morality plays from which Elizabethan drama developed? What of *Everyman*, with its personification of Death and other abstractions, and the *Interlude of the Four Elements*, a metaphysical argument in dramatic form? Or of

Lyly with his clustering divinities, allegories and symbols? What of Death and Revenge as personified in plays attributed to Kyd, and the highly symbolical and theological structure of Marlow's *Faustus*? Or Spenser and his extravagant use of symbolism, allegory and metaphysical speculation? This is the soil of Shakespearian drama. That Shakespeare more perfectly than other writers projected these essences into living and convincing figures is an additional merit: that is all. I use these arguments to show that, if the point is raised, it is I, not my critics, who see the Elizabethan Shakespeare objectively. The Elizabethan was a poetical age, and it is the poetry, which includes the symbolical effects I emphasize, that has endued Shakespeare's work with so extraordinary a power. This is one instance, or symptom, of a dangerous disease in the modern mind: we mask under a veneer of realism, intellectualism and objectivity an unfettered subjectivity leading to intellectual chaos; whereas loyalty to the imagination will lead to a convincing intellectual coherence. Here the process of false reasoning is clear. The Elizabethan period was poetical and symbolical whereas we live in a peculiarly unimaginative age. We have not seen the symbolisms in Shakespeare, and when they are pointed out we say, paying no regard to the evidence, that they are incompatible with the period of their creation. What we mean is that they are incompatible with the period of our criticism. Much the same has happened with our attitude to the Christian religion.

Intellect is a good servant, but when allowed to assume autonomous rights a most inefficient master. Immediately it lets the passions run riot, lending them its own authority. By putting primary faith in the imagination, however, we endue our intellectual activities with a power they cannot otherwise possess. Imagination is not simply emotional, nor intellectual; it results from a blending of emotion with intellect, the two creating a faculty which mysteriously controls both. Though difficult to explain in theory it is not necessarily hard to practise, at all events when contemplating poetry; and yet we must sincerely desire – trying alone is no use – to receive the message for which we are looking; there is an element of love in all imaginative apprehension. The critical faculty with a host of false associations is only too ready to prevent our focusing a fact in the imaginative world, and in an excessively intellectual age like the present it often succeeds. I therefore emphasize our need of imaginative understanding: first of the prophets and poets, and next of life itself.

Not only must we try to see symbolic literature with an imaginative apprehension if we are to find its more objective significance, but poetry and religious symbolism in general are themslves more objective approaches to reality than other less richly inlaid methods of expression, since they report not facts abstracted from their vital context but facts fused with a passionate significance. Being so closely in touch with reality, poetry is independent of the swiftly changing superficialities which currently pass for exact truth: it is significant, and 'significance' points to the future. Therefore, though great literature may be unpopular during the age of its birth, and might often be called subjective and fanciful within those limits, it is highly objective in terms of the unlimited future; and it is especially this futurity about high poetry that I wish to emphasize. All great work, in literature or life, is prophetic, and exists not in the past from which it arises but in the future to which it points and which it helps to create.

Today many minds refuse to grant the imagination the sovereignty to which its claim is hereditary. And yet not only in matters of religion and poetry, but even in the more intellectual pursuits, no primary excellence can be attained without transcending the ratiocinative process. I quote an example from chess which will be fertile to our inspection.

Most moderate chess-players, like myself, try to analyse at every turn the diverging ramifications of the next few moves. 'If I do this, he will do that, or perhaps that, and then I . . . Or if I do that, then he . . .'; and so on. The complications become swiftly infinite and the baffled mind makes a move in despair. Now a player of a much higher order, Mr H. P. Parsbo of Cheltenham, tells me that when making a decision he sees a whole movement simultaneously outrolled and leading to an ideal mate. He does not think in terms of a process but rather visualizes what he names a 'pattern' spread out immediately in space and time, or rather in space-time, and rejects moves that do not fit this pattern. This is clearly an aesthetic and creative, rather than an intellectual and analytic, method. He admits that there are no words to explain how such a mind-activity is possible, though it seems a simple faculty to the possessor. The good player tries not so much to play the game right as to prevent its playing itself wrong. Implicit in the laws of chess is always at any moment an ideal continuance which must be allowed to unfurl itself. There is however an important reservation to be made. Though he may select his move by an imaginative faculty, Mr Parsbo tells me, as one must expect, that he could at any time give reasons for his decision, playing out alternative variations step by step and demonstrating to a weaker player the faults in those moves he has rejected. This is certainly the true chess faculty; it is what M. Alekhine must mean when he says that he sees the pieces as 'lines of force'. When we consider the amazing feats a chess master can accomplish playing numerous simultaneous games blindfold, it is clear that no intellectual analysis of a normal kind could be adequate.

Though imaginative chess of this order may be beyond our intellectual comprehension, it nevertheless exemplifies a general law governing the relative powers of the analytic intellect and synthetic imagination in any field. That the finest mathematical faculty is intuitive rather than intellectual was witnessed by Henri Poincaré's well-known description in *Science and Method* of the way in which a long-sought solution seems to be worked out in the unconscious mind, the whole combination rising to consciousness when the pattern is perfected; the process corresponding to the chess-player's rejection of unsuitable moves.

The faculty which we are discussing is immediate and either visual or best expressed in visual terms; hence Mr Parsbo's word 'pattern'. It involves both the conscious and the unconscious mind, as is shown by M. Poincaré's description. For it space and time may cease to exist as such, otherwise it would be impossible to see chess-variations spreading across the board in space and developing move by move in time as a single pattern; and this pattern, since it contains elements both spatial and temporal, must be supposed to exist in some space-time continuum difficult to define. Such a faculty acts successfully and with ease where the labouring intellect is at a loss, yet it can at any moment demonstrate its rightness in intellectual terms, even though it may be impossible for the adept to explain the secret of his method to those not naturally initiated and attuned. Though to him it may be simple, there are no words by which he can explain it in terms of the theorizing intellect.

In my interpretative work I find myself in a similar position. One of my critics generously compares my book *The Imperial Theme* to the 'infinitely painstaking work in Eastern mosaics' and suggests that 'it would be harsh not to feel a kind of numbed reverence on account of the amount of human energy expended'. That reverence is misplaced. Except when actually at work on an essay I have kept no notes beyond what can be written at the back of my Shakespeare: my interpretations are the result of a simple and direct view of the plays. It is true that, until written out, the patterns described have not been clearly visualized, but it is also true that my work has developed along lines vaguely seen, though not always understood, from the outset. Before I knew how to do it or had any evidence that it could systematically be done, I asserted that a true interpretation would attend to the 'flesh' and blood' of poetry rather than the skeleton which is the logical content.[1] Similarly it was clear, however overpowering might seem the reasons against it, that Shakespeare's final plays must be regarded as immortality visions; but not till now have I worked out the defence against such reasonings. Sometimes I have asserted, with little evidence in my mind, that a certain imaginative association would be found throughout Shakespeare, only afterwards collecting suitable passages when proof appeared to be necessary; and so, though I have for long stressed the importance of the 'tempest' symbol in Shakespeare, it was not until I collected the material quoted in *The Shakespearian Tempest* that I was aware of its extent. My interpretations have unfurled with little effort and no hard thinking. That does not mean that they are the less trustworthy. Our chess analogy is helpful. However I may think my reasoning the safer with all its 'ifs' and suppositions, the imaginative player, seeing the ideal pattern as a single reality, wins. Similarly, by disregarding inimical theories, we can all focus hitherto neglected facts in the Shakespearian world. Seeing an already existent reality, we shall know that the fullest intellectual support can be relied on when defence is necessary, though intellectual reasonings will not themselves help to break new ground; they can consolidate a position, but cannot win it. Certainly an intuition that cannot defend itself in terms of intellect is of doubtful value: I tend to lose confidence in my chess expert's space-time pattern if he cannot at any point in his play demonstrate the dangers attending the move I should myself have chosen.

[1] This statement refers to my 1928 article on Shakespearian interpretation, now reprinted in *The Sovereign Flower*, Appendix E. [1960]

Poetic interpretation is also concerned with 'patterns'. I have elsewhere urged that we see the pattern of a Shakespearian play outrolled in space as well as in time. An easy play to visualize like this is *Timon of Athens*: on the one side a glittering world, rich garments, feasting, luxury and love; on the other, nakedness and hatred, a desert cave and the muffled thunder of the breaking seas. It should not be hard to visualize these as a simple contrast, as two areas of human experience; and yet some minds find it all but impossible; they cannot see such effects till they know whether Shakespeare 'intended' them. And how can we tell them? And would they believe us if we did? Sometimes a critic is more definitely hostile, as though you were to show a man a view from a hill-top, and after gazing at it for a while he were to turn round and say fiercely: 'I don't agree.' When I point out the vivid importance of the child-symbolism in *Macbeth*, one of my critics answers that 'in our experience of the play babies and their symbolic meaning matter hardly in the slightest'. I ask the reader to compare this statement with my quotations from *Macbeth* below (p. 45) and, remembering that traditional commentary regards the second child-apparition, his 'baby-brow' bound with gold, as only representing Malcolm, a young man of about twenty, to consider which interpretation does least violence to the text. To those who can adopt the imaginative view it is simple; to others, mysterious with the mystery that clouds the obvious. It is anyway both practical and fruitful; so that, after starting from the patterns in single plays and what I have called the Shakespearian Progress in those of Shakespeare's later years, it has been possible next to see the whole work of Shakespeare as a pattern of 'tempests' and 'music'; and in this book I attempt to visualize in outline the course of European poetic literature as a whole since the New Testament in a way that covers in its suggestion territories well beyond my actual reading and suggests the course our poetry should take in the future. Imagination unrolls the future, seeing it implicit in the present.

These interpretations seem then to exhibit characteristics similar to the intuitive methods we have reviewed in chess and mathematics. We may next suggest that the works which they analyse themselves owe their existence to some such faculty. The Shakespearian play is made of many inter-tissued suggestions in thought and imagery besides its more outstanding symbolisms, its action and the human persons who tread its stage. No amount of thought alone could have spun out the detailed perfections revealed to an intellectual interpretation; 'intellectual', since interpretation is neces-sarily nearer to the intellectual mode than is poetry, in that it attempts to relate the original simplicity to our labouring intelligence. Probably the writing of *Antony and Cleopatra* was to Shakespeare quite simple and spontaneous through use of a faculty similar to that of the chess adept cutting across the numerous difficulties we foolishly suppose to have been laboriously overcome.

The Shakespearian play is to be regarded 'spatially' as well as 'temporally'; we must be prepared to see it as a whole, presenting a massed area of corresponding units intermeshed with each other to build a system directly related to the story in which these units are also necessary links. Put more simply, each imaginative suggestion has a part to play in the story and a duty to fulfil to the 'atmosphere' as well. Both story and atmosphere are abstractions from the one unity, and fully to possess the play we must contain both in a single view. We may find it hard to explain how such a space-time seeing is possible, but it clearly exists. It is reported that Mozart saw, or heard, a complete work as a single whole before setting it down in the time-sequence of composition, and it is reasonable to suppose that *King Lear* was created in some such fashion. Nor does it matter whether or not we regard the original 'seeing' as unconscious, since that is only another way of saying that it was not intellectual or perceptive in the ordinary sense, the 'unconscious mind' being a paradoxical concept, an unknown quantity, the 'x' of our whole equation.

Space-time seeing has about it a certain forwardness, a prophetic element. My own work has unrolled without purposive direction, and yet with a continual assurance as though from a centre which could not lead me astray. Shakespeare regards the 'soul' as 'prophetic', and this 'soul' may also be equated with the mysterious 'nothing', or unconscious depths, incarnated in material shapes by the artist's technique (*Hamlet*, I. v. 40; *Richard II*, II. ii. 1–40; *A Midsummer Night's Dream*, V. i. 12–17; and see *The Wheel of Fire*, enlarged; XIII. 257–8; also pp. 27 and 41 below). A passage in *Richard II* (V. v. 1–66; see *The Imperial Theme*, XI; also p. 26 below) illustrates admirably this sort of growth: Shakespeare makes his imprisoned hero, in meditative mood, create a dream-world of the imagination similar to Shakespeare's own world of drama. Richard's thought-sequence next forecasts the progress of Shakespeare's greater plays at that time unwritten. This is not really strange. The one does not follow from the other; both unfurl from the same origin; they are small and great circles out-rippling from the same centre. That the space-time or creative reality should often be directly prophetic in temporal terms is inevitable, but only in temporal terms is it miraculous.

All this is very close to the chess-expert's ability to see intuitively the potentialities in a complicated position, seeing however not the myriad complexities which are to be rejected so much as the one simplicity to be adopted; instinctively ruling out at any one point all those moves which do not fit the simple pattern outrolling towards the ideal mate. I am myself conscious not so much of thinking out ideas as of receiving thoughts that come either from within or without, in meditation or conversation. The heading of this chapter was fixed before I had planned what to say. Just before starting it I had the conversation on chess which gave me my main direction, and that is my normal way of progression: I accept what fits, and reject what does not fit, my sense of significance. So too Shakespeare may be considered not so much to have thought out his effects as to have rejected those that did not fit his ideal pattern. He may not have been aware that his *Antony and Cleopatra* is full of vivid life-suggestions, but an impression of loathly disease or starvation – and there are many in Plutarch – would have immediately stimulated his sense of incongruity.

These faculties are all, in their way, prophetic: they see in full or twilight consciousness the future necessity thrusting up from the soil of the present, and reject all that hinders this necessary growth. They should be considered not as a 'thinking out', but as a conscious rejection of effects incompatible with the creative ideal in the soul, or unconscious mind, or imaginative intuition. The conscious intellect cannot create: it can only reject. Art is largely the rejection of incompatibilities whilst having regard to an ideal recognized first in terms of what it is not and realized after by the expression of what it is. Therefore the truly creative mind will be distinguished not so much by its memory as by its sieve-like power to forget, to reject, all that does not fit its creative purpose.

All poetry flowers from this 'second sight'. The poet is a 'seer' and a prophet, because he 'sees' something in the space-time world. This 'seeing' is not ordinary space-sight. It often appears to be independent of sight as usually understood, a mental reality only: the chess master can often play blindfolded with a facility not far beneath that of his usual play. Imaginative sight is not sight in the ordinary sense, and yet it can only be expressed in visual or aural terms. Hence poetic imagery is most important. We must however regard the images not in static isolation, but rather in their succession and interrelation: in the space-time world all pictures are dynamic. We must see a poem first as a rapid series of complex pictures; next, keeping the whole in our memory, try to possess its images in one expansive view without forgetting the series. Our aim should be to hold all the pictures in our mind simultaneously whilst not forgetting their sequence. The more richly we can do this, the more perfectly we shall recreate the reality to which the poem directs us. Poetry is a spectroscope refracting the one beam into a whole hierarchy of tints; or a sea whose ripples split the sun's light into a myriad sparkles. The original vision in great literature is difficult but vastly important: it is a sight of life itself in the space-time, which is the creative, dimension. The poet is accordingly the seer and prophet of creation.

Habitually we abstract from life, making two worlds, the inward and the outward. If we are emotionalists, we try to see the outer world as our instincts desire it; if we are intellectualists, we try to see it objectively without reference to our own desires. Both methods are liable to create pitiful abstractions from the real. The yet greater life is made from a continual allegiance to the inward desire and a simultaneous engagement of the intellect with the wider world. There is accordingly a middle and difficult path for us. We must preserve loyalty to our own more emotional intuitions, however they may appear to be denied; and yet we cannot, unless at our peril, forget the facts of life. We have to act in accordance with our inward pattern of ideal beauty while never forgetting the evil present or apparent in the world around us. In so far as we can blend these two approaches our ideal pattern is extended and becomes richer, and our knowledge of the world becomes more profound.

The greatest prophets, like the greatest poets, seem to have attained a high degree of correspondence between these two, the inward and the outward. It is as though the world they see reflects the pattern in their own souls; this is the cause of their assurance and of Jesus' assertion that the great God is a God of Love. They do not seem however to deduce their teaching logically from an inspection of external circumstances but rather to reject certain patent facts which would destroy their belief. Though Jesus' imagination played with profound understanding over good and evil phenomena, his actions appear to have been dictated by an intuition rejecting all evidence that his trust was vain. While his mind was recognizing the evil his actions were creating the good; and the result was a life more creative than any in history. Nor is it hard to see how this came about, how his acts could unswervingly obey an intuition to us not at all deducible from his world and indeed definitely conflicting with it, and yet clearly taking it into account.

Remember our chess-expert, and see Jesus playing with the white pieces of life against the black forces of death. The present position is the mental and political state of Judaea and the Roman World. The pattern he instinctively visualizes is not only the space-pattern of his own place and day. He rather sees – by nature he cannot help it – a quite different position outrolled simultaneously in present space and future time. Neither space nor time are distinct and in the space-time world both are transfigured. His pattern is still and solid, not subject to flux and variations, and yet composed entirely of them, itself dynamic, prophetic and creative. He does not think out his actions nor his words, but intuitively rejects those that do not fit the unwavering creative design on which his eys are fixed. Hence the unerring precision of his life. Though not focusing the future as an indefinite time-sequence with all its manifold possibilities and contingencies, all the things that may or may not happen, attended by the fears and doubts to which such thinking must give rise, he yet visualizes futurity as co-existent with the present, implicit in it, out-flowering from it, and makes every time the move that fits into this universal solidity. Like the chess-expert he makes sacrifices which to the less skilful seem disastrous; at the last he sacrifices the queen of his life, only the next moment to queen the pawn of death. So he lets his creative play unfurl itself with an inviolable artistic symmetry towards that ideal mate and final cause to which life itself is moving. Since his words and actions are expressions of that central creative power which is moulding the future of the world, they both foresee and help to create that future.

Seeing a simplicity in which present and future, fact and creative significance, are not distinct, Jesus often expresses himself in terms which baffle us. He knows that he has authority and that his justification is certain: this he may image in terms of his second coming, and if he appears to place this in the near future, we may say that his justification started within a generation at the birth of the Christian Church. What to him was an immediate reality is later unfurled in history, but he does not himself think in historical terms, since his mind works in a dimension from which history is a partial abstraction only. We must accordingly beware of limiting his statement: the second coming will have other meanings too. Jesus is expressing a simple insight in terms of a very complicated machine: the human intellect. He 'sees' something himself and continually urges men to 'see' with him, complaining that they have eyes but do not see, ears but do not hear. He speaks through a kind of poetry, poetry being the authentic language of the space-time vision, using images of the birds, the lily, the vineyard and fig-tree, harvests and the marriage-banquet. These are correlatives to his own knowledge, blending the space-world of sense-perception with the time-world of significant growth. His parables are more than stories; they are works of art where the spatial quality of the whole is as important as the time-sequence of events. Jesus speaks through imagery and example. He is less a teacher than a poet and an exemplar, creating the one pattern equally in his mind-pictures and the picture-drama of his life.

To him, men's difficulties are self-made. When death makes demands on us we are warned to 'leave the dead to bury their own dead' (*Luke*, IX. 60). Questioned about death, he answers, ' He is not the God of dead people but of living. You are far wrong' (*Mark*, XII. 27). How exquisite that last phrase! – and how simple the answer, so simple that even now we cannot understand it. Death is a delusion; no one was ever dead; a dead man is no longer a man and therefore cannot be even a dead man. It is very simple; the Grave-digger in *Hamlet* knows it (V. i. 145), but it is beyond Hamlet himself and beyond most of us. There are no dead. Jesus knows the answers to all these queries immediately because the questions are meaningless; his answer setting itself only to sweep away the rubbish that constitutes the question and leave people free to see what is before their eyes. In the space-time vision death cannot be real, for imagination cannot recognize a dead past, and there is no rigid distinction between the living present and the future. The future is implicit in the present, the present lives in the future and all extension is not in time or in space but in the space-time continuum. So death cannot be real: a space-time reality cannot be slain by time alone, since that would make the part more powerful than the whole. This is another way of saying that Jesus sees man, not as body or soul, but in a body-soul continuum: all dualisms are at root the same figments of the abstracting intellect. If we are to explain his miracles in terms of the intellect that denies them, we shall say that facts happen in the material order, whereas miracles happen in the real world made of body and soul, wherein neither are what we usually think them. Physical science traces the causality of disease in the material order; psychology does the same with the mind; but no science understands the body-soul complex, wherein alone is there any real causal chain. Suppose a man sees the shadow of a newly invented machine he has not met before laid out flat. The machine is started and he watches the play of shadows. What chance has he of reconstructing the original or explaining the interlinked causality of its working? A few outlines, that is all, may be hazarded. Medical science regards only such a shadow, its causal sequence is in the shadow-world. Whereas the actions of science must remain tentative and its assurance provisional, Jesus speaks and works in terms of the real machine of life. Miracles are simple facts, or acts, in the world of reality.

Everywhere in such imaginative matters the problem is the same. How can the expert explain when there is nothing to explain? All he can do is to point out facts and try to sweep away the false reasoning that clouds the sight. In my own experience, the most simple things have been the hardest to demonstrate; my critics reason in a direction exactly contrary to my own process; they complain that they do not see the picture to which they have turned their backs. I see facts in the poetic world and explain their significance; they cannot even see a fact until its cause, necessity and significance in their own false sequence is proved. I point out that 'tempests' often occur in Shakespeare's dramas in tragic contexts, and that I therefore regard them as symbols of tragedy. I am told in answer that tempests will be found in many writers in similar contexts, and that my contention is unsound. Observe the nature of this reasoning: 'Tempests are common, therefore they are uninteresting. What is uninteresting cannot be important. Symbols, however, are generally considered important. Therefore tempests are not symbols.' Yet tempests occur in nearly every Shakespearian play in tragic contexts: nothing can alter that. The imaginative apprehension sees a concrete reality and no theorizing can make it waver. Hence the confidence of those who wield it. But it may be almost impossible to convince the sceptical intellect, since there is no possible way of proving that a fact is a fact: we are down to rock bottom and no arguments can dig deeper. Any one train of false reasoning can, it is true, be beaten down easily, but another will rise in its stead. I am reminded of Dives in Hell who asks that he may revisit his brothers to warn them, and is told that if his brothers have not heard the prophets they will not believe, even though one rose from the dead (*Luke*, XVI. 19–31). It is profoundly true.

Or again, in interpreting a play I collect 'crown' references, pointing out that they suggest 'kingship'. A critic may object to a certain reference, arguing that it has no special symbolic meaning. He utterly mistakes my method. I can only explain it in terms of his way of thinking by saying that I follow the laws of imaginative chess and artistic creation in general in that, once I am on a certain train of imagery, I do not so much select suitable examples as reject unsuitable ones. If I find a reference to a ship I shall certainly not consider it suitable for my list of crowns, but when I find a crown reference it equally certainly does not deserve rejection. It may be necessitated by the story, apart from all symbolic suggestion: that has nothing to do with it, since I have already half-consciously sensed a blaze of crowns in the play and am to put down all quotations that support it. Imaginative work is positive whereas to search questioningly for anything is negative, implying a probability of absence. If I am wanting crowns I expect them everywhere, and am disappointed wherever I do not find them. We remember how the chess-expert does not search for the right move but rather rejects the wrong ones; for imagination has the ideal pattern already on its horizon.

My following chapters claim to derive from the prophetic imagination. Their ideas and interpretations are valuable, if at all, for two primary reasons. First, the pieces fit together into a cohering whole. For some months I have been, I suppose, rejecting unsuitable ideas, and this book is the residue. Second, it is positive, not negative; it points ahead, not back. I destroy nothing, but ask only that the visionary literature we possess be properly regarded, its own prophetic life be fulfilled in us. In our analogy from chess and our short inspection of the life of Jesus we have seen how the imagination exists in terms of the present and the future. Given a position, no chess-expert worries about the past moves; the position only exists in terms of its further evolution. To the imagination all things treasure their most glorious future within their present existence; they are 'lines of force' directed and co-ordinated towards victory. Imagination watches all life unfurling into futurity, seeing within the closed bud the yet invisible birth, the fiery and perfumed rose that is to be. Imagination is always prophetic; it is prophetic because it is creative; and it is creative because one of its parents is love.

PART I

General Theory

II

SYMBOLISM

THE word 'symbolism' indicates by derivation a 'throwing together'; it originally meant an agreement between two or more people as to the significance of an object. If we regard the symbol in isolation, this agreement between outsiders as to its significance will be reflected into a 'throwing together' of elements in the symbol itself; and it will be helpful to divide the elements into 'material fact' and 'emotional significance'. Britain's national flag is a rectangular piece of bunting, rather inartistically coloured. It contains however a wealth of associations. The history and future of Great Britain, the question of imperial right, the present state of British and world politics, all swarm within the modern mind contemplating this flag. A symbol is a passionate thing radiating dynamic ideas; and yet it is also remote and cold. Do we attach our own emotions to it? Yes, partly. But it is a symbol only by reason of the original fusion binding infinite and romantic associations to a limited object: it is a shape given to a chaos of fleeting intuitions and psychic forces, lending them focus and direction. Cold and remote with that remoteness that may often characterize the leader of men, it has power to liberate and use the fires in those minds to which it is addressed. And yet this power is only potential: it is not simply in the symbol or the contemplating mind but is manifest only in the fusion of both. So too a work of art, though in form still and cold, may be potentially alive with ever-new universes of meaning.

A symbol is more full of meaning than any ordinary statement can possibly be. The Christian Trinity is not only more true, but true in a completely different and more potent fashion than any logically formulated philosophy of religion.

A symbol may in all simplicity speak volumes. The Christian Cross does this. We may regard a logical statement as flat and two-dimensional, and symbolic utterance, or rather creation, as solid and rounded. Words may be symbols: in so far as they are poetic, that is creative, they have been born of a fusion of passion with fact and are accordingly symbolic. All imaginative writing obeys the laws of symbolic creation; it is first a living reality, only secondly a statement. It contains an infinity of possible statements. Shelley writes well of Dante:

> His very words are instinct with spirit; each is as a spark, a burning atom of inextinguishable thought; and many yet lie covered in the ashes of their birth, and pregnant with a lightning which has yet found no conductor. All high poetry is infinite; it is as the first acorn, which contained all oaks potentially. Veil after veil may be undrawn, and the inmost naked beauty of the meaning never exposed. A great poem is a fountain for ever flowing with the waters of wisdom and delight; and after one person and one age has exhausted all its divine effluence which their peculiar relations enable them to share, another and yet another succeeds, and new relations are ever developed, the source of an unforeseen and an unconceived delight.

> (*A Defence of Poetry*)

That is one of our grandest passages of aesthetic philosophy. Symbolic language, as Shelley says, is inexhaustible. But its riches, the riches of any symbol, will never be truly apparent while we regard symbolism as a secondary kind of expression; and when I say, here or elsewhere, that A is symbolical of B, I do not mean that A stands instead of B; rather that suggestion of B is inbound in A. Discursive reasoning is the handmaid of poetry and prophecy, not their master. Nor is metaphoric speech the fanciful and insecure thing it is usually considered, but rather the truest flower of verbal art.

'Only a metaphor' – and therefore the less true? Rather,

I should say, the more true. A metaphor is a perfect example of the symbolic process. Consider the lines:

> Such an act
> That blurs the grace and blush of modesty,
> Calls virtue hypocrite, takes off the rose
> From the fair forehead of an innocent love
> And sets a blister there; makes marriage vows
> As false as dicers' oaths . . .
>
> *(Hamlet,* III. iv. 40)

We have a complex woven of passionate thinking and visual apprehension. As Hamlet regards the Queen his mind contrasts the blushes of innocence, the rose and marriage vows with blurring ugliness, a 'blister', 'dicers' oaths'. This is, we may say, the primary impression in his mind. Also the abstract words 'virtue' and 'hypocrite' are contrasted. It is however dangerous to say that the impressionistic contrast is used merely in order to express the conceptual contrast of virtue and hypocrisy, since in such passages the former is the very stuff of poetry and may often pre-exist the poet's conscious development. The rose-blister contrast may be a richer expression of Hamlet's mind than the other.

In metaphor a concrete image is fused with a spiritual meaning and the result is poetic. A simile is an extension of the same process. We may even say that all language is, when powerfully used, metaphoric; and that when so used it will hold variations of meaning beyond the common-sense content, though this is there too. Poetry might be defined as words inflated by mind, if we allow 'mind' to cover emotion and thought alike. Nor must we too arbitrarily distinguish between emotion and thought; it might be argued that our virtue-hypocrite contrast, in Shakespeare's passionate context, draws on as powerful a passion as the more pictorial impressions. Poetic utterance may result from a blending of emotion and thought in one abstract noun, or a blending of either or both with a more concrete image. The one primary process is all we need to remember: a fusion of the subjective mind with words to create a potent and living utterance. With these reservations we may certainly say that the poetic result is usually rich in sensory impressions and emotional associations, these being inwoven with thought processes and logical statement. The result is poetry, words inflated by mind, symbolic speech; and this result contains meanings which may usually be best approached by regarding first the more striking sense-impressions.

Literary art is creation; there is a marriage of elements and a new birth. It is neither expression alone nor imitation, but a mingling of the two; neither subjective nor objective but both. Shakespeare has two passages to illustrate this. Here is one:

> I have been studying how I may compare
> This prison where I live unto the world:
> And for because the world is populous
> And here is not a creature but myself,
> I cannot do it. Yet I'll hammer it out.
> My brain I'll prove the female to my soul,
> My soul the father; and these two beget
> A generation of still-breeding thoughts.
> And these same thoughts people this little world
> In humours like the people of this world,
> For no thought is contented . . .
> (*Richard II*, V. v. 1)

In *The Imperial Theme* (XI) I have shown how Richard's following thoughts do actually pursue the rhythm of Shakespeare's later creative work. We can regard Richard as a lonely poet creating a dream-world comparable with Shakespeare's, and this creation comes about by a marriage of 'brain' with 'soul'. Brain is the more material faculty, covering intellect and sense-impressions; soul is the mysterious spiritual force, incapable of definition. From this marriage of the sense-world, the memory-world, with the soul we have a poetic creation. It is a marriage of the material and the spiritual.

To this our other passage is a valuable complement. I
refer to Theseus' words in *A Midsummer Night's Dream*:

> The poet's eye, in a fine frenzy rolling,
> Doth glance from heaven to earth, from earth to heaven;
> And, as imagination bodies forth
> The forms of things unknown, the poet's pen
> Turns them to shapes, and gives to airy nothing
> A local habitation and a name.
>
> (V. i. 12)

Poetic art incarnates in 'shapes' the vague 'forms' of the
spiritual world. These 'shapes' are earthly, they are images,
sensory impressions, words of any kind; the 'forms' are inde-
finable spiritual realities. The poet is said to glance 'from
earth to heaven'; by blending the heavenly or spiritual with
the earthly he accomplishes the newly incarnated birth of
poetry. The spiritual alone is a 'nothing' – a usual Shakespearian word for the 'spiritual' (see pp. 12, 41) – it has no
place, no meaning, no value until given its body. This
thought is implicit widely both in Christianity and Shakespeare, extending beyond aesthetic theory. 'Nothing' represents the dark and mysterious world of spirit corresponding
to Goethe's 'Mothers' (p. 112 below), and as such is powerful
for good or evil. Alone it may be dangerous to man, but
mated to shapes it is the vitalizing heart and inspired breath
that make words or actions glow with divine life. From this
harmonious marriage of elements is made the music of
poetic creation and creative life.

Poetic or symbolic creation is a microcosm of the larger
creation. Human birth in Shakespeare is conditional on a
similar marriage of elements:

> Why rail'st thou on thy birth, the heaven, and earth,
> Since birth and heaven and earth all three do meet
> In thee at once . . . ?
>
> (*Romeo and Juliet*, III. iii. 118)

Birth is synchronized with a marriage of 'heaven' and 'earth'.
An immortal spirit is encased in a fleshly home (*Twelfth
Night*, V. i. 247–8; *The Merchant of Venice*, V. i. 63–5).
Conversely, death is the severance of body and spirit. Romeo
addresses Tybalt:

> for Mercutio's soul
> Is but a little way above our heads,
> Staying for thine to keep him company.
> (*Romeo and Juliet*, III. i. 132)

Bolingbroke speaks to Mowbray:

> By this time, had the King permitted us,
> One of our souls had wander'd in the air,
> Banish'd this frail sepulchre of our flesh.
> (*Richard II*, I. iii. 194)

The colourings are various. Creation in *Genesis* is similarly
imagined as a union of the 'abyss', the waters, chaos, with
the 'spirit of God' (I. ii); and later God 'moulded man from
the dust of the ground, breathing into his nostrils the breath
of life' (II. 7). When body and soul are in harmony there is
reality and life; when severed, unreality and death. In terms
of these we see life, as we know it,[1] and death; creation and
destruction. Symbolic creation is a variation of the larger
processes of life.

I have suggested that the created symbol, or symbolic
language, may be regarded as solid, whereas un-poetic
language, or poetic language regarded only from its logical
and ratiocinative aspect, is flat. By this analogy we may view
the richness in meaning which Shelley claims to be a quality
inherent in poetry. Poetry is both paradoxical and symbolic;
symbolic as I have shown already, and paradoxical since the
thought-content may be contradictated by the associations,

---

[1] The reservation, which occurs in my original text, is necessary. See pp.
39, 49–50, 196–7, 330–2 below. [1960]

a process very clear in mournful poetry where the beauty of the language interpenetrates the pessimism of the thought. A symbol may change its significance from age to age and turn a new facet of its meaning to a new generation. Though the Virgin Birth in Christianity has for long functioned as an advertisement for asceticism, we may today find a very different meaning in it. In this book I prefer to talk of the Divine or Sacred Birth, which will suggest rather the divinity of birth and creation generally. It will be seen to elevate, rather than cast any aspersion on, the processes of sex and procreation. Nor is this irreconcilable with the older view, for to hold up virginity as an ideal is to raise sex to an infinite value. There are often easy answers to these apparent contradictions.

It may be objected that if symbols are so rich in meanings they must be valueless, since to mean anything whatsoever is to mean nothing. The answer is that symbols do not mean anything whatsoever; there is always a fixed boundary to their suggestion. The Union Jack is always to be related to the British Empire and says an infinite number of powerful things about the Empire to which it refers. Similarly the Divine Birth says an infinite number of things about the divinity of a certain birth. A symbol is both finite and infinite: it is a channel rendering dynamic those ideas and passions which, like a river breaking its banks, would without some lateral impediment cease their swift course onward and spread their vitality to waste in every direction. Symbolism is accordingly creative. Therein lies its morality.

Art and morality appear at first to conflict and it is dangerous to attempt any too facile an equation. The more instinctive emotions such as love, hatred and ambition find varied expression in Shakespeare and are the main substance of his tragic work. It is precisely the breaking free of passionate instincts in the protagonist that gives the poet his chance. We shall therefore consider a peculiarly challenging unit: no theory that does not cover such an instance will prove finally satisfying. I select one from *Timon of Athens*:

> Hate all, curse all, show charity to none.
>
> (IV. iii. 536)

No one living in a Christian community will call that a moral statement; and yet it is a gem of poetry. The poet has married words to a powerful emotion, or we may say that he has 'incarnated' his emotion in words; and in this very marriage and incarnation consists the only true morality of art. Moreover, if we consider this line as a unit, we see that the poet has subdued his emotion to a limited number of words; in which surrendering of instinctive and unlimited power to a confining purpose we shall find an analogy to the moral life. Goodness is always an incarnation; it is creative. The word 'virtue' holds, or used to hold, many suggestions, many echoes, of creative power. The process is this: the invisible and infinite passion is married to a limited and concrete expression – the limit is always necessary – and from this marriage is born an art-form. Here it is a single line: it might be a single word, scene, play, or novel. The morality of art lies in its creativeness, which implies incarnation and limitation.

Wherever we have a satisfactory artistic whole, we may apply this reasoning. There is usually a sense of power compressed, as in Wordsworth's lines in *The Prelude* on the statue of Sir Isaac Newton:

> The marble index of a mind for ever
> Voyaging through strange seas of Thought, alone.
>
> (III. 62)

The limiting function of the line-unit is very evident here: it helps to charge each word, not very exciting words themselves in the second line, and as we read the charge is liberated, exploded, a pistol shot reverberating into the infinite. So always in poetry thoughts and passions are married to words and images, actions or persons, to create a new whole the more powerful for the compression and sacrifice necessary to subdue vast psychic forces to the limits of the particular medium. In all highest literary creation there is this marriage of the spiritual to the material. The original impulse has to burn through some hard, often intransigent, material, either realistic events or some close analytic thought: the fancy is not free to play as it will. Dante's philosophic and historic references and Shakespeare's faithfulness to his sources serve to illustrate this. Goethe's *Faust*, perhaps, suffers from this very lack, since in the second part there is little outside authority to fetter his intuition. Nevertheless his expression is in other respects very concrete and impersonal. Without this impersonal element, this limiting material, there is no creation.

The artist works in terms of repressed and sublimated instincts. Were human existence as perfectly harmonized as the instinctive and disciplined life of animals, there would be less need for art; nor, indeed, much scope for thought or even language, which all derive from a tension between desire and realization. Human consciousness as we know it functions in terms of insufficiency, and art seems not only to derive from this very insufficiency but to exist in order to remedy it. It appears then that in so far as the artist satisfies his desires he can dispense with art; in so far as he is forced to repress and sacrifice them, he will tend to liberate them by artistic expression, surrendering them to marriage with words, images, stories. Whether in art or life, submission and control are necessary: technique is the morality of art, just as morality is the technique of life. Nor can we argue from particular biographies of artists that art is, if not immoral, certainly unmoral. Many poets have lived immoral lives. Even so their desires may have been excessive and their art results not from the satisfaction but rather from the dissatisfaction of those desires. The patterns of art reflect the patterns engraved on the mind by its pain and frustration. What we enjoy, we enjoy, and there is an end of it; what we hunger for and cannot find, this we possess in another sense, stored with eternal things. Art is an earnest of heavenly riches. And it is highly moral: for art is the surrendering of instincts to a material medium and universal purpose, with all that that implies; and morality is the surrendering of instinct to an end sanctioned by a judgement which regards the future as well as the present, the community as well as the individual. A moral action expresses instincts in terms of the world beyond the individual; an immoral act is one whereby the individual carves for himself regardless or witless of the laws of the created world. Both art and morality are each, in their own way, a fusion, a marriage, of the subjective mind with an objective universe. Finally, the close relation of the moral and artistic modes will be evident from one further consideration. Morality seems to depend on the concept of 'will'. Now the further we pursue analysis of instinct and behaviour, the less reality can be attributed to the moral will: at the extreme, the concept vanishes; it has no reality apart from the essences it orders; it is rather an aspect of those essences when harmonized. The artistic parallel is exact: form without content is meaningless; form is one aspect of essences in harmony and under analysis is found to exist not here nor there but in and through the organic whole. The harmonies of art are thus born from and induce a harmony of being: art and morality converge.

The making of a symbol or of poetry is not only a fine way of expressing difficult things; it is a highly moral act. The only immoral art is bad art. And not only is poetic creation a moral act; it has a definitely moral result; it purges and purifies. Though passions and desires are raised, no passions or desires are raised that are not in the same act satisfied. The marriage of elements that makes a symbol or a poem awakes a corresponding harmony in the recipient.

Let us consider again our simplest instance of poetic creation, the making of some symbol by 'throwing together' in lively marriage some spiritual essence with a sense-impression. The pains and troubles of our earthly existence derive either from our seeing an external fact or facts without being able to focus any dynamic significance therein pointing us onward, or from some passionate desire unfitted to any shape, person, or line of action that may release and sanction our energy and urge to creative life. Whenever and wherever, for however short a space, we find these two worlds, the inward and the outward, the human and the natural, in harmonious relation, then is our sense of significance and purpose recaptured. But when these two fall apart, we are separated from our world and unhappy, seeing around us a barren and stony stare in the world of manifestation, a field strewn with corpses of the late romantic joy, while within us burn unquenched fires of desire, Satan torments, conflicting and inwardly tempestuous. So the symbol, in which significant emotions are blended with some concrete image, is potent to save. This is why Jesus spoke in parables. He is the great king of metaphoric speech. What is his teaching? We do wrong to abstract a superficial ethic from his words. Rather he points us to the lily, the birds of the air, the vine, the marriage-banquet. We are to let our instincts pursue the joy, the rhythms of growth, the creative luxuriance, the blessed peace of these. In symbol, he preaches the symbolic life. He would have us blend our life with the life around us, incarnating our instincts along the creative rhythms of nature; he would have us live our metaphors. The process which is at the heart of metaphor is the most important element in Christianity. The Incarnation is itself one gigantic metaphor whereby the divine Logos is married to a human form. And Jesus calls us to metaphoric action: he would have us realize a harmony whereby the human and the natural are blended; and in this marriage we recognize the divine.

And yet, in the moment when, in art or any romantic joy such as love or mystic sight, a symbolic potency is achieved, we do not normally use the term 'symbol'. From our lower consciousness it is a necessary term, denoting the two worlds that have been 'thrown together', but when that marriage is actualized we forget that there were ever two worlds to be reconciled; we know then that they were never in reality distinct. What is a symbol to intellectual enquiry is a simple sight and fact to the romantic sight. The symbol exerts a power whereby we are brought to a state beyond the categories of analysis. It is of little interest to a man who is properly in love to say that he has satisfactorily symbolized his sexual desires. Even philosophically we can explain this, since when two elements are blended to produce a third, that third will hold a significance apart from its constituent factors. A child has its own inviolable individuality, and Christ as incarnate God is at once more than man and more than God.

Such then will be our understanding of poetry and religious symbolism. It may be objected that by giving the word 'symbol' so wide a content, covering all poetic expression, I have robbed it of its specific and usual meaning. This is true. But then I claim to be showing, here and elsewhere, that there is more to be found in our poets than has hitherto been supposed, and in so doing to be extending the symbolic richness of the poetic world. It is true too that I often select dominant symbols, abstracting them from their setting and regarding them as entities; and this may seem an arbitrary act. Certain elements however in any art-form will clearly be more symbolically powerful than others and to an intellectual analysis these will necessarily seem more important; and so in my treatment here of Dante and Goethe I shall select impressions of the circle, the rose, of fire and water and mountains. The perfectly receptive reader would need no interpretation, but neither would the perfect scientist need any science. Moreover it is natural in reading to miss important suggestions by limiting a particular poetic effect to its position as a link in the narrative. We should rather be prepared at any time to see any one piece of a poetic pattern as symbolic in its own right, radiating power over and beyond its place in the story, and if we do this we find riches unguessed in all our greater works. There is nevertheless a useful distinction to be drawn between elements which are natural to the story and pregnant to imaginative inspection as well and those which are addressed more particularly to the romantic vision without appearing to make contact with the usual processes of the world. These latter I call 'direct symbolism'. When in *Macbeth* Duncan's horses are said to have eaten each other, we have an event outside natural law; it serves a poetic but not a realistic purpose. We shall find in the New Testament events which appear to be of a similar order. But there is no rigid bounding line. In imaginative writing direct symbolism flowers from the symbolic world of its growth, rooted in that world and inseparable from it. It is always most important for our understanding of the world it grows from.

My interpretations of Shakespeare bear the same relation to their original as does the science of Christian theology to the Bible. In both dominant symbols are abstracted to further our understanding. From the one I have taken the tempest-music opposition; from the other, theologians have derived the Trinity. These tune our minds to understanding in a way otherwise impossible. In this book I shall again often abstract from the created whole of an art-form certain persons, impressions, images, treating them as symbols, as units poetically conceived and created, in order to channel the fine frenzies of poetry and prophecy to our use and raise our minds to a plane where they may the more fully receive the all but ineffable dreams of great art. And they in turn will next raise us to life itself. The Biblical narrative is a

III

THE SHAKESPEARIAN ART-FORM

SHAKESPEARE saw poetic creation as growing from a union of earth and heaven or brain and soul (pp. 26–7); and his own theory may be used to assist our understanding of his dramatic structure and dramatic philosophy. The one process of poetic creation is repeated from step to step. It occurs in choice of a word, in the making of a scene, the building of a whole work. I have already referred to the temporal and the spatial elements in Shakespearian drama; we might provisionally call them the story and the imaginative design; or the plot and the philosophic significance; and so on. Exactitude is impossible but we can agree that there is much thought and feeling inwoven with the action. The poet entwines his mind with the story he uses, incarnating his thoughts and feelings in the material before him. Soul and body are finally close-knit in poetic life.

We can distinguish the Shakespearian artist from the newspaper reporter by saying that the latter presents only one of the two elements necessary to art. He tells us the facts and no more. Shakespeare is interested not only in facts but also in their significance. The one gives us a series of memorized incidents, the other a dynamic and living experience. Therefore the Shakespearian play is not realistic in the usual sense. It is not like events we remember, and our knowledge of the world is almost entirely a matter of memory; rather it is like experience itself. The plays are vivid experiences, to be lived through and judged not as life-memories but as life, not as a distillation of experience but as experience. Memory falsifies experience, abstracts from it, while the unique and immediate actuality eludes us: nothing is so mysterious as the actual and all our poets and prophets labour to draw the veil which shuts us from the life we live. Either we remember the fact without its significance; that is what gives us science. Or we reason about the significance abstracted from any living fact; that is what gives us philosophy. These two worlds, the material and the spiritual, are unreal. The immediate reality, intractable to intellect, is made of both, transcends both, and the Shakespearian play, so finely welding fact with significance, earth with heaven, reintegrates, recreates, the actual, the world of experience, the reality of life.

It is true that some writers, such as Tolstoy and Chaucer, have the magical gift of presenting fact or incident in all simplicity yet so washed with spiritual light that they may claim to recreate the whole glory of the actual, even of actual experience, without so much trafficking with intellect. Tolstoy in his novels and short stories shows great mastery in this kind. They are not written like a newspaper report, and yet they are not interwelded at every point with the author's profound thinking, or at least this does not appear. At its best, such writing is magical and factual at once. We are in a very different world when we turn to Dostoievsky or Herman Melville. In *Moby Dick* there is an interweaving of a realistic tale with a mass of philosophic speculation, the two being perfectly married in the whale-symbol; for the White Whale is by far the more terrific as a symbol of natural enmity by reason of the meticulous and laborious descriptions which habituate us to whaling in general and all its ramifications. In Dante and Thomas Hardy there is, or appears to be, a more static philosophy, not so modified at every turn by the action. Dante employs a Christian philosophy, Hardy a personal pessimistic intuition which was fairly consistent throughout his life. The Melvillian or Shakespearian writer however has scarcely any static philosophy; the thinking is so closely interwoven with each narrative in turn that you cannot readily tell whether it is being applied

THE SHAKESPEARIAN ART-FORM

to the tale or suggested by it. We have accordingly three types of literary artist: the Dantesque, where philosophy and narrative seem fairly distinct; the Chaucerian or Tolstoyan, where the one is so perfectly incarnated in the other that no distinction seems possible; and the Shakespearian, set between these two, where we watch the process of marriage and resultant incarnation continually being acted before us, the philosophy appearing to vary according to the work in hand. Now, considering that the two elements, fact and philosophy, are ultimately false abstractions from the real, it will at first seem that the Chaucerian writer is by far the most valuable, directly introducing us to reality. But this conclusion is misleading.

First, we must see that, whether we like it or not, there does exist a mass of philosophic lore; we cannot help thinking things out, and this thinking is a major part of a thoughtful man's life. Moreover it is equally natural to us to abstract and memorize facts drained of spiritual significance. This dualism is at the root of all evil, it is a gaping wound in man. Religion and poetry, all symbolic creation, are concerned with healing this wound, and that cannot be done by neglecting it. The sick, not the healthy, need a physician, and a physician who understands sickness. Therefore the most important works are those which may be felt reintegrating the two worlds that have fallen asunder. In them we are aware of a contest, an intellectual activity wrestling with the story; two vast forces, their Titan limbs enmeshed and the naked muscles so swelling under the strain that in this antagonist activity both philosophy and story are presented with greater power and meaning than they would otherwise possess. We have outgrown our childhood and are not yet entered into Paradise. To wrestle with our God, or the God within us, is necessary.

Wherever we find these two elements in a work of Shakespearian quality, we shall find nevertheless that the final creation transcends its constituent parts and exists not as spirit or materiality but in that spiritual-material continuum which alone is real. Both philosophy and story cease to exist as such in the result. This miracle is done before our eyes, in terms of what we know, our pain and frustration, our questions and pitiful abstractions. Though *Macbeth* on every level gives us a sense of conflict, the conflict is always being resolved in the poetry. The Shakespearian play is ever active, ever in process of new creation and re-creation, and dependent on us to take part in its vital movement and redeeming purpose. It is not a copy of experience, it is itself experience. We burn through it; it is purgatorial. Thus, superficially unrealistic and not very close to the factual, that is to the contours of life as we remember events a year, a week, a second past, it is yet most realistic as direct experience, its giant and inhuman figures blurred by nearness, by psychic currents, the actual impending event, by the terror or beauty of the immediate. A Tolstoyan novel is like a distant range of hills, rhythmic contours switch-backing against the sky; with *Moby Dick* or *Macbeth* we ourselves enter those dark ranges, lost in their circuits, climbing darkly up, unknowing, unseeing, dim giants around and above; but the reward awaiting our ascent is great, and the panoramic vision we expect of infinite value.

In organic life every part of the organism presents a facet of its controlling and infusing principle. We shall next observe how the spirit-matter dualism is reflected in the art-content as distinguished from the creative process. Art, being itself creation, has creation for its theme. Destruction in some form will tend to make the action, creation to close it. Two worlds will be first separated and then joined.

Our extreme example is *Macbeth*, with its violent disjointing of the spirit-world from nature. This spirit-world is grim: we have Hecate and the Weird Sisters, Banquo's ghost, the air-drawn dagger, apparitions, dreams, miraculous portents. The play is crammed with spirit-essences and dark with impending death. At the extreme this death-reality is a 'nothing': 'nothing is but what is not' (I. iii. 141). This 'nothing' may be linked to the 'nothing' to which the poet gives a 'local habitation and a name' (p. 27). It may be either pleasing or fearful. It is the 'nothing' of eternity towards which Timon moves:

> My long sickness
> Of health and living now begins to mend,
> And nothing brings me all things.
>
> (V. i. 191)

Richard II, thrown back on the pure negations of an inward mysticism, in his lonely despair feels that

> Nor I nor any man that but man is
> With nothing shall be pleased till he be eas'd
> With being nothing.
>
> (V. v. 39)

Richard is severed, like Timon, from all incarnate joy. But this 'nothing' is also the soul's 'nothing' of the Queen's foreboding earlier (*Richard II*, II. ii. 1–40); dark, abysmal, mysterious. It is eternity abstracted from time, meaningless until incarnate, the mysterious Mothers of Goethe's *Faust* (p. 112 below). When this severance takes place, both time and eternity are meaningless and unreal. In *Macbeth* the spirit-world is insubstantial and the world of nature, severed from its infusing principle, is formless and inorganic. Nature's laws are upset: horses eat each other, the owl preys on the falcon, there is hideous tempest and the earth quakes. We have our body-spirit dualism starkly apparent: colour, shapes and life-forms disorganized against naked spirit void, dark, and uncontrolled; conflict, chaos and death. In Macbeth himself we see an aspiring and ambitious spirit untuned to creative action in the world-order. All evil is to be related to such a severance, all good to the opposing harmony. Shakespeare's sense of murder as a body-spirit severance (p. 28) may be extended on the planes of ethic, aesthetic and metaphysic. This is the way with Shakespeare: his words, his theory and practice of art, his plots and metaphysic, his thought and action as both dramatist and poet, all are one. They all obey the laws of destruction and creation; of death and life; of tempest and music. Hence the harmony, minute and massive, of Shakespeare's work.

This is not an idea arbitrarily applied to *Macbeth*. It is rooted in the play's texture and similar patterns are found elsewhere. *Julius Caesar* is on a more optimistic plane but there is the same disjointing of spirit and nature, with similar results. 'Spirit' is a thickly scattered word, and its sense-equivalent is 'fire'. The spirit-world of *Macbeth* is murky, though shot with fire; *Julius Caesar* is full of fire. In Shakespeare evil and destruction involve the laying bare of spirit. We see the protagonist horribly aware of unincarnated spirit in *Hamlet*. Events tear the superficial coverings of life from Hamlet's eyes; tear also the superficial consciousness from his mind; and leave him a naked soul, confronting the naked soul of man. All this is expressed from the start by the resurrection of his father's tormented soul, nakedly unincarnate, hideously immortal. In *King Lear* deceptive appearance is agonizingly withdrawn, a deceptive consciousness dethroned and Lear himself, accompanied by the naked Tom, reaches self-knowledge through the fantastic leaping devils of lunacy, knowledge of himself and of the world. In these dramas there is a lurid, extravagant, bizarre spirit-world fearfully exposed as the world of manifestation is stripped of its garments and naked spirit revealed. Such is the wrenching apart of spirit and nature, but the action always moves towards a recreation, a rebirth, a new harmony. In *Timon of Athens* the tinsel glitter of civilization and humanism is torn away to leave mankind naked to the imprecations of the naked Timon. 'Naked Spirit' is in Shakespeare all but correlevant to evil. He is the great poet of incarnate life.

I do not intend, however, to underrate Shakespeare's good spirits; his angels and the gods in his final plays. They are creations of a different order; they are not ghostly. We can have supernatural effects where there is no evil, but no profound study of evil without supernatural effects.

We may observe an upward progress from *Macbeth* to *Antony and Cleopatra* and thence to *Pericles*. In *Macbeth* spirit and nature are roughly disjointed; in *Antony and Cleopatra* spirit infuses, inflates nature beyond natural boundaries till our natural world seems divine; in *Pericles* we have a vision of Diana, in *Cymbeline* of Jupiter. *Antony and Cleopatra* gives us a peculiarly unified experience in that it needs no religious symbolism beyond its paradisal humanism. There the two worlds are subtly blended and the one purely supernatural effect is the mysterious music (IV. iii. 12) which may itself be taken to heighten our impression of this harmony. But the poet in his later plays allows himself gods and goddesses, showing them as agents of harmony from above the world of man. In *The Tempest*, they are introduced into the Masque, though with slight autonomy. Prospero commands them at will. But what of Ariel? Prospero controls both Ariel and Caliban: here the excessively spiritual and the excessively earthly are shown under human control. The spirit-nature harmony is always our ideal, though it need not preclude the possibility of divine beings, conceived as self-sufficient personalities in contrast to ghosts which are only hideous abstractions from the human. Shakespeare's dramas show first the conflict, then the blending, of these elements.

An earlier play may serve further to illustrate the regularity with which Shakespeare's patterns obey the law of incarnation. In *A Midsummer Night's Dream*, as I have demonstrated in my extended analysis of it in *The Shakespearian Tempest*, we find fairyland and humanity in disorganized contact. There is disorder among the fairies, caused by their excessive aspiration towards mortal favour, and among mortals caused by their excessive aspiration towards the fairy consciousness of love. There is a complex and hazardous interthreading of fairy and mortal life, until they are symbolically satisfied by the union of Bottom and Titania. The two worlds finally embrace to music on the bridal night when for the lovers spirit and body are in perfect harmony, and the fairies bless their union in Theseus' palace. Theseus stands over the action as a man in whom discords are resolved. He shares with Bottom and Oberon the dominance of the drama, refusing to believe in the frenzied imaginations of lunatic, lover, or poet (V. i. 2–22). His poetry is incarnated in life. He is almost a Christ-figure possessing the Christ-harmony.

We have examined the body-spirit dualism in the artistic process and also in the resultant action. At every level we find a dynamic interaction of two elements either antagonist or blending in marriage. I have called the plays 'experience': they are experiences of the poet's mind interacting with his world and of the reader who submits himself to them. Now experience itself always involves a dualism. I use the term primarily because it holds powerful suggestion of both a subject and an object; a mind, or spirit, and a material environment. It denotes that reality existent in the interaction, whether in opposition or in harmony, of a conscious unit with some outer event, which can, if we like, be considered always material, in order to preserve our spirit-matter dualism the more neatly. It is quite legitimate to do this, since the material and the spiritual must both be present and the purely spiritual essences may be considered to exist in the subject's mind. It will be clear from our arguments hitherto that only in such experience can we expect any absolute reality. We here come up against a curious but necessary inference. If experience alone be real and neither the experiencer nor the experienced have complete reality, we see at once that reality is extra-human or super-personal; related to humanity and human action, but never limited to one person. The resultant from any organic mingling transcends the constituent parts; and so human experience is more than human, indeed it becomes superhuman. In it we touch the divine. True, this rather makes of the divine an everyday affair, but so it is. All religions and all art are purposive towards awaking our sight to the miraculous life which we live, to immediate experience. This exists in terms not of matter or of spirit, but of both; or rather in the matter-spirit continuum which transcends its elements and corresponds to the 'eternal life' of the Gospels.

The plays of Shakespeare show us heroes in dynamic relation to their environments. But the hero and his world are not rigidly separate: they are interdependent. Disorder in the state and disorder in the hero's mind balance and depend on each other. This relation, the play's essence, is transmitted to us most purely by the imaginative effects in the style and particularly by the more direct symbolisms.

In *Macbeth* the three Apparitions that appear to Macbeth (*Macbeth*, IV. i) together constitute a microcosm of the play's statement. This is the first:

Thunder. First Apparition: an armed Head.

This shows us a hideous dislocation, a mockery of the human organism; but it is also iron-plated and menacing. It reflects the absurdity of Macbeth's murderous acts. He is the head of the community, absurdly severed from the body, Scotland. And he is dangerous. Also this symbol throws forward to the end, where Macbeth's own head is to be severed from his body and brought before Malcolm. The destructive force is finally self-destructive. Against this death-force life is marshalling its champion:

Thunder. Second Apparition: a bloody Child.

From the bloody agony of death is born the other blood-agony of birth; from the soil of destruction springs the plant of creation. This apparition symbolizes the pangs of creative life, forcing to birth a saviour from out the bloody fields of death. Here is that saviour, that saving life:

> Thunder. Third Apparition: a Child crowned, with
> a Tree in his hand.

This is the baby royalty of life, the Life-Child victorious, sceptred with the Tree of Life. So Macbeth addresses it:

> What is this
> That rises like the issue of a king,
> And wears upon his baby brow the round
> And top of sovereignty?
>
> (IV. i. 86)

These apparitions all appear to thunder, suggesting tempest and conflict; and then the procession of future kings appears to music. This miniature drama tells us more of the play's meaning than any psychological analysis of the protagonist. He is not all important; but his relation with his environment, his experience, is. That relation is one of a death-life conflict, and here we have it. It is important to realize that such direct symbolisms reflect the total meaning in any art-form of Shakespearian quality. Other examples from Shakespeare could be given: the animal references in *King Lear*, the fiery spirits in *Julius Caesar*, and the continual tempests accompanying tragedy everywhere; the handkerchief in *Othello*, the music in *Antony and Cleopatra*; in the later plays the divine beings, Diana, Apollo's oracle, Jupiter. The essential experience at the heart of a play will be bodied into such symbolism, usually supernatural.

The nearer a play approaches to a vision of good essences the less conflict there will be, the less jarring and nerve-racking will be the experience and consequently the less of supernatural phenomena and direct symbolism will be required. Direct symbolism serves to cement the gaping apart of the two worlds: the sharper the dualism or conflict, the more direct symbolism is necessary. *Macbeth* is rich in such symbolism; and so is the New Testament. In *King Lear* there is less. *Antony and Cleopatra* has none but the music we have already noticed. The experience here is love, the reality is love, the protagonists are 'in love with' each other. The love-reality is reflected in the imagery of the play, but there is no powerful supernatural symbolism except the music. Though active opposition is strong there is no deep-rooted and cataclysmic conflict, and the amount of direct symbolism varies according to the violence of the conflict. What is good is natural and needs no violent and unnatural effects, and so a love drama will be more quiet than a crime drama. In the final plays there are divine symbols, as in the New Testament: evil is again vividly present, if only to be vanquished. *Antony and Cleopatra* gives us a sudden flash of sight, but we cannot live in that world long and fall back on more natural implements of thought.

It has been my aim to show that the Shakespearian tragedy may be considered as a blending of two elements; that the vision it exposes is a vision of life as itself composed of two such elements; and that the experience of the protagonist, like the experience of the poet or reader, is similarly to be regarded as of two-fold origin. I have stressed the importance of direct symbolism as binding the two worlds within the drama and pointing the meaning of the action. We now pass to apply a similar examination to the New Testament.

IV

THE NEW TESTAMENT AS
AN ART-FORM

WE may suppose, not unreasonably, that to a final judgement creative living is on a higher plane than creative art. Goodness must come before poetry, incarnation in life before incarnation in words. To compare giants with each other, Jesus, if we are to believe the New Testament, must be to us a greater than Shakespeare whose life, however good or bad it may have been, is forgotten and therefore now irrelevant. Jesus lived the perfectly incarnate life; that is, the perfect life, since all evil is to be regarded as an imperfect incarnation of instincts.

'If we are to believe the New Testament'. But why should we? Much of it appears to be 'only symbolism' and fails to reach the standard of factual narrative attained by the newspaper reporter. Our final authority for believing in Jesus is the New Testament, and that we shall not today properly understand without a recognition of its artistic qualities.

Poetry is an organic creation born of a spirit-matter marriage, and being organic it presents on every level the same ruling principle. It deals in creation on the analogy of life. Its subject is life and therefore also the antagonist to life, death. Creation is the theme and process of creative literature, life and death the recurring subjects of poetic life: such is the organic quality of poetry. Now consider the New Testament as an art-form. Its subject is the Incarnation of the mysterious Logos. It has a most powerful child symbolism in the Divine Birth, with an opposing death in the Massacre of the Innocents. Incarnation, birth, and life are its beginnings and the personal life narrated shows a perfect incarnation of spirit in the world-order. The book announces a marriage of Heaven and Earth. Such then being the essences within, or at the heart of, the organism, we expect the whole, like the Shakespearian art-form, to reflect a process of incarnation. By considering this process we shall tune our minds to resolve many difficulties.

We may regard poetry as an abstraction from life; a more perfect, because more concrete, abstraction than factual narrative on the one side and philosophy on the other, but still an abstraction. Moreover history, being a highly selective and organized product of the world-memory, though less highly organized than poetry, is more real than a series of unrelated facts. Both poetry and history are creative abstractions from reality. Neither by itself will be final, and their fusion can give us a still closer approach to reality. Just as the Shakespearian philosophy is enmeshed in a Plutarchan story to give us poetic creation in *Antony and Cleopatra*, so some impersonal poetic quality has been fused on a yet higher plane with history to give us the New Testament. Its subject is incarnation; its technique is also incarnation. The world of poetry blends with the world of history to create a whole greater than the work of any single poet, poetry being now not the completed product but only one of its factors. Life events and their fullest significance are blended: we face essential life, only one degree below the actual.

The world of myth is close to that of poetry. The New Testament has many correspondences with ancient myth. The sublimation of a hero is usual in mythology. The semi-divine birth of Arthur reminds us of the Gospels and Aeneas' mother was a goddess. Such myths represent instinctive reactions to experience presented in terms of the fact-value integration. Fact and value correspond to the past and the future respectively; integrated, they create immediate experience; and only in such integration and immediacy can we know our life and immortality. The truly creative mind in any field will tend to select past facts with a view to their future significance, rejecting the rest as irrelevant. But it is often hard to do this. As culture advances the dualism opens. We cannot receive myths as true since they are not historical facts and we find little help in history since it has no significance for the future. We do not want to fall back to our childhood, as individuals or as a race; nor could we, if we wished to. There is a necessity and a purpose in the dualism which we endure. Nevertheless the truth that life is greater and more divinely ordered than our lower consciousness allows, the truth that all human experience is super-human, is reflected in these myths. Therefore a yet richer integration must be our hope, incorporating the purest poetry with the critical and historical faculty. Such an integration we may find in the New Testament.

The story of Jesus is dramatic. To point this quality I shall notice shortly just one facet of the Shakespearian art-form, observing its similarity to the Gospel narrative. The Shakespearian tragedy often has some such rhythm as this: first, concord, feasting, music; next the tempests and discords of tragedy; then a short period of happy or resigned or pathetic calm and beauty, usually accompanied by music, generally broken or in some way interrupted, about the fourth act; and, finally, the concluding disaster. Here I draw attention to the hush that preludes the gathering strength of the last wave. There is a pause, a whispering stillness, like the sultry silence before typhoon.

Romeo, just before he hears news of Juliet's death, is meditating on a dream of a miraculous love-consummation beyond the grave; and Richard II in his prison meditates and hears music, just before he is murdered. In *Hamlet* the Gravedigger's songs and Hamlet's lyric prose over Yorick's skull build an interim of melodic calm. Desdemona has her 'willow' song. A deathly serenity breathes through the tortured silences of Lady Macbeth's sleep-walking. Brutus solaces his anguished mind with the boy Lucius' music, enjoying a momentary peace before the intrusion of Caesar's ghost. In *King Lear*, music accompanies the love-reunion of Lear and Cordelia. In all these, there is a hint, a delicate suggestion, of some unutterable purpose. The inevitable and crashing conclusion is aureoled with an angelic sweetness cast ahead by these sacred moments.

Other writers share this intuition. There is Faustus' dialogue with the Scholars in a lyric prose recalling Hamlet's, just before the end of Marlowe's *Doctor Faustus*. In Webster's *The Duchess of Malfi* the over-glooming arch of tragedy drops its approaching shadow on the scene where Delio and Antonio listen to the ominous reports of the echo. They stand beside 'ancient ruins' with a 'reverend history', ancient religious ruins (V. iii. 10–12). In *Tess of the D'Urbervilles* Thomas Hardy sets the stage for his fourth act at Stonehenge by relics of a past religion, Angel Clare telling Tess that the ruins are Druidical remains and that she lies on an altar. In these two sombre works there is a deathly peace before the peace of death, and in both ruins suggest the eternal. In both *Wuthering Heights* and *Moby Dick* the protagonist before the end unburdens his lonely soul to a companion; Heathcliff to Nelly, Ahab to Starbuck. There is no real communion: the unutterable cannot be told. In *Moby Dick*, it is a calm morning, a still sea and a summer breeze, inviting to sanity and land and home. After raising Starbuck's hopes, Ahab pursues his course towards the White Whale and death. We recognize that the suffering may not be shared, and have feeling of a purpose and a necessity in the undeviating course which the story pursues.

Consider again our impressions: a communion with some mysterious calm and submission to an unbending fate; a peace before death; the incommensurability of the hero's consciousness with that of his companions; a sense of eternity as a living presence in the drama. There may be a parting of lovers, friends or servants, as in *Romeo and Juliet, Richard II, Julius Caesar, Timon of Athens* (IV. ii) and *Antony and Cleopatra* (IV. ii), and with these we may compare the Last Supper. But the incidents to which I have referred recall rather the moments of lonely prayer spent by Jesus in communion with the eternal will the night that he was betrayed, his disciples wearied and sleeping, poor comrades to his purpose. Each of our tragic heroes in turn endures a miniature Gethsemane.

In the Gospel narrative we see Jesus himself with full consciousness of all the implications of the action which no one person in our other drama possesses. We, but not Lear, have a sense of approaching doom while he is reunited to Cordelia; Ahab never knows precisely why he must kill the White Whale; and so on. This is a primary difference: Jesus as a person corresponds to the art-form of the poet. He is in himself the incarnation the poet accomplishes in art. He creates in his imagination his own poetry and then acts it, making himself protagonist in his own drama. Shakespeare's tragic heroes may sometimes be regarded as figures of a Christ-like endurance and martyrdom. Timon is in this way a Christ-figure, so is Richard II, the analogies being pointed in the text (I. ii. 51; IV. i. 170). *King Lear* has strong Christian affinities and the comparison is supported by Lear's crown of flowers. But there is this difference. Shakespeare's heroes meet tragedy through a certain partiality in themselves, whereas Jesus is complete; he is a figure of righteousness, whereas the tragic protagonist is always, in some degree, at fault. Morality is incarnation and the poetic protagonist cannot be shown as himself possessing the full incarnation possessed by the art-form. He can be only partially moral, the morality existing not in any one person, but in the whole drama. This difference in the protagonist marks the extra dimension of incarnation which the New Testament possesses over the Shakespearian play.

Though Jesus may be said to correspond to the art-form of a Shakespearian play, yet he does also remain protagonist in a wider context which we may best regard as an art-form created by the Divine Artist. The New Testament is a divine poetry in that it blends the poetic world with the world's history, as the human poet blends his private philosophy with a narrative. We have seen that it contains essences closely correspondent to those found in mythology and art. That some of it is directly historical is reasonably clear. I shall next observe how these two elements may be considered to blend.

In the Shakespearian play we may distinguish three sorts of event: those which are necessary as story-links, but cannot be considered to hold any imaginative significance beyond this; those which are purely symbolic; and those which show a blend of the imaginative and the realistic. In the New Testament, where the divine imagination is interlocked with history, we must expect again three orders of event: some which are factually true but imaginatively non-significant; some which are symbolical but factually false; and others which are both true to fact and imaginatively cogent. Though we can easily recognize that these three orders of event or idea are contained in both the Shakespearian drama and the New Testament, individual judgements will disagree in any exact allotment. I do not intend to make any dogmatic statements as to which events in the New Testament are impossible. Here are a few which have caused trouble: the Virgin Birth, the Voice of God from Heaven naming Jesus as His Son, the Temptations by the Devil, some of the more startling miracles, the bodily Resurrection of Jesus, the Ascension into Heaven. I suggest that some of these are unlikely to have occurred as facts: a newspaper reporter would not have observed them. But a fact, as usually understood, is a pitiful abstraction from living experience and we need not deny that these events may have been in some sense actualities, immediately true to qualified recipients: their truth lies in the order not of the factual, which is always dead, but of the actual, which is living. The miracles are variously improbable as 'facts', pseudo-natural or easy to understand. I am referring always to the modern mind, which in its sharp separation of facts and values creates a distinction which can hardly be valid. However, since the New Testament has a supreme meaning for us precisely because of, and in order to close, this very rift opened between Earth and Heaven, we may and should think in terms both earthly and heavenly as freely as we choose, such receptivity being the condition of understanding.

The New Testament shows us a convergence of two lines: the line of value and the line of fact, that of poetry and that of history. A maximum of historic truth is wedded to a maximum of poetic splendour. Nor is it in any way surprising, nor does it in any way detract from the wonder of this Incarnate Logos, that some elements in our tale are purely symbolic. Our two lines do not only converge; they cross, and it is this crossing or interpenetration that is important. Parts of our drama are both historically true and symbolically significant; some of it is historically true and symbolically unimportant; some of it symbolically true but historically false. We have not a static picture of the incarnated Logos but rather a dynamic experience of incarnation, a sense of the world-order being interpenetrated by the divine. Every time a sensitive mind re-reads it, the book recreates itself afresh. It is a silk shot with dazzling colours as you turn it to the sun; it sparkles; it is dynamic, a living organism, an inexhaustible well of life. Were every single event in the New Testament factually true, it would be nearer biography than poetic creation. 'The life and letters of the Christ': the suggestion sounds ludicrous. Or it might be purely poetical and would then be no greater than *King Lear*: it would be too fanciful, or spiritual, and would bear no relevance to history. We are aware not of a temporary dislocation of the world-order by the heavenly but of an interpenetration, a divine marriage, an incarnation. This principle of incarnation applies not only to the central figure of the organism, Jesus, but to the whole book. The living evidence of its authority may be said to be directly dependent on the historic falsity of some of its facts.

There is yet another aspect from which we may the more richly understand these varied and powerfully direct symbolisms. We have emphasized Jesus' morality in contrast with that of the Shakespearian protagonist. The Shakespearian hero is immoral in that he aspires to a partial ideal. Even Macbeth may be said to sin only through an improper direction and co-ordination of instincts themselves good: all crime is pathological. So too with the aspirations of other tragic heroes: Brutus' quest of honour, Hamlet's idealism, Angelo's puritanism, Lear's grasping love, Timon's craving for an earthly paradise, Coriolanus' pride, Cleopatra's consuming love for Antony; all are, in their way, fine. But we usually feel that these heroes have failed to incarnate their desires on the most creative level. Now though Jesus seems to be fulfilling the required conditions, he cannot properly be said to have incarnated his instincts in harmony with his society. He is shown as conflicting with his surroundings, and to be too far beyond one's time may appear as immoral as to be behind it. But the creative incarnation of instincts works in terms not only of the present but of the future too: it is creative in time as well as in space. Therefore it is important that Jesus' influence should be shown as pointing forwards. Strictly speaking the Gospels alone leave us with a Jesus who is immoral; in the wider context only, a context including the Acts of the Apostles, the Epistles and the Book of Revelation, do we realize the creativeness of his life. We may remember how we saw Jesus (p. 15) visualizing a pattern of which he himself was a part, and how his actions were calculated in terms of that pattern's present and future development.

We must not limit our attention to Jesus the man, nor even to the Gospels, but see him rather in relation to the whole New Testament. It is dangerous to fix attention on the Shakespearian protagonist alone; the play's essence is to be seen in the relation existent between the hero and his environment; and this essence, transcending any one individual, is reflected in direct symbolisms, usually supernatural. Similarly Jesus is not to be regarded as a lonely God on earth: he is divine, the Christ, not in his own right as a person, but rather by right of his convictions, words and actions together with the reaction to these of other men. This is our way to understanding of the Divine Birth, the Voice from Heaven at Jesus' Baptism, the Transfiguration, the Resurrection and Ascension; of the interpretative and highly symbolical gospel of John; the coming of the Holy Spirit or, as I prefer to call it, the Sacred Life; the mystic experience of Paul and his later Herculean evangelism; the birth of the Church and the theology of the Epistles; and finally the prophetic Book of Revelation pointing its beam into the darkness. In terms of these the New Testament expresses the living relation of Jesus to the present and future world of men. This relation, rather than any one figure, is the Christ, who thenceforward exists potentially within the experience of all men. This human experience is a derivative of the great experience which made the New Testament; the experience of the Divine Principle in terms of Jesus and his influence; the experience of the great God of Life in terms of Man.

The New Testament compresses the very essence of life. There is surely no other book like it in the world, for nowhere else do art and history so combine to create beyond themselves. The nearest thing to it is the Shakespearian play, and only by seeing it on the analogy of Shakespeare can we understand how it comes to hold a truth and a power un-paralleled elsewhere. There is no question of belief or unbelief: the New Testament is a living reality.

I answer one final objection. It might be argued that, how-ever we may reason, the New Testament has not the minute poetic exactitude of the Shakespearian play, and that this lack in the work of the Divine Artist is, to say the least, curious. But the New Testament has to integrate the world of history and value in a sense hardly done by Shakespeare. Shakespeare's is primarily a poetic world in that it is a poet's world. The New Testament is composed by different authors, and for this very reason its records, though clearly the less minutely intercorrespondent with each other, are the more evidently the result of some organic principle working in human terms yet transcending any single human person. Divergencies and contradictions are a necessary part of such an organism, and we need not be put out by discrepancies within the Gospels and the surface differences in the philo-sophies of St John and St Paul: Browning adopted a similar technique as a road to truth in *The Ring and the Book*; and really all drama does the same, in that its persons express conflicting aspects of the central theme. Only so can a super-human truth be told in human terms. The New Testament is always very human as well as divine. God is not writing a book to drop from Heaven so that man may have all his difficulties resolved; it is as though Life itself were travailing to create it in terms of human experience.

I have tried to show that the New Testament is neither throughout poetry nor history but a blending of the two. Often it reads like a work of art and yet we are simultaneously aware that actuality is so stamped on it that there can be no fiction. We also find jagged pieces, either crude fact or heightened symbolism, that at first appear to spoil its pattern either as art or as history; and I have tried to show why these are necessary and even essential. If we still do not like the more symbolical qualities, we may consider that, if a Divine Author is to make a book about Jesus, He is far more likely to create in the style of the Shakespearian artist – surely as near to divine artistry as anything human we can conceive – than as a newspaper reporter. Or again, if we do not like the rough facts and discrepancies in the book, we might remember that the divine art-form will not necessarily conform to human ideas of neatness. We instinctively like our gardens, their lawns and marbled pools; their paths, flower-beds and fountains. This is nature narrowed to human dimensions; and such is the work of Shakespeare. But the primeval forest, the volcano, the prairie, desert and steppe, the mountain cataract and restless ocean, these obey different laws and are part of a pattern whose exact artistry we cannot readily define.

V

CREATIVE NEWNESS

POETRY is to be thought of as 'creation', its qualities of 'expression' and 'imitation' being only facets. The word 'poet' means 'maker' and in the Middle Ages 'maker' was a usual term for 'poet'. To regard poetry as creation is not new in theory, but the implications which follow are revolutionary. For creation is new, and it points ahead. Jesus' life was a unique creation in that it showed a perfect incarnation of spirit in the world-order and therefore necessarily pointed beyond the world-order of his day, penetrating into the future and carving its way into the thought and actions of subsequent generations. We have supposed creation to result from a marriage of two elements, with destruction as a separation of those elements, severing spirit from body. If we apply these thoughts to our poetic product, we see how much past criticism has, by its attempts to reverse the poetic process and resolve the poetry into its constituent elements, been essentially destructive. Conversely, to regard poetry as always new will lead to a creative interpretation, pointing not to the past but to the future. We have hitherto been viewing creation mainly as a process; I ask now that we contemplate it as a product.

All creation is miraculous. A new entity is formed that was not implicit in the elements whose marriage led to its birth, and it may be necessary to call in categories of the supernatural to explain the mystery. Shakespeare defines both human birth and poetic creation in terms of an earth-heaven marriage (pp. 27–8). When the spiritual element in creation is equated directly with the divine, this category includes the miraculous element in creation which is conditioned by the spirit-matter marriage contained. Sometimes we shall do well to regard the divine as an over-ruling principle, sometimes as simply a factor. Both God and man in the Old Testament have qualities which we today might call evil, but it is really only the separation of God and man that is evil: the God-man relation is out of joint. In the New Testament harmony is restored by the Incarnation, or perfect Creation. Whenever a God-man harmony is realized, an Incarnation is accomplished and the Christ — who must not be too rigidly limited to the historical Jesus — is born again. The Church has significantly recognized Incarnation as the heart of reality.

Dante's *Divina Commedia* often discusses the mystery of creation. We are told that Francis chose a bride and made her his for life. The bride was 'Poverty':

> Their concord and glad looks, wonder and love,
> And sweet regard gave birth to holy thoughts.
> (*Paradise*, XI. 70; Cary's translation;
> p. 95 below)

So they gained 'hidden riches'. The creative life is imaged in terms of human love, marriage and birth. The good life is creation. Creation has peculiar properties:

> Spirit, substantial form, with matter joined,
> Not in confusion mixed, hath in itself
> Specific virtue of that union born,
> Which is not felt except it work, nor proved
> But through effect, as vegetable life
> By the green leaf.
> (*Purgatory*, XVIII. 47)

The poetic product has just such a 'specific virtue' born of a union and its 'virtue', or power, is conditioned by our receptivity. Notice the 'vegetable life' and 'green leaf': Dante's poetry is vividly naturalistic. Elsewhere we have a distinction of 'substance' and 'informing virtue' as the elements of creation (*Paradise*, VII. 130–4). The Sun imprints heavenly virtue on earth and 'doles out time with his beam' (*Paradise*, X. 25–9). Creation is not only a union of elements, but also 'new':

> . . . love is that inclining,
> And a new nature knit by pleasure in ye.
> (*Purgatory*, XVIII. 26)

Natural laws themselves – it might be better to say 'natural laws as we usually think of them' – cannot create. There is always a descent of the divine, of divine newness. In a difficult piece (*Paradise*, VIII. 126–50) Dante explains that nature, if she were not ruled by Providence, must for ever produce men no different from their parents:

> Were it not
> That Providence celestial overruled,
> Nature, in generation, must the path
> Traced by the generator still pursue,
> Unswervingly.
>
> (VIII. 138)

The lower nature alone cannot accomplish creative newness. Or we might say that nature properly understood, being essentially creative, is miraculous. This is why the Christian religion, in describing the perfect or essential man, tells us of his divine birth. Birth and creation, if we are not to falsify them, must contain a miraculous element.

There is really no process of creation: it is miraculous and immediate. Dante has a dazzling passage on its timeless quality (*Paradise*, XXIX. 13–35). The Creator, 'beyond time's limit' and 'inhabiting his own eternity', unfolds his 'eternal love' into 'new natures like unto himself':

> . . . nor before,
> As if in dull inaction, torpid lay;
> For, not in process of before or aft,
> Upon these waters moved the Spirit of God.
>
> (XXIX. 20)

'Creation' is immediate (XXIX. 26–31) and therefore set beyond our intellectual categories, beyond time. In talking of it we may, and often must, refer to its origins and so reduce it to a causal and therefore a temporal process, but this is only a provisional necessity; and if it be objected that the New Testament itself thinks in terms of incarnation and therefore of time, I answer that all high prophecy speaks largely in terms of the intellectual fallacies which it aims to remove. On every level the breach between the spiritual and the material is bad; a moral evil, an intellectual falsity, a technical weakness. All art, all prophecy, is concerned with healing this wound. A divine being comes to visit man to reunite him with God; that would not be necessary had there been no severance. The New Testament both reminds us of this severance and points us to reintegration; it would lift us beyond time, and introduce us to immortality, which is essential life. But to think in terms of the integration while using language which does not suggest it may be dangerous, leading to a neglect of the mysterious element in creation. A baby is not to be considered the result of a purely 'physical' process since 'purely physical' to our minds holds a very limited content. So Dante describes how the 'babe' comes from the 'animal' (*Purgatory*, XXV. 64):

> Know, soon as in the embryo, to the brain
> Articulation is complete, then turns
> The primal Mover with a smile of joy
> On such great work of nature; and inbreathes
> New spirit replete with virtue, that what here
> Active it finds, to its own substance draws;
> And forms an individual soul, that lives,
> And feels, and bends reflective on itself.
> And that thou less mayst marvel at the word,
> Mark the sun's heat; how that to wine doth change,
> Mixed with the moisture filtered through the vine.
>
> (*Purgatory*, XXV. 70)

Notice again the lively comparison concluding a theoretical passage: Dante is rich in natural suggestion.

Dante emphasizes the divine element in creation. The universe is a tree whose life is 'from its top' (*Paradise*, XVIII. 26). In a pregnant passage (*Paradise*, II. 111–48) we hear that creation is sown from above. From one heaven to the next beneath the divine seed is propagated:

> Thus do these organs of the world proceed,
> As thou beholdest now, from step to step;
> Their influences from above deriving,
> And thence transmitting downwards . . .
>
> (II. 120)

The 'sacred orbs', the stars and planets, are as 'mallets' in the hand of the great 'workman', inspired by 'blessed movers'. The glory of the skies takes the 'image' and 'impress' of the 'deep spirit' which moves them. This impregnation of the stars by the divine is associated directly with the organism of man:

> And as the soul, that dwells within your dust
> Through members different, yet together formed,
> In different powers resolves itself; e'en so
> The intellectual efficacy unfolds
> Its goodness multiplied throughout the stars.
>
> (II. 133)

'Virtue' – which means creative power – is said to 'enliven' the various bodies with which it is 'knit' – 'as life', we are told, 'in you is knit'. So,

> From its original nature full of joy,
> The virtue mingled through the body shines,
> As joy through pupil of the living eye.
>
> (II. 142)

Elsewhere Dante tells us that the created product varies according to the degree of 'lustre' imparted by the higher reality, that all natural and human birth is to be thought of in this way, that artistic creation is of the same kind and that the perfect example of creation is recorded in the New Testament:

> Descending hence unto the lowest powers,
> Its energy so sinks, at last it makes
> But brief contingencies; for so I name
> Things generated, which the heavenly orbs
> Moving, with seed or without seed, produce.
> Their wax, and that which moulds it, differ much:
> And thence with lustre, more or less, it shows
> The ideal stamp imprest: so that one tree,
> According to his kind, hath better fruit,
> And worse: and, at your birth, ye, mortal men,
> Are in your talents various. Were the wax
> Moulded with nice exactness, and the heaven
> In its disposing influence supreme,
> The brightness of the seal should be complete:
> But nature renders it imperfect ever:
> Resembling thus the artist, in her work,
> Whose faltering hand is faithless to her skill.
> Therefore, if fervent love dispose, and mark
> The lustrous image of the primal virtue,
> There all perfection is vouchsafed: and such
> The clay was made, accomplished with each gift
> That life can teem with; such the burden filled
> The Virgin's bosom . . .
>
> (*Paradise*, XIII. 57)

The Incarnation is the perfect Creation: but all human and natural birth, all artistic work, are lesser sorts in the same kind.

This thought of creation being vitalized from above rather than from below is important, and in so far as we think in temporal terms it is safer to place its cause not in the past but in the future. Morality is to be in harmony with God; that is, to be in harmony with the heart and origin of creation. We are not to derive 'justice' from any 'created good', but rather act in 'consonance' with the divine (*Paradise*, XIX. 82–7). This is why, acting from the great origin, true righteousness will appear itself original and new, and is always creative. The divine emphasis in Dante's thoughts on creation is to be related to the simple truth that creation is always new, drawing its life from above, not from below; and pointing us rather to the future than to the past.

Birth is new and miraculous. Those alchemists who looked for a miraculous discovery in the Middle Ages saw that it must come about in terms of a marriage and a new birth. Goethe's *Faust* has a passage on alchemical theory and on it A. G. Latham writes a note:

> In this passage Faust describes processes still familiar to the chemist, in the fanciful jargon of the alchemists. The *Red Lion* and the *Lily* are chemical substances, possibly preparations of gold and silver respectively. To these are attributed different sexes. They are 'wedded together' in a retort, which is the first 'bridal-bower', under the influence of the uniform heat of a 'water-bath'. Then the retort is exposed to the naked flame, and thus the newly-wedded pair are driven over as vapour into the receiver, the second 'bridal-bower', where, if the experiment has been successful, a richly-coloured sublimate is formed. This sublimate, resulting from the union of the two, is regarded as their offspring, and is known as the Young Queen. It is in fact the Philosopher's Stone, which transmutes base metals into gold, and is a panacea for all diseases.
>
> (Goethe's *Faust*, Everyman Edn. (see p. 105 below); 166)

Homunculus, one of the most powerful life-symbols in Goethe's poem, comes from a medieval laboratory. The medieval mind was instinctively attuned to the harmonization of science and poetry. The Renaissance divorce was necessary, but a new integration lies ahead.

The New Testament is a wonderful reality, but as soon as we start to reason as to its origin, or the origin of certain of its events, we begin to question its authority; and it is to this sceptical consciousness that I have addressed my examination of the artistic process. But we cannot stop there. Having accepted the book as a marriage of elements, blending the historical and the imaginative, we must next see it as a new birth, as a product transcending its factors. It is in this sense that all art-forms are authentic pieces of life: the creative mystery burns from them.

To think too rigidly in terms of the artistic process may be very dangerous. It paralyses interpretation, which depends on a recognition of creative newness not only in theory but in practice. Much fallacious thinking has been levelled against my Shakespearian interpretations. People ask whether Shakespeare can be considered consciously to have 'intended' this or that effect which I emphasize; or point out that by failing to have regard at every point to Shakespeare's source – the story on which he builds – I wantonly impoverish my work. These arguments form no contact with my interpretations, since it is essential to my method to regard the art-form as transcending particular sources and intentions. In art such as Shakespeare's numerous rays of truth, historical narrative, contemporary stage technique, the author's personal experience of men and manners, his thought and passion and the emotions of the real people who once trod the earth and whose story the poet recaptures, all are as rays to which the poetic act is as a lens, concentrating them in one burning point, transforming a passive light into an active heat, burning into reality, into the future, dynamic and penetrating. The result is different in quality and power from its supposed causes; and such, on a still grander scale, is the New Testament. If we limit our receptivity by continually remembering that this effect was necessitated by out-worn stage conditions, that by the story the poet is using, and so on, and let these hamper our appreciation of effects which might otherwise be considered rich in significance, we are committing the greatest of blunders. We are continually un-making the poet's creation. Such critics will try to place themselves at the poet's elbow, to catch and isolate the thought he is putting into the poem, to unthread his personal philosophy. It cannot fortunately be done and if it could it would tend to destroy rather than interpret the work of art.

If interpretation were to extract from the art-form only the thought or emotion put into it deliberately and consciously by the poet, together with any other essences that pre-existed or in some other way were independent of the creative act, it would be valueless. Moreover, it would suggest that the poet might have done better to express his thoughts directly rather than entangle them in irrelevancies, and would thus constitute an attack upon poetry itself. We will suppose, for the sake of simplification, that *Antony and Cleopatra* is a creation resulting from two elements, one consciously personal and the other objective. Now, though my interpretations of *Antony and Cleopatra* in *The Imperial Theme* emphasized respectively the 'spatial' and the 'temporal' aspects, yet this was an interpretation not of any such integrated elements as I have just noted but rather of separate aspects of the completed creation; and this completed creation was transcendent to the poet's conscious mind and the source or sources on which he worked. Interpretation does not aim to extract what was originally integrated. It does not try to reverse the creative process but rather receives the whole creation as a unique reality pointing to the future, and then does the best it can to interpret in whatever terms seem most adequate this magical and mysterious reality. Though it will recognize, if asked, that there are undoubtedly subjective and objective elements within the work under inspection, it will never let thought of either repress the awakened imagination. Only by having regard to the true nature of poetic creation and by refusing to be fettered by false reasonings will interpretation produce valuable

results. Then, respecting the laws of creation, it will be itself
creative.

In my previous chapters I have certainly argued in terms
of causality, and have admitted two constituent elements in
creation. But I have done this in a general and vague way,
and in the interests of the created whole. Whether looking
ahead or back I start with the art-form itself. This is quite
different from the criticism that compares Plutarch's *Antonius*
with Shakespeare's *Antony and Cleopatra* in order to note
which words and incidents are added by Shakespeare, and
next boldly regards these as more significant than the rest;
and correspondingly refuses to allow the fullest possible
symbolic meaning to an event which comes directly out of
Plutarch. By becoming constituent to a new whole, every
part is dynamically changed. Creation is a multiplication of
elements rather than an addition, and you cannot solve the
mystery of poetry by a subtraction sum. Provided that we
know what we are doing we may accordingly enlist thought of
the artistic process positively in service to the created result,
but never negatively to impoverish it. The created whole
must always remain our starting point and central concern.

As this is a matter of great importance and one which in
practice is nearly always neglected, I shall next refer to some
helpful passages from other writers. Here is the first, from
Jan Smuts' *Holism and Evolution* (1926):

> A poem or a picture, for instance, is praised because it is a 'whole',
> because it is not a mere artificial construction, but an organic whole,
> in which all the parts appear in a subtle indefinable way to subserve
> and carry out the main purpose or idea. Artistic creations are, in
> fact, mainly judged and appraised by the extent to which they
> realize the character of wholes.   (V. 98)

Organic life has peculiar properties:

> If an external 'cause' is applied to an organism or a living body it
> will become internalised and transformed, and will be experienced

as a stimulus, which in its turn will be followed by a response. The response is not the mere mechanical effect of the cause, and this is due to the complete transformation which the latter has undergone. In the moment which elapses between stimulus and response a miracle is performed; a vast series of organic changes is set going of which comparatively little is known as yet. The inorganic becomes organic, the alien stuff of the environment is recreated into the stuff of the living organism . . . Anything passing through the organic whole thereby becomes completely changed. Any action issuing from it has the stamp of the whole upon it. The procedure is transformative, synthetic, recreative, holistic, and the result is 'new' in one degree or another.   (VI. 135–6)

Finally:

> That is the essence of a whole. It is always transcendent to its parts, and its character cannot be inferred from the character of its parts.   (XII. 341)

The truth could not be better stated.

Browning tells us that his poem *The Ring and the Book* is the result of his own mind's activity at work on an old tale:

>   . . . thence bit by bit I dug
> The lingot truth, that memorable day,
> Assayed and knew my piecemeal gain was gold, –
> Yes; but from something else surpassing that,
> Something of mine which, mixed up with the mass,
> Made it bear hammer and be firm to file.
> Fancy with fact is just one fact the more;
> To-wit, that fancy has informed, transpierced,
> Thridded and so thrown fast the facts else free,
> As right through ring and ring runs the djereed
> And binds the loose, one bar without a break.
> I fused my live soul and that inert stuff,
> Before attempting smithcraft . . .
>
>   (I. 458)

'Fancy with fact is just one fact the more'. Again:

> What's this then, which proves good yet seems untrue?
> This that I mixed with truth, motions of mine
> That quickened, made the inertness malleable
> O' the gold was not mine . . .
>
> (I. 700)

This helps us to understand the New Testament. The power and value are unquestioned, yet it 'seems untrue'. But it is true in an even more concrete sense. 'Is fiction which makes facts alive, fact, too?' (I. 705) the poet asks. The implied answer is, 'Yes'. He goes on to explain that man may 'project' his surplusage of soul in search of body, but must have something to revivify if he would create; that though breath cannot light a 'virgin candle', it can yet fan a dying flame. He is true to both aspects of creation, subjective and objective. The gold was not his, but he moulded it; the fancy was his but it needed material beyond itself on which to work. The final result is as much a fact as those facts that went to its making. It is more: it exists in the realm not so much of the factual as of the actual; it is a creative act.

Here is another pregnant passage from Browning's *Abt Vogler*. The musician is regarding his work as an earth-heaven marriage:

> to match man's birth,
> Nature in turn conceived, obeying an impulse as I;
> And the emulous heaven yearned down, made effort to reach the earth,
> As the earth had done her best, in my passion, to scale the sky:
> Novel splendours burst forth, grew familiar and dwelt with mine,
> Not a point nor peak but found and fixed its wandering star;
> Meteor-moons, balls of blaze: and they did not pale nor pine,
> For earth had attained to heaven, there was no more near nor far.

Browning recognizes that there is a miracle within the creative arithmetic:

> But here is the finger of God, a flash of the will that can,
> Existent behind all laws, that made them, and, lo, they are!

And I know not if, save in this, such gift be allowed to man,
  That out of three sounds he frame, not a fourth sound, but a star.

So an historic detail or piece of traditional symbolism in the New Testament, a phrase of Plutarch's in Shakespeare, a piece of scholastic logic in Dante, may be in their context rich with a significance derived from the new whole they help to build; and a final interpretation regards the symbolic rights of every part, however humble, knowing that each holds a meaning not its own but none the less powerful for that. Each part is splendid by reason of its vassalage to the whole; like liveried servants or soldiers or priests of God, whose uniforms endue them with extrinsic rights.

It may seem that by regarding art as so impersonally miraculous and refusing to regard it as a personal revelation I impoverish its appeal. Surely there is a sense in which Shakespeare's work is Shakespeare's? There is. *Macbeth* represents an experience of conflict, and the experience was Shakespeare's. But a vivid experience is not a personal philosophy nor even an 'attitude to life'. Moreover, it is conditional on the objective world, it is a fusion of the mind with that world. A man cannot create, nor have any experience, without some objective reality; for even poetic images, dream-shapes, one's own body, all must be considered objective to the experiencing centre. Herman Melville writes well on this necessity of creation:

The world is for ever babbling of originality; but there never yet was an original man, in the sense intended by the world; the first man himself – who according to the Rabbins was also the first author – not being an original; the only original author being God. Had Milton's been the lot of Caspar Hauser, Milton would have been vacant as he. For though the naked soul of man doth assuredly contain one latent element of intellectual productiveness; yet never was there a child born solely from one parent; the visible world of experience being that procreative thing which impregnates the muses; self-reciprocally efficient hermaphrodites being but a fable.

(*Pierre*, XVIII)

We must allow the poet to have the advantage on his side; his soul contains 'one latent element' of productiveness; in Shakespeare the 'soul' impregnates the 'brain' (p. 26 above). The spiritual or psychical reality is the more decisive factor. In Dante the divine element covers the final miracle of the spirit-matter union incommensurable with its parts. Creation comes from above rather than from below; its cause is in the future rather than the past, the poet's mind rather than his material. Though Browning fused his 'live soul' and the 'inert stuff' before attempting 'smith-craft', yet he himself is the 'smith': Prospero is master of both Ariel and Caliban. But the poet writes from the imaginative consciousness, the consciousness of the actual rather than the factual, discussed in my earlier chapters, and in this consciousness, to which the act of composition raises him, he is more than man as usually understood, and may after descending from creative work and returning to his normal consciousness forget things which he knew in the act of composition. Therefore the poet's sources or supposed intentions must never be allowed to interrupt or modify our interpretations.

The essence of an artistic creation is newness and its every part is to be seen not in relation to its origin, the whole from which it has been abstracted, but in relation to the whole into which it has been integrated. Only by not asking at every turn whether this or that is Plutarch or Shakespeare can we be receptive to these new relations. The 'not asking' is implicit in a creative response. A final interpretation will no longer draw any distinction between direct symbolism and realistic narrative. Hitherto we have been wandering darkly among the mysterious woods and hills of poetry, and that has its own fascination. Now I ask that we be prepared to see our territory as a landscape; we have come out of the woods and overlook them from a mountain height. No longer shall we have regard to any process, but the work of poets and the New Testament alike will be accepted in their own right. For all this applies too to the New Testament. I have shown how some vast poetic beam is there seen playing on the world of history. It has been useful in order to relate this mysterious book to our sceptical minds to regard it as two lines, poetic and factual, crossing and diverging. But we cannot stay there: we must next see it as a completed and perfected whole. We must no longer ask at every turn whether the events are historically true or pieces of direct symbolism, though these provisional distinctions have been valuable, and we can return to such analysis when we wish. The New Testament transcends those categories of poetry and history, imagination and fact, which it fuses together. Here again we must not ask, and this 'not asking' is the condition of a creative understanding.

In my next chapters, I take seriously, as creative visions truer today than when they were written, some works of admitted strength: the New Testament, the poetry of Dante, Shakespeare and Goethe. But I do not search for what was originally intended, by man or divine author, in these works: I show what they can, and therefore must, mean to us today. I shall, however, expect many criticisms that would invalidate a profound interpretation of a symbol by referring to that symbol's 'cause'. It is a current blunder to think that, when we find a cause or supposed cause for anything, we have limited its significance. The reasoning, in so far as there is any, is puerile, since things do not exist alone and the only past cause of any one event must be supposed the whole state of the universe the instant before. Moreover poetry exists not in the historical order but in the real world, and in terms of that only can it be said to have any cause. It is an event in the life-stream of the actual from which biography and history are abstractions; its causes, if it has any, are hidden. A succession of molehills rise one by one, but each is not caused by the preceding one, but by the mole which we cannot see. This hidden life is creative and its cause is in the future, not in the past: the mole has a purpose. Yet we go on refusing to face the creative visions of poetry and every time, if asked our reasons, we are driven to false arguments in terms of history, sources, intentions, false causes of one kind or another. Poet after poet swings by in his fiery chariot, while we sit down to write his biography, analyse the influences that directed his work, interpret vision in terms of neurosis, find reasons for this and that, until the poetic substance is dead in our hands, mutilated limb by limb, slain by causality. It is not so bad as that, you will say. But wait till you have read further, and see if arguments do not rise to your mind, as they would to mine did I let them, suggesting that a certain meaning cannot be applied to a symbol with whose derivation it seems incompatible.

I ask then that we face the literary product, rich in meanings, potent to heal and save, a life-giving sun. We are as buds refusing the hour of their unfolding. I ask that we let poetry work its way with us, relax ourselves to its mastering and creative strength, think in terms of symbolism rather than logic, the future rather than the past. All great work is of the present and the future, not of the past: we must recognize its virgin birth. If we search too anxiously for its origins we shall be like one who, looking in a pool, troubles the still mirror by stirring up the sediment beneath, and sees his true reflection turned first to a dancing antic shape with hideously elongated sideways grin, next quickly and mercifully befogged and dissolved in the rising mud. That is what has happened in Shakespearian studies. It is the same with the Bible. Neither Shakespeare nor the Bible are out of date: in both we can see, if we will, the true image of the modern world. Let art be as a still mirror. Or as a drama. How can a man in the wings of a theatre, with machinery around and above, looking from a ridiculous angle on to the stage, hope to receive the subtleties of an expert producer? I ask that we sit rather in that first circle of the mind to which all poetry is directed.

PART II

Poetic Interpretations

VI

THE POET'S PARADISE

ALL poetry is concerned with creation and life and being so concerned speaks necessarily of destruction and death: at the extremes we have death-visions and life-visions and the most intense poetry is found at these extremes. The poet responds to the glories of the created universe, its contours and colours. He sees, too, its significance: every image is dynamic, a present and picturesque fact pointing to its own potential splendour. The poet is always seeing through the shapes which present themselves to us to that whole more concrete and physical, more rounded, reality whose significance is ultimate. All poets are as men in love; but they know too that there is death. We have at one extreme impressions of disease, disorder and destruction; sin, cynicism, loathing; darkness and death. Set over against these are physical beauty in nature or man; concord in the community; romantic valour and love; birth and creation; light and life. Poetry urges us to know our life, to own it, to live it; and to do this it speaks through symbol and parable; through images of flower and harvest, the trees and beasts of the field and air, the infinities of sea and sky, the profounder infinities of human birth and human love. To possess this glorious life, to find union with it, man hungers inwardly, too often insatiate and starved. Dark poetry tells of loneliness, thwarted longing and death; and to this dark poetry we must give a wide and understanding sympathy, that we may see how it blends into the poetry of paradisal life.

Details are changeable, essences persist. Old English poetry is burdened with woe; and Chaucer, though happiest in a middle path where neither ecstasy nor despair find place, yet does not shirk the knowledge that tragedy overwaits all

human adventure. With the Renaissance, when so fine a
blaze is ignited revealing new vistas in the poetic and the
actual world, this very fire serves often to cast a deeper
gloom, a more dread abysmal fear, than any in our earlier
literature. The stage of seventeenth-century imaginative
prose is draped in black. Donne preaches a death-philosophy,
seeing the best men most cruelly tortured, and warning mankind not to forget the dissolution that awaits them; a
Christian faith lighting those cavernous glooms with its
candle, fluttering uncertainly in the vaulted dark. Sir Thomas
Browne's solemn cadences are enlisted against the darkness.
That darkness, by the slow revolutions of his planetary
thought, shows at last its obverse of light and we listen as
the arithmetic of language tells out the answer to our equation of death:

> There is nothing strictly immortal, but immortality; whatever
> hath no beginning, may be confident of no end – which is the
> peculiar of that necessary essence that cannot destroy itself.
>
> (*Hydriotaphia*, V)

The immortality he would assert is parasitic on thought of
death with little positive life-conviction. This Christianized
age in our literature is paradoxically a very death-like period,
and it is not strange to find its soil bringing forth Robert
Burton's *Anatomy of Melancholy*.

The Augustan period is less intense, the imagination is
more relaxed, and the finest works of Dryden, Pope and
Swift tend towards satire, a mode which reacts from the
partiality, the littleness, the faults of human life, but scarcely
plunges into those universal glooms and dark profundities
that vitalize the most powerful death-literature. When inten-
sity returns, we have Gray's *Elegy in a Country Churchyard*,
and the Romantic Revival with its fiery strength, its ambitious
hope, its obverse of despair. There is no grimmer poet than
Tennyson: his work is loaded with those deathly glooms and

nightmare fears that are nevertheless the spade and rake to
dress the gardens of Paradise. In Carlyle, in Melville, in
Hardy, today in Eliot, the death-consciousness paradoxically
creates its wondrous poetic life.

Death-literature is born from an intense life-desire. It
concentrates rather on what is not than what is, and desiring
the one it hates the other. Powerful death-visions will often
be dramatized in stories whose action presents an ambitious
and aspiring protagonist, who reaches out for the impossible
and creates his own destruction. All satanisms in literature
or life arise from an imagination not tuned to creative life,
a too ambitious aspiration towards paradise, a leap into the
future regardless of the present.

Milton's Satan is proudly equipped in mind and body.
He falls from ambition, from knowing his own merit and
striving to give it place and approbation. Through this sinful desire to too great a pre-eminence he quickly loses
grandeur and strength. The loathsome horrors of the death-
consciousness are allegorized in Satan's companions, Sin
and Death. Sin is both his child and his harlot; she is born
from his head and by her he has a child, Death. Evil is born
from an introverted and unnatural self-concentration and
Death from a further incestuous union. In Byron's *Manfred*
a change is apparent. The Romantic Revival stresses the
divine spirit in human aspiration. Manfred dares both spirits
and gods rather than submit his tameless soul to any yoke:
he challenges Arimanes on equal terms. He lives agonizedly
in memory of past sin and ideal striving; time is a rack on
which he is stretched, tugged in a conflict between past and
future. A loathly fear is in him associated with some hideous
evil, some sexual horror; and yet too a divine face, like one
he wronged, intermittently threads the poem. Death approaches, and he meets it with scorn. Guilt-stricken but
unrepentant he redeems himself by faith in his own self and
its nameless ideal. Our satanic heroes grow less dark, and

in Shelley's *Prometheus Unbound* the rebel becomes the saviour of mankind.

Through these impressions of guilt, horror and death shine fleeting glimpses of a purpose. In Melville's *Moby Dick* Ahab enlists his strength against the White Whale as cause and symbol of his suffering. And yet the evil may be thought to originate in Ahab himself. The issue is not clear; in these visions it often is not clear. In Emily Brontë's *Wuthering Heights* Heathcliff, like Ahab, is set on revenge. Both have been wronged by life and they attempt to right the balance. Plunging reckless into the dark, they obey a purpose hard to formulate. Rejecting repentance for his deeds, Heathcliff tries to explain, just before his death, that his hope is now all but in his grasp: 'I tell you I have nearly attained *my* heaven; and that of others is altogether unvalued and uncoveted by me' (XXXIV). We may suppose that he wins Catherine in death. Few heroes are darker than Heathcliff, and yet none more clearly is impelled by and moves towards love. All evil is the thwarting of a love, as all death is the thwarting of life.

In the Old Testament death and evil are closely related, sin bringing death and banishing man from Paradise. There is a relation of sin to sexual instinct in that Adam is tempted by Eve and that both become newly conscious and ashamed of nakedness; and also, as in the *Faust* stories, to man's hunger for knowledge. Knowing evil, he henceforth suffers the death-consciousness from which all our satanic literature derives. In the Old Testament man builds his Babel with reckless pride and the result is disharmony, disunion and misunderstanding; but at Pentecost the Holy Spirit restores that lost union of man with man (*Genesis*, XI. 1–9; *Acts*, II. 1–13). The symbolism of language and 'tongues' (pp. 123, 332 below) is powerful in these incidents, speech being the bond of union.

We do well to think first of books, not of authors' opinions or of protagonists, and whenever we focus a death-quality to relate it to equivalent impressions elsewhere. Vast masses of our greatest literature unroll the same statement, showing that man and his universe are out of harmony and that this dislocation takes the forms of sin, evil and death. The sin is not wholly and only man's; it exists rather in the inharmonious relation between man and God, or man and nature, and either may appear to be the evil force. The God of the Old Testament seems sometimes as much at fault as man. Evil is not really applicable to units at all: it exists only in and through a relation. In the Old Testament it is the God-man relation that is out of joint and therefore evil. So too with death: no man can himself, as a man, be dead, but faced by the loss of what he loved he experiences a sense of death. Or he may while alive for yet other reasons be seen to live a death-in-life. Death is a state of being, an inharmonious experience. Satanic literature, in various forms, recreates such experiences.

However powerfully we find these death-visions expressed we must regard the evil as relative; either as a disharmonious relation or, which amounts to the same, as a good force misdirected. Dante can help us here:

> 'Creator, nor created being, e'er,
> My son', he thus began, 'was without love,
> Or natural, or the free spirit's growth.
> Thou hast not that to learn. The natural still
> Is without error: but the other swerves,
> If on ill object bent, or through excess
> Of vigour, or defect. While e'er it seeks
> The primal blessings, or with measure due
> The inferior, no delight that flows from it
> Partakes of ill. But let it warp to evil,
> Or with more ardour than behoves, or less,
> Pursue the good; the thing created then
> Works 'gainst its Maker. Hence thou must infer,

That love is germin of each virtue in ye,
And of each act no less, that merits pain . . .'
                    (*Purgatory*, XVII. 87)

'Thou hast not that to learn'. It is true: the poet knows this,
by this alone he writes, expressing dark and bright essences
with like joy in his work. All evil is a search, a desire, an
unincarnated longing. Our dark heroes strive for a nameless
unincarnated ideal: the abstract craving of Marlowe's
Faustus, the unruly self-pride of Satan, Manfred and his
elusive aims, Ahab and his introverted hate against that
thing which the Whale symbolizes but which it yet is not,
Heathcliff with his cherished revenge and ghostly Cathy.
In so far as man fails to incarnate his life-desires his agony
writhes inwardly, casting blackness into his universe. In
Macbeth and *Julius Caesar* evil takes the form of discarnate
or naked spirit. Shelley sees himself in *Adonais* (xxxi) as tormented through having looked 'on Nature's naked loveliness'. The Earth-Spirit in Goethe's *Faust* (p. 112 below)
strikes fear. In the old myth Actaeon, seeing Diana naked,
is turned into a beast, and devoured by his own hounds, like
Sin in *Paradise Lost* whose womb is gnawed by the loathly
creatures she has borne. There is no hell comparable with
sight of a paradise unattainable. The Holy Spirit may be
equated with Satan in so far as it can be supposed to seek,
but not find, incarnation. Evil is the reflection in the material
world cast by the brooding Spirit of God that ever demands
more, and still more, incarnate life.

I assert two main streams in our literature: the lurid
Phlegethon of Death and the bright Eden-waters of Life.
Most poets work in both modes, passing through a deathly
period to visions of essential life. This life is the paradise
of the love-consciousness, and whatever the paradisal poet
presents is vitalized by the elixir of romantic sight, so that
his lovers, his birds, his trees and flowers are radiant: they
flame and burn with a thousand sparkling joys, alight

with a sacred joy. This is the paradisal naturalism of the poets.

The Middle Ages are rich in erotic perception and human idealization. The lover sees a divine ideal in his lady; the devotional love-lyrist addresses a romantic appeal to the Virgin Mary. Medieval literature with its elaborate Christian allegorization and romantic feeling often approaches the marriage of poetry and Christianity which it is my present purpose to forward. But in England we have no paradisal literature on a comprehensive scale until the Renaissance. Our original Teutonic stream had been much altered by the Romance influence; the Medieval tradition was still further altered by the new learning. As we inspect this amazing revival we can suggest that its 'cause' was a 'marriage'. The Medieval and Christian tradition meets a strong and masterful lover in a newly arrived Hellenism. But a renaissance is a 'rebirth'; and any birth is different from its causes, and never wholly implicit in them. The Renaissance is therefore, like all sudden creations, a miracle and a mystery: a sudden blaze of life. In English literature we can detect elements Hebraic, Christian, Medieval and Greek. The chivalric ideal is blended with Platonic philosophy; medieval alchemy, astrology and medicine interpenetrate the new science; the universe is variously Ptolemaic or Copernican. Classical deities are as powerfully impregnated with poetic belief as any symbols from orthodox Christianity. These appearances are to be observed, but they do not take us far in explanation. All we can say is that we find a strongly heightened life-apprehension. The poetry is best considered to flower directly from this.

The Elizabethan poet does not decorate his thoughts with classical references; his mythological persons are alive, he possesses them as truly as any Greek, and they blend with his English setting. He has a sense of physical beauty and a delight in pastoral that is today unrecapturable. He was often in paradise; an earthly paradise. Such a paradise exists whenever man, contemplating a present actuality, finds his spirit wholly blest in that communion, without further desire or unrest. A similar paradisal poetry flowered at the Romantic Revival but only Keats retrod the slopes of Arcadian delight with Elizabethan ease.

The romantic vision sees a spirit-flame blazing in the actual, as did Blake in his 'Tyger', whether this actuality be man, woman, child, bird, beast or flower. It is felt to be alight with spiritual and prophetic significance. In poetic imagery impressions of 'light' and 'fire' correspond to the concept 'spirit', and so those poets who are most spiritual present a blaze of light. The visual correlative is perhaps arbitrary: in mystical experience there is probably no 'fire' or 'light', though these terms come in to help description. The poet experiences something vividly together with its vital significance, and since to say what he has to say it is not enough to describe the thing alone, he shows it as fiery with the brilliance of a splendid creation. God appeared to Moses as a burning bush (*Exodus*, III. 2). The extremes of paradisal and death poetry are usually expressed in terms of vivid light and absymal dark, though this darkness may be lit by lurid flames.

Some poets are reluctant to over-illuminate their poetry. Keats and Shelley form an interesting comparison. Shelley's world scintillates and flashes with innumerable brilliances; it is spiritual, ethereal, volatile and swift. Keats writes for all our senses, the sight, hearing, touch, taste, smell; his descriptions have a more rounded perfection, his poetical world is more solid. His nature is mostly of earth: the ripe vine, the flowers at his feet as he listens to the nightingale, the green-robed senators in the woods, all are close, real and magical, but always warm and asking to be touched and smelt. Keats' world is rich in both sombre and happy impressions. His *Ode to a Nightingale* is typical. One stanza is full of horrors, the setting is dark, a wood by moonlight: the final effect is both happy and sad, but with an over-mastering beauty and a rich magic surpassing light.

I therefore draw this distinction within our paradisal world. The natural tendency is to express the highest poetic glory in excitable light-imagery, but there is a yet more perfect poetry, whose wonder is nearer to the normal yet no less beautiful. Whereas the first tends to a visionary ecstasy the latter embraces reality with all the senses and is more calm. It is less spiritual in that the spirit-world is so perfectly incarnate in the poetic act that little light-imagery is needed to balance our habitual blindness. It glows and blushes, but never flames. Some lines from Blake's *Auguries of Innocence* will make this distinction clearer:

> God appears, and God is light,
> To those poor souls who dwell in night;
> But does a human form display
> To those who dwell in realms of day.

Where effects are mainly paradisal, the first thing to look for is the amount of fire and light generally: the more of such imagery is being used, the more attention is being given to the spirit-world as apart from the world of creation.

In poetry the depths are paradoxically on the surface. My remarks are not drawn from any intellectual inferences as to the poet's mind or the process of his art; they derive from a plain and simple regard to surface impressions. Poetry by its very nature embodies what we call, perhaps wrongly, its content. In so far as we are receptive to these impressions we shall find our poetic understanding enriched, and to further that understanding we must watch for impressions of life and death and see how they intertwine and contrast with each other.

Death and horror may invade nature, as when to the heroine of Webster's *Duchess of Malfi* the sky seems 'made of

molten brass' and the earth 'of flaming sulphur' (IV. ii. 27).
Wide areas of our literature are covered by Milton's lines:

> Through many a dark and dreary vale
> They pass'd, and many a region dolorous,
> O'er many a frozen, many a fiery Alp,
> Rocks, caves, lakes, fens, bogs, dens, and shades of death,
> A universe of death, which God by curse
> Created evil, for evil only good,
> Where all life dies, death lives, and nature breeds,
> Perverse, all monstrous, all prodigious things,
> Abominable, unutterable, and worse
> Than fables yet have feign'd, or fear conceiv'd,
> Gorgons and Hydras and Chimaeras dire.
>
> (*Paradise Lost*, II. 618)

In Tennyson's *The Palace of Art* the poet tells how he builds
his home of lonely vision but how instead of bringing him
joy it brought horror and despair. Here is a sample:

> But in dark corners of her palace stood
>   Uncertain shapes; and unawares
> On white-eyed phantasms weeping tears of blood,
>   And horrible nightmares,
>
> And hollow shades enclosing hearts of flame,
>   And, with dim fretted foreheads all,
> On corpses three-months-old at noon she came
>   That stood against the wall.

His soul feels a supreme horror, a sense of evil, a guilt:

> She, mouldering with the dull earth's mouldering sod,
>   Inwrapt ten-fold in slothful shame,
> Lay there exiled from eternal God,
>   Lost to her place and name;
>
> And death and life she hated equally,
>   And nothing saw, for her despair,
> But dreadful time, dreadful eternity,
>   No comfort anywhere.

The hero of *Maud* suffers a living death:

> Dead, long dead,
> Long dead!
> And my heart is a handful of dust,
> And the wheels go over my head,
> And my bones are shaken with pain,
> For into a shallow grave they are thrust,
> Only a yard beneath the street,
> And the hoofs of the horses beat, beat,
> The hoofs of the horses beat,
> Beat into my scalp and my brain . . .
>
> (II. v.)

In Wordsworth's *Immortality* ode a negative consciousness is compared to 'the darkness of the grave'.

For a paradisal contrast we may turn to Spenser's bridal-song, *Epithalamion*. There is to be music, the pipe, tabor, timbrels, dances of 'damsels' and 'boys', all praising 'Hymen'. The lady appears as 'Phoebe', her eyes like 'sapphires', her body a cluster of splendours; forehead of ivory, cheeks like the blush of apples 'rudded' in the sun, lips as cherries, her breast a 'bowle of cream' with paps as 'budded lilies'; her snowy neck a 'marble tower', her whole body a 'palace fair'. What riot of purified sensuality! The woods ring to the joyousness of it. But through all this shines a diviner sugges-tion, 'the inward beauty of her living spright'. The day is 'holy'. The bright evening star appears in the east, a 'fair child of beauty, glorious lamp of love', leading the host of heaven with its 'golden crest'. The Bride is decked for nuptial pleasures, and bedded in lilies and violets with 'silken curtains', 'odoured sheets' and 'arras coverlets'. She is like Maia in Tempe, on the flowery grass. Paradisal impressions cluster to honour this marriage-song, this hymn to Life itself. On this night all satanic things are banished. Horrors of death and nightmare are barred. No 'lamenting cries nor doleful tears' are to sound, there are to be no 'deluding dreams' nor 'dreadful sights'; housefires, light-nings, evil spirits, witches, the owl and raven – the *Macbeth* world – are banished from this nuptial hour. And the poet prays for marriage blessing and marriage fertility, first to Cynthia, Juno and Hymen, and then to the higher heavens, the realm of blessed saints, pagan mythology blending naturally into Christian grace.

So Spenser creates his paradise on earth. In a more spiritualized vein Shelley's *Epipsychidion* dreams a love-consummation of excessive wonder. This love will be rich as 'the trees of Paradise' (387). He will enjoy so ideal a union with his 'bride' (393) that love will endue them with powers greater than death:

> . . . more strength has Love than he or they;
> For it can burst his charnel, and make free
> The limbs in chains, the heart in agony,
> The soul in dust and chaos.
>
> (404)

They will sail in a bark whose 'nest' is to be a 'far Eden of the purple East', a 'Paradise'. There nature's radiance itself shines with a lover's brilliance:

> Till the isle's beauty, like a naked bride
> Glowing at once with love and loveliness,
> Blushes and trembles at its own excess . . .
>
> (474)

All is here immortality, immediate, deathless, utter union and communion, a burning day-spring and inconquerable life. In *Prometheus Unbound* Asia, corresponding to Dante's Beatrice, is seen in radiant transfiguration. There is music, then a song. A 'Voice in the air' is heard singing:

> Life of Life! thy lips enkindle
> With their love the breath between them;

And thy smiles before they dwindle
    Make the cold air fire; then screen them
In those looks, where whoso gazes
Faints, entangled in their mazes.

Child of Light! thy limbs are burning
    Through the vest which seems to hide them;
As the radiant lines of morning
    Through the clouds ere they divide them;
And this atmosphere divinest
Shrouds thee whereso'er thou shinest.

(II. V. 48)

Again, observe the light-imagery.

I offer an example of what I have already suggested to be a more perfect kind of poetry, blending life and death with the positive principle dominating. Here is a stanza from Keats' *Ode to a Grecian Urn*:

Ah, happy, happy boughs! that cannot shed
    Your leaves, nor ever bid the Spring adieu;
And, happy melodist, unwearied,
    For ever piping songs for ever new;
More happy love! More happy, happy love!
    For ever warm and still to be enjoy'd,
    For ever panting, and for ever young;
All breathing human passion far above,
    That leaves a heart high-sorrowful and cloy'd,
    A burning forehead, and a parching tongue.

Observe how sober the expression of 'boughs', 'leaves' and 'spring'; the exquisite melody of the third and fourth lines; the vividly physical imagery in the last line; the yearning for a love which is peace, an ideal love suggested, not by personal emotion or vision, but by a very tangible Grecian Urn; the longing for a perfect love, the knowledge of death, the creation of a warm poetic life. And observe, too, the absence of fire or light imagery. In this kind Keats is a master.

Our basic effects function independently of period or religious belief. At moments of high optimism poetry speaks naturally of light, love and flowers; colour will embroider the page and bright images sparkle. Contrast today the impressions in T. S. Eliot's *The Waste Land* and *The Hollow Men* with those in *Ash Wednesday* and *Marina*, to observe death-imagery, darkness and blindness, chaos and disorder giving place to happier and brightly coloured impressions, to the white-robed lady, 'brown hair over the mouth blown', the rose, 'blue' of larkspur and flowers generally, to birds, fountains and sea, to music and sweet scents, in *Ash Wednesday*, and to bird-song and children in *Marina*. Whenever the mind is in union with its world, or some part of that world, we have what Wordsworth in his *Immortality* ode called the 'vision splendid', the vision of saint and lover and poet; and this will express itself in natural and human imagery. Crashaw, who addresses a violent eroticism to the Virgin, does much the same as Shelley whose Emilia Viviani in *Epipsychidion* becomes transfigured by love. We are to forget the process and see only the result, wherein both poets blend the divine and the human, and in very similar fashion. Dante is really little more eschatological than Shakespeare. One incarnates an eschatological world in natural imagery, the other presents the actual world under poetic idealization. If we say that Dante is the more spiritual, that will be mainly because his work blazes with far more fire-imagery than Shakespeare's. All our well-worn words, Paradise, Eden, Elysian Fields, all our sense of immortality, are interpretations of immediate life-experiences. There is nothing more ultimate than love and life and all poetry, all religion, works in their cause.

Wordsworth, in his preface to *The Excursion*, writes:

> Beauty – a living Presence of the earth
> Surpassing the most fair ideal Forms

Which craft of delicate Spirits hath composed
From earth's materials – waits upon my steps;
Pitches her tents before me as I move,
An hourly neighbour. Paradise, and groves
Elysian, Fortunate Fields – like those of old
Sought in the Atlantic Main – why should they be
A history only of departed things,
Or a mere fiction of what never was?

All paradises and radiant actualities are one: poetry may
bring paradise to earth or see earth as paradise. Its function
is to wed man to his own life, and the marriage is Paradise.
This is how the marriage is performed:

For the discerning intellect of Man,
When wedded to this goodly universe
In love and holy passion, shall find these
A simple produce of the common day.
– I, long before the blissful hour arrives,
Would chant, in lonely peace, the spousal verse
Of this great consummation: – and, by words
Which speak of nothing more than what we are,
Would I arouse the sensual from their sleep
Of Death, and win the vacant and the vain
To noble raptures; while my voice proclaims
How exquisitely the individual Mind
(And the progressive powers perhaps no less
Of the whole species) to the external World
Is fitted: – and how exquisitely, too –
Theme this but little heard of among men –
The external World is fitted to the Mind;
And the creation (by no lower name
Can it be called) which they with blended might
Accomplish: – this is our high argument.

The thoughts correspond to those developed in my early
chapters. Wordsworth asserts that true life exists when the
mind and its object are in love-unison. This union is, as he
says, 'creation'.

The poetic world suggests that man has developed a faculty that banishes him from Paradise. This endues him with a sense of sin and death and causes unrestful aspiration and desire. Lust and crime reach forth, desiring: all evil deeds arise from unrestful aspiration. But as English literature unfurls the dark thing is turned slowly to the light, and in the Romantic Revival we feel the essential splendour of all human aspiration. The desire is good, though action be unwise. All evil is a kind of lust. Sin is an introverted and pervertedly imaginative state. Both sin and death arise in our minds from an unruly pushing forward, jostling the present to catch an impossible future. Death arises from life-desire as lust from love-desire. But whenever desire is housed in present and immediate forms, life-forms, love-forms, a paradise springs from the desert, and streams interlace the parched sands. Whenever a poet's imagery delights us, it creates for us such a paradise, the present fact glows with meaning; and this is so whether it be dark or bright. Death-literature is great as that of which it is the obverse, because it is itself that obverse, made of life-desire. Satanisms are as creative as paradisal visions. In lyric the best poetry is perhaps Keats', where death and life are variously shaded petals on one rich flower.

VII

RENAISSANCE PROPHETS:
DANTE, GOETHE, SHAKESPEARE

I

The line numerals of my references to the *Divina Commedia* are those of the translation by H. F. Cary, which I am using throughout.

IT is usual to suppose that Dante's great poem *La Divina Commedia* is permeated so thoroughly with scholasticism and contemporary reference that it cannot be understood without considerable learning. But in so great a poem whatever has been integrated will derive vitality from the whole which is its new setting; and that whole is not readily antiquated. Dante's poem is weighty with imaginative effects. The philosophic and historical references find their places in the imaginative scheme, and when seen like this their significance is not hard to understand.

The poem is in three parts: *L'Inferno, Il Purgatorio* and *Il Paradiso*. It narrates Dante's progress through Hell, Purgatory and Paradise. What are we to say of these if we do not ourselves believe in any so rigid an eschatology? In what sense can an admirer be said to accept Dante's attitude and conviction? We can suggest first that the whole is to be regarded as Dante's personal spiritual progress from an evil to a blessed state; but this alone does scant justice to the firmly objectified system to which he introduces us and in which he himself believed. Therefore we must blend our facts, and say that the poem expresses Dante's experience of an objectively conceived evil and grace. We need not believe what Dante believed but we must believe in his belief, tuning our minds to his experience. Then we shall see that the people he finds in Hell are there because he sees them as

95

Hell-forces. Persons are not evil: evil is a relation, a reciprocity. Dante's progress through Hell shows Dante's experience of evil in terms of people he knew or books he had read and we can follow his Hell-experience without agreeing to his judgement on pagans. All poetry must be read like this: the constituting elements grow out of date in a year, an hour, a minute, but the experience symbolized is dateless. Dante's *Inferno* is such an experience endued with poetic immortality.

Of the poem's three divisions the *Inferno* is the best known and probably the easiest to follow. We have grim life-forms: monsters, reptiles, harpies, furies, minotaurs, mastiffs and so on. There is a forbidding naturalism: jagged crags, rocks, dark abysms and desert sands, mud and slime, rivers of blood, torrents and cataracts, fiery rain, fog, whirlwind, storms, earthquake. Tempests and shipwreck occur as in Shakespeare. We find both agonizing fire and freezing cold. It is a dark starless world lit by hungry tongues of red flame. Trees are horribly human, suffering when their leaves are torn. The human figures are men raving, cursing, weeping, without end or hope. They suffer in varied undignified postures, head downwards with only the legs appearing above ground, fixed in separate fiery compartments like tombs, their heads reversed so that they see backwards only, or condemned incongruously to hold their decapitated heads while speaking. It is hideous, incongruous, ludicrously horrible. They are whipped, flayed, pronged; stung by hornets and scorptions; buried in mud and slime and down-beaten if they show their faces. Or their limbs are disjointed, scattered. They are naked – this is noted continually – begrimed, mutilated. It is a dark, impossible, nightmarish Hell; a hideous living distortion, a prolonged death. It is Dante's expression of the death-experience. True, it is presented in terms of live beings, but this is inevitable since you cannot write long on nothingness. And indeed there is no nothingness and what we call death is always a living experience parasitic on life. Absolute death is inconceivable. Death ultimately means agony, horror, incongruity, chaos, despair: this is what Dante paints.

The *Purgatorio* grows in brightness as the progress ascends. In Hell we have fire: flames of wrath and torture flicker, casting black shadows among its crags and round its deepening circles. The Mount of Purgatory is like our human world with light and darkness alternating. The sun's position is noted canto by canto and its appearance discussed. Some of the persons have their eyes stitched up and grope in darkness. There are many references to sight, eyes and light. God is a 'high sun' (VII. 26); Virgil, Dante's 'luminary' (VI. 29); and love a 'flame' (VI. 38). The ascent from Hell to Paradise is one from raging fire to sunlight and thence to a diviner blaze. Often in Purgatory we have a sweet naturalism. Spirits approach nervously like sheep: the simile is beautifully developed (III. 78). Country life provides exquisite imagery. Virtue winnows good from evil like chaff (XVIII. 65) and good fruit is not gathered from an ill plant (XX. 42–5). Statius says that the 'sparkles' of the *Aeneid* were the 'seeds' of his own poetic 'flame', and calls it 'a celestial fire that feeds unnumbered lamps' (XXI. 94), typically Dantesque phrases blending fire and creation. Dante and his guide Virgil come to a wonderful tree of 'goodly fruitage' (XXII. 129), and from it come voices counselling temperance. It is a purgatorial tree whose unreachable perfumes and fruits are an agony to the sufferers, inflaming them with desire (XXIII. 56–69). There is both a heaven and a hell in these sweet suggestions. Paradisal joys are desirable and right, but evil warps the true instinct. The highest desires may be imaged in terms of food and drink: wisdom is a pleasing 'fruit' (XVII. 85); the holy river Eunoe is a 'beverage' (XXXIII. 136); Beatrice allays Dante's 'thirsting', or hunger (XV. 75); she is a kind of food (XXXI. 129). All is finely naturalistic and physically described and when the Terrestrial Paradise is neared we have a radiant nature, an ecstatic joy, a riot of sense-splendour. They pass the wall of fire and Dante is in the Terrestrial Paradise.

This paradise is beautifully drawn for us. It is a 'celestial forest' breathing 'delicious odour'. The 'feathered choristers' warble there (XXVIII. 1–14). Birds are vital constituents to Dante's paradisal imagery, beautifully and sweetly imagined in their wheeling or aspiring flight. At the wall of fire Dante's desire is like a 'young stork' that lifts its wing for flight, and then drops it afraid (XXV. 10). This earthly paradise is a glorious nature with bird-song, soft airs, sweet odours and rippling waters. Here Dante finds the lady Matilda by the 'yellow and vermilion flowers', a human radiance crowning the radiant nature. Her eyes shoot 'splendour' on him as she smiles a welcome. It is a paradise of love-sight and the trees rustle with a strange music. He is afraid. But she tells him to fear nothing, for this is a place of 'laughter unblamed and ever-new delight' (XXVIII. 56–98). Dante's Paradise is one where sense-joys are consummated, not rejected.

And then comes Beatrice, the love-ideal of his youth. The poet elaborates his tale, height by height, to this moment. The stage is set, the Terrestrial Paradise meticulously imagined, other ladies are her harbingers. A 'lustre' shines, there is music in the 'luminous air' (XXIX. 14–21):

> Before us, like a blazing fire, the air
> Under the green boughs glowed . . .
>
> (XXIX. 32)

There is a procession: first 'seven trees of gold' which are next seen to be 'tapers'; behind, a tribe in whitest raiment. The poet beholds

> The flames go onward, leaving, as they went,
> The air behind them painted as with trail
> Of liveliest pencils . . .
>
> (XXIX. 73)

Next come 'four and twenty elders', singing. These are followed by four animals 'each crowned with verdurous leaf', each with six wings plumed, the plumage full of eyes (XXIX. 81–91) and a triumphal car drawn by the Gryphon, half-bird, half-beast:

> The members, far
> As he was bird, were golden; white the rest,
> With vermeil interveined.
>
> (XXIX. 108)

The procession symbolizes the Old and New Testaments and the Gryphon, half-bird, half-beast, the union of the divine with the animal nature and therefore the mystery of the Incarnation. Nymphs circle in dance, one ruddy like 'clear flame', the next 'emerald', the third snowy white. There are seven figures wearing not lilies like the first troop but roses, till it seemed 'that they were all on fire above their brow' (XXIX. 117–46). Crowned and garlanded with burning roses. Flowers are scattered, there is music, and dance. As sunrise from breaking clouds, so from this cloud of fire and song, of many-coloured dance and flowers, appears Beatrice in white veil, with wreath of olive, mantled in green and robed in 'living flame' (XXX. 33). The beauty is too great, and Dante falls in contrition and despair.

Then he drinks in the wonder of her eyes which reflect the mystic Gryphon. Through Beatrice's eyes he contemplates the mystery of the divine interlocking the natural. The *Purgatorio* blooms with a glorified nature whose trees and flowers burn with the flame of life, the green flame of trees, the red flame of the rose, the white ray of the lily. It is a paradise both pagan and Christian. The air is perfumed, the cheek fanned by the brush of an unseen wing, the kiss of a Gospel thought (XVII. 66–8). Through sense-forms so sweet we approach the feast, the viands and rich fruit, the nectar, of Paradise. Now Virgil gives place to Beatrice;

poetry to romantic sight. No poet presents a more glamorous erotic vision than Dante; none rates higher the arrow-flame of love. Beatrice is all but equated with the Christ.

The *Paradiso* is made from a glorious naturalism, a blaze of fire and light, circling dance, and Beatrice. These are interthreaded with profound thought and historic figures of grace: Solomon, Thomas Aquinas, St Peter, Justinian. We experience an ascent through various spheres, the moon, sun, planets, stars, to the final vision ineffable. All is still miraculously sensuous: never are we left in a void. Dante always creates with life-forms, sense-forms, and even in his own vast blaze of light his images are never dissolved. These are our main imagistic impressions: food, trees, foliage and flowers; fishes and eagles; fire, eyes, arrows; love and light; the rose; circlings of all kinds, dance, music and song. There is swiftness and an especially spinning motion, a whirlflame of concentrated, top-like, static speed. The poem expands those brief ecstasies known by flashes on earth; it prolongs the lightning paradise of a rose's perfume, the swift arrows of lovers' glances; such experiences are expanded to a whirling yet peaceful blaze of sweetness enjoyed and possessed.

Nature is still important. The warmth of Christ is a force which 'gives birth to flowers and fruits of holiness' (XXII. 47) and St Peter as founder of the Church 'set the goodly plant' which, once a stately 'vine', has since become 'unsightly bramble' (XXIV. 109). Dante is a 'leaf' of a tree whose root is his ancestor (XV. 84). The paradisal progress is an ascent to the topmost branches of the universal Tree. They are in the fifth sphere, of Mars:

> On this fifth lodgement of the tree, whose life
> Is from its top, whose fruit is ever fair
> And leaf unwithering, blessed spirits abide . . .
>   (XVIII. 25)

Later they move from 'branch to branch' and approach 'the

topmost bough' (XXIV. 114). The universe is one vast, paradisal tree: the Tree of Life. The Terrestrial Paradise has been left behind in the *Purgatorio* and natural phenomena might seem to be necessarily left behind too; but without them there can scarcely be any poetry nor any vividly experienced Paradise. Henceforward a gigantic naturalism flowers from our paradisal blaze.

Natural imagery is born from a supernatural setting. Fishes are often charged with optimistic suggestion in poetry. They suggest a darting and glinting motion and like birds may accompany love-thoughts. Here is an example where the appropriateness of the figure measures the value of the symbol:

> As in a quiet and clear lake the fish,
> If aught approach them from without, do draw
> Towards it, deeming it their food; so drew
> Full more than thousand splendours towards us,
> And in each one was heard: 'Lo! one arrived
> To multiply our loves!' and as each came,
> The shadow, streaming forth effulgence new,
> Witnessed augmented joy.
>
> (V. 97)

As in the *Purgatorio* we have many bird-impressions. Eagles are important in both sections. There are the angelic 'falcons' with 'verdant plumes' who vanquish a serpent like the serpent of Eden (*Purgatory*, VIII. 103); the falcon symbolizes aspiration (*Purgatory*, XIX. 64); an Eagle denoting the Roman Empire battles with the holy chariot, the Church (*Purgatory*, XXXII. 105–16). The eagle suggests majesty and aspiring power. Dante in sleep is lifted up the Mount of Purgatory as by 'a golden-feathered eagle' (*Purgatory*, IX. 18). In Paradise eagles are vivid. Beatrice gazes on the sun 'as never eagle fixed his ken' (I. 46). The Empire is an 'eagle', 'the bird of Jove,' or 'God', with 'sacred plumes'

(VI. 1–8). The celestial lives are imaged as a flock of birds:

> And as birds, from river banks
> Arisen, now in round, now lengthened troop,
> Array them in their flight, greeting, as seems,
> Their new-found pastures; so, within the lights,
> The saintly creatures flying, sang; and made
> Now D, now I, now L, figured i' the air.
>
> (XVIII. 67)

Thus is 'blazoned' the phrase 'Diligite Justitiam'. The specks of fire then separate like 'sparkles' shaken from a flaming brand and arrange themselves into an eagle form:

> And when each one
> Had settled in his place; the head and neck
> Then saw I of an eagle; livelily
> Graved in that streaky fire . . .
>
> (XVIII. 98)

These myriad lives form into one vast organic life:

> Before my sight appeared, with open wings
> The beauteous image.
>
> (XIX. 1)

Each is a 'ruby' reflecting the sun. The beak of the bird speaks, and afterwards, like a 'falcon', it 'rears his head and claps him with his wings' (XIX. 33). Again it waves its wings, 'labouring with such deep council' (XIX. 93). The Eye of the Eagle, the part that 'sees and bears the sun in mortal eagles' (XX. 29), demands attention. The fires 'glittering in mine eye', it says, are 'chief of all the greatest' (XX. 32). This towering poetry is closely interwoven with thought and speech from the blessed lives. Soon after there is a golden ladder with 'splendours' descending, like rooks that speed to the fields at dawn, while some 'wheel around their airy lodge': so seemed 'that glitterance wafted on

alternate wing' (XXI. 29–36). Never did the bird-imagery
so sacred to the poetic imagination receive so resplendent an
expression as here, as the blessed make one towering bird of
Paradise, the Eagle of Life.

Or these happy lives form themselves into a wreath or
crown. Crowns and wreaths are favourites in the *Purgatorio*
and the *Paradiso*. So the blessed make a crown with Dante
and Beatrice the centre: three times 'those burning suns'
circle them (X. 73), and then another company out-circles
them and both circles revolve, blending motion to motion,
song to song (XII. 1–5). They are next wreaths of roses:

> About us thus
> Of sempiternal roses, bending, wreathed
> Those garlands twain . . .
>
> (XII. 16)

They sing of the ultimate mystery of the Trinity and the
Incarnation. There are other roses. Holy words raise assurance 'full-blossomed' in the bosom 'as a rose before the sun'
(XXII. 54). Beatrice once asks Dante why he gazes at
her and does not turn to the 'beautiful garden blossoming
beneath the rays of Christ', for here, she says, 'is the rose
wherein the Word Divine was made incarnate' (XXIII. 71).
In form of a rose-circle Dante creates one of his finest
visions. He sees light flowing like a river and a wondrous
land of flowers like 'rubies chased in gold' (XXX. 67). The
divine light spreads out in a circle and all beings up-risen
from earth form themselves into a resplendent rose. 'Into
the yellow of the rose' Beatrice leads him (XXX. 122–7).
And then again he views it as one whole:

> In fashion as a snow-white rose, lay then
> Before my view the saintly multitude . . .
>
> (XXXI. 1)

Angels like a 'troop of bees' cluster to where their 'fragrant
labour glows', then rise and stream back again, their faces

'of flame' and wings 'of gold' (XXXI. 6–17). The Rose is the
Christian Church; the Church is a flower, or again a 'fair
bride' (XXXII. 114). Love and the rose are correlative to
the poetic imagination. So brimful of the very perfume of
erotic delight is Dante's Christianity.

This rose-circle and the circling wreaths blend with other
circles and circlings. Dante's great poem is built round
circles. Hell is divided into circles and the purgatorial ascent
is made in spiral circlings. Throughout the *Purgatorio* there
is circle-imagery, the sun's disc and the moon's, birds
wheeling, dancers circling, the universal spheres revolving.
There are crowns and wreaths and the smaller circles of
lovers' eyes. In the *Paradiso* the impressions are more
powerful. The celestial lives move with 'whirling speed'
(XVIII. 38). Spirits may be 'little spheres' (XXII. 22). This
is typical:

> I had not ended, when, like rapid mill,
> Upon its centre whirled the light; and then
> The love that did inhabit there, replied . . .
>
> (XXI. 71)

The 'light'. Sometimes he calls them 'splendours'. One of
them and its companions all cluster 'into one' and roll upward 'like an eddying wind' (XXII. 95). They are imagined
in spinning motion like the revolving spheres they inhabit:
they and their heavenly spheres are never properly distinct,
as the 'sweet harmony' of their voices sounds among the
'wheels' of Heaven (VI. 129). The paradisal ascent is one
from sphere to sphere, and Dante's final vision, at the end
of his poem (XXIII. 107–31), is a triple circle enclosing
a human form, recalling that other mystery, read earlier
(pp. 99, 206, 229) in the circles of Beatrice's eyes, of

> Three persons in the Godhead, and in one
> Person that nature and the human joined.
>
> (XIII. 23)

Man with all his conflicts is mysteriously one with the divine harmony.

And all this is related to Beatrice. She is the condition through which it is visualized. Though 'fulminating streams of living radiance' play round us and we are 'swathed and veiled in dense impenetrable blaze' (XXX. 50), this solid blaze is one with her blazing beauty, the radiance of her smile and 'laughing eyes' (X. 58) is beside us. The fire-imagery lends splendour to her and she to it. Herself she blazes with immortal sight, her glory increases as they rise, and light and still more light sparkles in her eyes and in her smile. Once she tells Dante that, did she smile, his 'mortal puissance' would be turned to ashes (XXI. 4–11). The erotic vision is one with the divine: in it the incarnate Logos is reflected, the dualism of the Gryphon resolved, the relation of man to the cosmic harmony apprehended.

II

My page references to Goethe's *Faust* apply to the old Everyman edition translated by Albert G. Latham. The numerals run as follows: Prelude & Prologue, 1–10; Part 1, 11–163; Part 2, Act I, 179–242; Act II, 243–305; Act III, 306–356; Act IV, 356–390; Act V, 390–422.

Dante's poem is a poem of fire: the hungry flames of Hell; the varying lights of Purgatory; the solid blaze of Paradise. But we have also seen how skilfully the poet incarnates his spirit-world into natural forms. Goethe's *Faust* is still more strongly naturalistic. The poem is rough and chaotic: it expresses the experience of a lifetime, speaking in terms of Renaissance aspiration and the erotic intuition, looking back to ancient Greece and surveying man's future. The final ideal is that of creative work, and the whole is crowned by a Christian immortality. Historicity and time are indeterminate, the experience only is important.

First I outline the drama's story. Faust is old and weary of study; for life only he longs; abstract thinking has served him ill, and he is on the point of suicide, when Easter hymns recall him to life. By magic he summons Mephistopheles. Though fiery bright and a cheery soul Mephistopheles is our negative force. He is a spirit of denial (10), 'the spirit that denies' (40), all created life he would recall to the 'void'. He opposes 'light' and the 'bodies' it proceeds from and illuminates, preferring darkness and chaos (40). 'Light' is accordingly to be associated with 'bodies' and creation, Mephistopheles with chaos and destruction: we might say that flames incarnate in bodies is light. Creation wins continually from Mephistopheles, life multiplying itself in earth, air and water, and 'flame' only remains his own; he is a 'Son of Chaos' fighting against 'Creative Might' (41). Faust scorns him, yet accepts his aid, confident that nothing the devil gives will satisfy him. So he embarks on his course, which starts with a romance. Though he ruins Gretchen, experience of love arouses noble thoughts and attunes him to the 'glow of Heaven' (118; p. 209 below). This love-ecstasy is absurd to Mephistopheles, who only recognizes lust, and Gretchen's tragedy ensues. Faust's life-desire slays life's richest flower, his first life-adventure causes a death.

Nature's re-creative powers redeem him from despair and he is next at the Emperor's Court. There is a court Masque, followed by a vision of Helen, and the union of Helen and Faust.

Part I has shown us the limitations of an unfettered instinct: Part II shows art as a substitute. This Masque presents figures of pastoralism and Greek myth leading up to the appearance of Poetry as Boy-Charioteer, and ends in a conflagration. It is followed by the vision of Helen, typifying the Greek ideal of Beauty. To present this vision to the Emperor Faust has to descend to the Mothers, the discarnate origins of life and creation. This section of the poem corresponds to the Renaissance.

The vision does not satisfy Faust. He would find a Helen that does not vanish and goes to Wagner, his old pupil, who is at work on a medieval experiment, seeking the principle of Life. Wagner succeeds, and creates Homunculus. Homunculus, the furthest creation of medieval science, serves to lead Faust to Helen, but he does not as yet properly 'exist' (284–5, 293–4); he is a fiery spirit awaiting incarnation. He desires the Hellenic quest on his own and after much searching and after deciding to exist through water rather than fire, finds his ideal, Galatea. Galatea comes drawn in a car, with a wondrous procession, just like Beatrice, except that this is a sea-ceremony. A hymn is sung, honouring water whence 'all things' are 'created' and ocean as 'life-giver' (304); the radiant vision draws near; Homunculus spills out his life-flame in ecstasy, anointing Galatea with his own brilliance; and another hymn is sung, this time to Eros who marries Homunculus' fire to Galatea, Queen of the Waves:

> To Eros the empire, whence all things first blossomed!
> (305)

All the elements are praised in turn. Fire and water are at peace. It is a powerful climax.

Meanwhile Faust meets Helen. Medievalism blends with the Hellenic ideal, and gives birth to Euphorion. Euphorion is the child of the Renaissance, as Homunculus of the Middle Ages, and is associated with Byron (351). In unfettered aspiration he dies while too rashly scrambling up mountain cliffs, and Faust and Helen part. These scenes covering the Renaissance and the Romantic Revival are radiant with Hellenism, a glorified nature and a powerful erotic vision. Helen, while she is present, is absolute Queen, and even Lynceus, who seems to represent the medieval Church, admits that he has failed to see her because her light blinded him.

Two other sections only can be recorded.[1] Towards the close Faust devotes himself to creative and altruistic work, and at death rises up mountain ranges to reunion with Gretchen, for only by such romantic blessedness can man rise to Paradise. It was the same in Dante. At the conclusion paganism gives way to Christianity but the Christianity, as in Dante, recognizes the sovereign rights of the Eros:

> Here the ineffable
> Wrought is with love.
> The Eternal-Womanly
> Draws us above.   (422)

The greater Renaissance poets approach Christianity through the erotic intuition.

We have a vast nature, chaotic, often seemingly discordant, but ever-active and dynamic; a seething, torrential and creative energy. Goethe gives us 'creative Nature limned in vivid imagery' (13). The poet, he tells us, can show the 'one sweet harmony' (4) of the whole built of a myriad discords – 'into the whole how all things weave' (13). His imagery, like the creative nature it paints, is never static. 'With growth and with travail the earth is a-thrill' (27). 'Is' – everything is vividly and dynamically immediate: 'The vale is a-bud with the boon of hope' (27). All is motion: 'Doth not the world in all its streams sweep on . . .'? (51). Again:

> How from the window of the chancel there
> Upwards the never-dying lamp doth glimmer!
>
>   (126)

It is all a 'changeful weaving' (15); jewels 'flash with myriad hues prismatic' (191) and watch-fires 'shoot red flames

---

[1] The poem's narrative details have been admirably elucidated by A. Gillies in *Goethe's Faust*, 1957. The war which follows the incidents corresponding to the Romantic period may be placed as a forecast of twentieth-century world-conflicts. See *Christ & Nietzsche*, II, and *The Golden Labyrinth*, X.

athwart the night' (258). To Goethe motion's charm out-splendours static beauty:

> Self-blessed is Beauty — cold and listless,
> 'Tis grace alone that makes resistless.
>
> (271)

'Might, tumult, frenzy' (359) beat in his world and he loves cataracts 'in thousand twists and turns swift-plunging to the vale' (388). Cataracts are especial favourites. The Walpurgis Night is a swirling ascent, Faust and Mephistopheles speed by on black horses; in Part II there is continual change, an interthreading dance of elements, conflicting, blending, creating.

The poem roughly corresponds to Dante's Purgatory. Though it contains satanic and paradisal elements, its stage is earth and the conflict purgatorial. It is characterized by mists and mountains. The moon is 'misty' (138), there are 'misty vapours' (219), 'cloud wreaths' (220), a 'vaporous cloud' (254). Here is a stage direction: 'Mists spread abroad veiling the background and the foreground too, at pleasure' (325). Faust appears from out of a cloud and then watches it float away (356). Even if we have morning, it is the 'morning's misty haze' (367). We are often in a world of mists and clouds. Rocks and mountains are everywhere. Here are some stage directions: 'Woodland and Cave', 'Rocky Cove of the Aegean Sea', 'High Mountains', with 'a mighty, jagged rocky summit' (111, 291, 356), and at the end 'Mountain Ravines, Forest, Cliff, Wilderness' with 'Holy Anchorites scattered up the mountain-sides, having their dwelling in rocky clefts' (415). The Harz Mountains are the scene of the Walpurgis Night festival (133). Vast cliffs, forest-clad mountains, grand and rugged nature generally, are impressed on our imaginations. Faust would like to hover round 'mountain-caves' like a spirit (12). The 'rugged pine-clad highland' is dear to Goethe (32), 'upwards and onwards'

(32) is his poem's theme, and mountains are its symbols. Seismos boasts of his mountain-making prowess (275–6). The battle in Part II is waged largely in terms of mountains: 'great are the mountain's forces' (370). Goethe's nature is vast and powerful. Plunging torrents, sprouting verdure, hills thrown up from the furnaces boiling at earth's centre, turbulent seas, shifting mists and clouds and glinting sunset skies, all are constituent to creation's ever-changing glory.

One important dualism persists through Goethe's nature-thought: fire and water are opposed. Both are active forces, but whereas water is more gently creative, fire is satanic, fierce and unrestful. Faust speaks of 'this fire within my bosom flaming' (103), Mephistopheles 'fans' in his heart 'devouring' fire (112) for Gretchen, and Mephistopheles' lust is a 'flame' (282). Mephistopheles, the satanic principle, is dressed in red (46). Many of his tricks are associated with fire. In Auerbach's Cellar wine is turned to 'the flames of Hell' (72). In the Witch's Kitchen there is a cauldron 'over the fire' and from it 'a great flame bursts out and flares up' (75, 80). The Witch 'splashes' flames towards Faust with a ladle: 'splashes' is typical, since Goethe often sees fire as liquid. Mephistopheles is himself a 'monstrous birth of filth and fire' (122).

In the Masque at the Emperor's court we watch a curiously interesting rhythm. First, simple and picturesque nature is suggested by pretty rustic figures and persons of Hellenic myth; next, art in general, civilization and greed prompted by the gold-mining gnomes (216), are dramatized; third, there is a fiery conflagration. Metallic wealth is 'golden blood', which seems to 'boil and bubble' (212), a 'well of fire' and 'froth of pearl' mixing 'flame and foam' (218). The fire 'crackles' (219), maskers seem to burn, the Emperor himself burns, it is a disastrous termination to the gaiety. Luxury and greed sully nature's happiness and desecrate art.

Nature, art, a greedy civilization: it is a descending sequence. Goethe writes the moral:

> O Youth, O Youth, wilt never thou
> In the pure measure of joy contain thee?
> O Majesty, wilt never thou
> All-powerful, yet let Prudence rein thee?
>
> (219)

The fire of lust is quenched by 'misty vapours' and 'cloud wreaths': water conquers fire, 'softly steaming, smoothly welling', asserting itself over 'spirit-malice' (219–20).

This is a persistent opposition in *Faust*. In Part II we have an argument concerning the relative importance of fire and water in the creation of mountains (284–5). Mountains are symbols of high power in Goethe, as heroes of the natural world. Anaxagoras supports fire, Thales water. The pigmies and cranes fight it out. Pigmies and mine-folk, the gnomes of the Masque (216), are associated with fire, metals and mountains. Mephistopheles and Faust argue too: Mephistopheles supports fire, insisting that the mountains are creations of hell-fire, but Faust will not complicate his intuition of nature's serenity by such subterranean questionings however his companion may urge the importance of the abysmal flames and Moloch's hammer (357–8). The heroic battle in Part II (362–81) is won for the Emperor by mountain waters and mountain fire: the mine-folk are called in by Mephistopheles for the occasion. Faust is mainly interested in the cascades, whereas Mephistopheles is more interested in the fireworks. Faust uses the victory for his own advantage, and boasts of the mountain's fiery forces: often he profits by Mephistopheles' fire, usually regretting it afterwards.

The mine-folk and their smithies and metal workings suggest hard metal as against organic nature, and sometimes gold, arousing the fires of greed (216–18). They correspond to deep instincts. Mountain spirits may symbolize that which is behind creation, the Shakespearian 'nothing' (pp. 27, 41 above), unincarnated eternity. Whatever passes in the world above is shown them by their 'spirit-power' in the 'eternal silence' (370). Much the same is told us of the 'Mothers' to whom Faust goes for Helen, fleeing from the 'existent' into the 'unfettered realm of Form' (231). This is a spiritual and fiery quest, the key he takes being lit 'with flames' (230), and we are told that it is more dreadful than any voyage over the ocean's billows. The spirit-principle in both Shakespeare and Goethe may be felt either as fire or as a dark nothingness, Goethe's 'nethermost abyss' where are 'forms of all things that be' in 'the Eternal Mind' (231). This is the land of the Mothers. All these related impressions, including the mountain mine-folk, correspond to unincarnated spirit, whereas water suggests organic nature. After the Masque, Mephistopheles observes that the Emperor has survived fire and next offers a conquest of the sea (221): continually we find the two together in association or contrast.

Fire is not necessarily satanic. Wherever there is a violence in man or nature, we may have fire. Faust's love for Gretchen was a fire. After the disaster he sees how he sought to kindle 'the torch of life' and was penned in 'a sea of fire' (182), and from this image he passes to the 'cataract', the transition marking an important change of direction. He will turn his back on the fiery sun, and

> The cataract, that through the gorge doth thunder,
> I'll watch with growing rapture.
>
> (182)

Wherever we have essential power of life nakedly apprehended, there may be fire. The Earth-Spirit early in the poem appears in fire: 'A ruddy flame flashes. The Spirit appears in the flame'. It is a 'creature of Flame', and strikes fear in the beholder (14–15). This is the naked beauty of Nature dangerous to man, the naked loveliness that Shelley writes of

(p. 84 above). Homunculus, an unincarnated spirit always searching to be born, is likewise fiery. He 'flashes' (252); his 'glass hums and flashes mightily' (259). The creation of Homunculus is an adventure into the life-origin itself. Homunculus is a spirit of aspiration and fire: so is Euphorion. Euphorion's fiery love causes the maiden he would win to turn to flame: she 'bursts into flame and flares aloft' (348). He shakes the fire from him; fire of his own passion.

Goethe is working at the fiery life-principle, man's aspiration and desire, his longing and inevitable failure; whenever love or any desire is hasty, it may be associated with fire. Not that Goethe desires peace. A static paradise is no paradise to him, and his well-loved cataracts may themselves be equated with turbulent passion: 'I am the cataract', says Faust, seeing that his desire seems fated to crash ruinously down on Gretchen's life (115). Faust thirsts always for life and still more life, and the poem as a whole labours to turn this life-fire into organic and creative action. Water is creative; fire, unless wisely directed, destructive. Goethe's use of these impressions is explained by a Shakespearian passage:

> Methinks King Richard and myself should meet
> With no less terror than the elements
> Of fire and water, when their thundering shock
> At meeting tears the cloudy cheeks of heaven.
> Be he the fire, I'll be the yielding water:
> The rage be his, while on the earth I rain
> My waters; on the earth, and not on him.
>
> (*Richard II*, III. iii. 54)

The life-fire forces Faust to destruction; his love-fire ruins Gretchen, his ambition-fire sets Philemon's cottage in luridly described flames. Poetry may be a substitute, an outlet for the life-fire: in the Masque the Boy-Charioteer personifying poetry dispenses 'flamelets' to those he favours, splashing them with fire (209–10). But the last word is with creative action, with water rather than fire. Faust at the close turns his attention to mastery of the ocean, draining a marsh. He is opposing water, but water and fire are alike passionate forces, to be controlled. Water is docile at the last: fire, at the last, is a torment, and so described by Mephistopheles at his final discomfiture (409). Our poem opposes the wisely creative life with fiery passions; nature's grand surfaces with the subterranean forges and smithies that throw them into place; outward form and the blazing inner life; water and fire. Water is given the poet's explicit favour, but fire makes the poem. In the Masque, where the gnomes and the nymphs suggest the fire-water opposition, the gnomes claim that 'at bottom' their 'purpose' is 'kind' and friendly to 'good' men (216). Mephistopheles, the scarlet-robed fire-principle, is essential to Heaven's plan and is employed by the Deity to awaken man to action (10). The only doctrine that fits our paradoxes is that of incarnation, of the creative life, incarnating in creative action the life-fire which, not properly projected, brings destruction.

Goethe's mighty poem is rich in paradisal passages. The word 'paradise' itself is frequent. Sometimes we have ordinary nature-description, radiantly expressed; sometimes a transcendental vision in natural terms. Early in Part I Faust meditates on the cosmic splendours that his own life cannot grasp (13) and later Voices sing to him of an ethereal and watery paradise (43–4). As Faust wakes in Part II he sees a glorious prospect: 'A very Paradise about me lightens!' (181). That is typical. There is the paradisal Hellenism and sea-paradise of the Classical Walpurgis Night. Water-paradises are emphatic and the river Peneus important at one point as a stage setting. A radiant Arcadia is prophetically described towards the close of the 'Helena':

Pan shields them there, and Life-nymphs there in legions
In the moist cool of bushy clefts dwell free,

> And striving yearningly to higher regions
> Rears itself, branchwise, crowded tree on tree.

(339)

Here all men are healthy, content, immortal:

> The blooming child to fatherhood unfoldeth
> By favour of this limpid day;
> We stand amazed, and still the question holdeth
> If men, if haply Gods, are they?

(339)

It is a prophecy of man become divine in union with essential life. Such radiant paganism is set against a dark medievalism. Homunculus, intoxicated by an Hellenic water-paradise, addresses Mephistopheles:

> The North thy heritage is.
> Thy birth was in the misty ages,
> The waste of priesthood and of chivalry . . .

(254)

He is only at home 'in the murky', says Homunculus. Yet Goethe's poem is interthreaded by Christian thought. There are Faust's childhood recollections, springing to mind as the Easter music breaks into his darkened life. Part I is impregnated strongly with Christian feeling and at its close angelic voices assert Gretchen's redemption. Most of Part II is pagan and Hellenic, but it ends with a Dantesque ascension. The story melts into the divine at either end: there is the Prologue in Heaven and Faust's ascent to Paradise while Mephistopheles is tormented by a hailing shower of roses.

So Goethe, in his own mighty fashion, blends pagan and erotic intuitions with Christianity. He writes of nature and man's place in nature, of creation and creation's miraculous strength. The Emperor throughout is a weakling and spendthrift, and his court is to be contrasted with the grandeurs of nature and the simple sweetness of human life when in harmony with the laws of creation. There is continual suggestion of simple and erotic human happiness; of country music, song and dance. The poem tingles with eroticism and the thrill of life and birth. Goethe does not favour a flashing and sophisticated civilization, richly robed and crowned with temporal glory, though he makes a fine poetic use of clothes: Mephistopheles is in red and gold with a cock's plume in his cap (46), Faust in medieval dress for his union with Helen, Euphorion's mantle and lyre are left after his spirit flames upward. The suffusing atmosphere is one of natural simplicity and natural grandeur. Life, nature, creation and the Eros are the main themes. Life is both turbulent and creative. Love, beauty, birth bubble up, irrepressible; a mighty life pulses in this mighty song, a multitudinous and mountainous life-force. Two main principles emerge: the fire-principle and the water-principle. The one is fierce, violent, hasty; the other sometimes turbulent, yet on the whole more gentle, soothing, creative. Both are necessary: often they blend. Mephistopheles is himself part of God's organic scheme, fire seethes at the mighty heart of the mountain. The conclusion is this: that, following nature, the fires of life be incarnated in creative action.

III

Shakespeare steers a middle course. Whereas Dante stresses the divine and Goethe the natural, Shakespeare as certainly stresses the human. Dante is a poet of both hideous evil and life so blazing that it becomes pure, almost solid, light; Goethe the poet of nature and fire; Shakespeare, though he uses a full range of imaginative effects, the poet of humanity. Like Goethe he writes primarily in terms of nature and man, and like Dante steadily faces both the ultimate evils and the radiance of victorious love. Dante attains a perfect and circular harmony at a certain sacrifice of truth to the chaotic nature of experience, whereas Goethe attains a certain truth to nature with a sacrifice of intellectual harmony.[1] Shakespeare holds the balances, his whole universe revolving on the tempest-music opposition. Tempests suggest nature, music the divine. Between these two the Shakespearian drama is enacted and they, nature and the divine, correspond roughly to the works of Goethe and Dante.

Shakespeare's nature ranges from tempests and thunder, raging seas and fierce beasts to paradisal impressions of soft airs and water, as in the description of Cleopatra on Cydnus in *Antony and Cleopatra*. Both aquatic and aerial life-forms, vivid in *Antony and Cleopatra*, occur in other idyllic contexts, corresponding to the fishes and birds in Dante's Paradise. Sun, moon and stars overwatch man's drama and its action is attuned, from time to time, to music: at the limit, we hear 'the music of the spheres' (*Pericles*, V. i. 231). But the central concentration is human. To Shakespeare, at the top of his vision, the human is the cosmic, the cosmos itself becomes human. Cleopatra's dream-Antony is the universe, her universe an Antony; Prospero is a kind of God and yet Prospero is as surely man. Shakespeare is the mighty poet of incarnate life.

Because Shakespeare puts faith in man and man's civilization, he vitalizes his drama with effects of feasting, raiment and gold. Feasting as in *Timon of Athens*, *Macbeth* and *Antony and Cleopatra*, is often important; in *The Tempest* a banquet is a dominating symbol. But food may suggest equally life and greed. As in Goethe, where the luxury of the court is powerfully satirized, so the court of Denmark in *Hamlet* is soiled by inordinate festivity. Rich clothes are likewise important. In the early romances Shakespeare satirizes extravagant fashions; Macbeth, who seizes a glory he cannot

---

[1] And yet modern physics, with its revelation of circularities within the atom, appears to support Dante. [**1960**]

own, is absurdly possessed of a title that sits on him as 'a giant's robe upon a dwarfish thief' (V. ii. 21). But Cleopatra dies in her 'best attires', and at her dying says

> Give me my robe, put on my crown; I have
> Immortal longings in me . . .
> > (*Antony and Cleopatra*, V. ii. 282)

Throughout Shakespeare crowns are impregnated with poetic power.[1] Pericles at a pinnacle of Shakespeare's dramatic experience, calls:

> Give me my robes. I am wild in my beholding.
> O heavens! bless my girl.
> > (*Pericles*, V. i. 224)

There is Hamlet's 'inky cloak' (I. ii. 77), and Prospero's mantle.[2] Nakedness is symbolically important: the nakedness of Edgar in *King Lear*, Lear's own intention to be naked as he, and, most powerful of all, the naked Timon repudiating civilization from the frontiers of death. Goethe, like Shakespeare, is, as we have seen, rich in raiment, in spite of his naturalism. Dante shows his sufferers in Hell as naked, but his Paradisal lives are either clothed radiantly or seem to blaze with a fiery nakedness waiting to be uplifted 'lightly' in the 'new-vested flesh' (*Purgatory*, XXX. 15) and 'garments' (*Paradise*, XXV. 129) of the body they are to receive.

There is much gold in Shakespeare. Gold may, like clothes, be repudiated as worthless, even as poison; or it may

---

[1] Shakespeare's royal symbolisms are discussed throughout *The Sovereign Flower*.

[2] I should also have mentioned the clothes of the wrecked people in *The Tempest* undamaged and even, with intimations of immortality, 'fresher than before' (I. ii. 218; II. i. 65–8). Prospero's symbolic mantle was well discussed by Colin Still in *Shakespeare's Mystery Play*, 1921; reprinted as *The Timeless Theme*, 1936. [**1960**]

be used to point the richer gold of essential life. 'There is thy gold', says Romeo to the Apothecary,

> worse poison to men's souls,
> Doing more murders in this loathsome world,
> Than these poor compounds that thou may'st not sell.
> I sell thee poison; thou hast sold me none.

But it is yet a life-force, too. He continues:

> Farewell: buy food, and get thyself in flesh.
> (*Romeo and Juliet*, V. i. 80)

The incident forecasts *The Merchant of Venice* and *Timon of Athens*, where gold symbolism holds a similarly ambivalent, and primary, importance. Gold, jewels or any rich merchandise may be used to suggest the spiritual riches of love (*The Shakespearian Tempest*, II. 65–73; V. 222–3). Dante's Paradise has rubies, emeralds and pearls, and the divine grace is as 'hidden riches' (*Paradise*, XI. 75). The flash of wealth illuminates Goethe's drama, but its fires turn to a blaze of greed and an incitement to decadence and evil. Throughout our greater poets, riches have two directions: they may either serve or oppose essential life.

The plays from *Hamlet* to *Henry VIII* are, at their most powerful, death visions and immortality myths. *Hamlet* and *Macbeth* both emphasize death. *Hamlet* is weighed down by loathly horror, disease-imagery, and death; the play starts with a ghost, there is a graveyard scene. In *Macbeth* death is an active, rampaging force, with hell loosed murderously on earth; *King Lear* and *Timon of Athens* are purgatorial; and *Antony and Cleopatra* emphasizes Elysium (IV. xii. 51) and a love negating death. In *Pericles* and *The Winter's Tale* the protagonist is separated from his wife and loses his daughter; both he thinks dead; the loss is associated with tempest, the restoration with music. Shakespeare's final plays are impregnated with religious vision and transcendentalism. These, with the plot of loss and reunion and their powerful child and nature symbolism, make them, more powerfully than most happy-ending romances, dramatic statements of immortality. Here too we find elements Dantesque and Goethean. There are two primary human life-symbols in poetry: the lover and the child. Dante, whose Paradise expands primarily the romantic love-intuition and who is little concerned with the temporal process as a process, sees the divine in terms of Beatrice. Goethe, to whom the creative process as a process is more important, is concerned with both the lover and the child: hence his many important birth-themes, Gretchen's child, Homunculus, Euphorion. Goethe's world is one of up-thrusting, blossoming life, a creative world. If we now turn to *Pericles* and *The Winter's Tale*, we find that the miraculous restoration of Thaisa or Hermione corresponds to Beatrice's restoration to Dante, or Gretchen's final restoration to Faust, whereas the return of the lost child, Marina or Perdita, will suggest the victorious power of creative love within the temporal process. Dante and Goethe in different ways stress the importance of creative living; and Shakespeare's final plays are myths of creation.

Shakespeare's world is multitudinously varied. Christian eschatology entwines with a pagan naturalism and both with themes of empire and world-glory. The histories show us the pangs of national evolution; the romantic comedies blend humour with a paradisal eroticism; the tragedies analyse death-forces, the final plays celebrate life's conquest over death. The most powerful impressions emerging, apart from tempests and music, are those of human love and human birth; and their opposites, evil and death. Shakespeare, like Dante and Goethe, approaches the divine through the romantic ideal incarnated in his Juliet, Portia, Desdemona, Cleopatra, Thaisa, Hermione, Imogen and Queen Katharine. Love is irradiated by religious and Christian metaphor and love-themes often entwined with religious events and persons such as Friars. *The Tempest* sums up the Shakespearian universe. The contemplative peace and philosophic forgiveness of suffering age in Prospero blends with the new and young marriage-joy of Ferdinand and Miranda. In *Henry VIII* the poet speaks not through pagan deities as in the other final plays, but through a Christian symbolism. He returns to a national rather than a philosophical and personal theme, and becomes a national and political prophet, like Isaiah and Virgil and Dante. As in Isaiah and Virgil, we have a child: the child Elizabeth. Like Goethe's *Faust*, Shakespeare's work develops through the romantic ideal to a Christian symbolism.

I shall now offer two essays on the New Testament. St Paul's Epistles and the Gospels may be interpreted as I interpret poetry; they employ the usual poetic life effects, including the erotic symbol, recurring as marriage; but they point further to a wider union and a deeper and more enduring music such as Shakespeare touches in *The Tempest*. My aim is to reveal these richer essences too often neglected with a neglect which sometimes leads to dangerous statements as to the death-philosophy of Christianity. There are dark effects, death-impressions, certainly, but that is because the New Testament, like all poetry, is fighting for life against death. If ever a book had a message of life, it is this. And yet we are tempted by a perverted Christian teaching and many false associations to talk and think of its death-philosophy. We might as well talk of the death-philosophy of a richly laden fruit-tree.

VIII

MANKIND IN GLORY:
AN ESSAY ON ST PAUL

I

IN studying the New Testament we must resist the tendency to regard Jesus in isolation and also the tendency to undervalue those of its events which appear supernormal. If we insist on reducing it to prosaic thought, we shall fail to focus its meaning, since it is pointing us to more exciting matters. We must see the whole book as an expression of a resplendent force and creative energy tapping new power, new life, for men. This life is embodied in a number of vivid life-impressions and to this mesh of pictorial language and pictorial event we must give close attention. Though Jesus will be the most important single person in our drama, his true importance will not be apparent till we recognize not only the poetic quality in his own life and words but also its reflections in the actions, letters and prophecies of his successors.

We have already drawn a distinction between poets who use vivid fire or light imagery and those whose words have a less scintillating excitement, a more natural bloom. Both modes serve a purpose and both are found in the New Testament. We have the Keatsian imagery of Jesus' words in the Synoptic Gospels, but where the writer describes some visionary fact, there may be a blaze of light such as Jesus never himself uses in his parables. St John, an interpretative writer, intellectualizes the imagery of the other Gospels, heightening and translating it; and St Paul both interprets by close reasoning and uses images of glory. 'Glory' is not a word to be associated with Jesus' own imagery; he is more

Keatsian, more natural, more homely. But the more interpretative books are necessary to our understanding. We shall
therefore start by reviewing St Paul's approach to the
Christian fact, his explanation of it and his message. After
that we shall pass to St John and thence to the Synoptic
Gospels.

The Acts of the Apostles describes some marvellous events.
A new power has entered the world. We have a description
of its coming at Pentecost:

> They saw tongues like flames distributing themselves, one resting
> on the head of each, and they were all filled with the holy Spirit –
> they began to speak in foreign tongues, as the Spirit enabled them
> to express themselves.   (*Acts*, II. 3)

In this fire all differences are melted. It is an intoxicating
elixir: the bystanders think that 'they are brimfull of new
wine' (II. 13).

The miracles done by Peter are striking; he wields the
power of Jesus himself, dispelling death-forces. Stephen's
martyrdom is dramatic. Being 'full of grace and power' he
performs 'wonders and miracles' (*Acts*, VI. 8). He is all but
transfigured:

> Then all who were seated in the Sanhedrin fixed their eyes on him,
> and saw that his face shone like the face of an angel.
>   (*Acts*, VI. 15)

He accuses the authorities of being 'uncircumcised in heart
and ear' and of resisting the holy Spirit. He is as one
possessed:

> He, full of the holy Spirit, gazed up at heaven and saw the glory of
> God and Jesus standing at God's right hand.   (*Acts*, VII, 55)

They take him out and stone him, but death marks no failure:
from Stephen's death is raised up Saul's, or Paul's, prophetic
life, as from Jesus' death this whole life-inspiration has arisen.
Every death is the sowing of another seed to enrich the

harvest. Paul, who has been ardent with threats of slaughter against the disciples (IX. 1), is visited by a vision:

> As he neared Damascus in the course of his journey, suddenly a light from heaven flashed round him . . .   (*Acts*, IX. 3)

The light is 'dazzling', to use his own word elsewhere (*Acts*, XXVI. 13). He is converted and starts his mission. The Divine choice was well placed.

Henceforth we see Paul in various tribulations, imprisoned, tormented and shipwrecked, yet ever active with a mighty strength, possessing a purpose which turns all impediment to a spurring hope, all failure to inspiration. He is the ambassador of life, serving his master the great – in Peter's phrase – 'pioneer of life' (*Acts*, III. 15). In argument with the authorities, in disciplining the new church, in policy of any kind, he is supreme. At any difficulty he is like Dr Johnson in an argument; he just overturns it. As soon as he is converted, his theological training makes him a frightening antagonist:

> Saul became more and more vigorous. He put the Jewish residents in Damascus to confusion by his proof that Jesus was the Christ . . .
> (*Acts*, IX. 22)

They plot to make away with him, but he is equal to all occasions and escapes in a basket. When he tries to join the disciples they are, not unnaturally, suspicious and 'afraid of him' (*Acts*, IX. 26). He must have been a formidable personality. When he is imprisoned in Macedonia there is an earthquake and we find him doing his best to reassure the jailer. The jailer and his family are converted to Christianity and the praetor sends orders that the prisoners are to be released. Paul stands on his dignity and refuses to go:

> 'They flogged us in public and without a trial, flogged Roman citizens! They put us in prison, and now they are going to get rid of

us secretly! No indeed! Let them come here themselves and take us out!'   (*Acts*, XVI. 37)

The praetors go to 'appease' them and 'beg' them to leave. Paul and Silas take their time, visiting their friends, and go away at their leisure.

These incidents are characteristic. It is as though Paul is grown-up, trying to make children behave themselves. There is danger, just as Gulliver may be in danger among the Lilliputians, but it is an unfair contest. Paul is equally at home in practical affairs and theoretical reasoning. In Greece he comes on an altar inscribed 'To an unknown god'. This calls forth his declaration that God is not 'unknown', nor an abstract entity to be set in shrines and carved by human art, but rather the great God of Life itself:

> The God who made the world and all things in it, he, as Lord of heaven and earth, does not dwell in shrines that are made by human hands; he is not served by human hands as if he needed anything, for it is he who gives life and breath and all things to all men. All nations he has created from a common origin, to dwell all over the earth, fixing their allotted periods and the boundaries of their abodes, meaning them to seek for God on the chance of finding him in their groping for him. Though indeed he is close to each one of us, for it is in him that we live and move and exist – as some of your own poets have said.   (*Acts*, XVII. 24)

He is 'breath', 'life'; the life we live. Paul urges the Greeks to awake, to know their own essential life. His creed is sublimely humanistic. Observe his apt reference to Greek literature, his education giving him an advantage the original disciples did not possess.

When he is in difficulties with the Roman authorities, he makes use of his Roman citizenship:

> Then those who were to have examined him left him at once alone; even the commander was alarmed to find that Paul was a Roman citizen and that he had bound him.   (*Acts*, XXII. 29)

He makes equal use of his Rabbinical learning, splitting his
Jewish accusers into two parties by his claim to be a Pharisee
suffering for his Pharisaical beliefs (*Acts*, XXIII. 6–9).
While in Roman custody he gets wind of a plot and per-
suades the Roman commander to have him safely removed.
Tertullus accuses him before the governor Felix:

> The fact is, we have found this man is a perfect pest; he stirs up
> sedition among the Jews all over the world and he is a ringleader
> of the Nazarene sect . . .   (*Acts*, XXIV. 5)

Paul defends himself. Felix postpones his decision and talks
to Paul, who makes the best of the opportunity:

> He sent for Paul and heard what he had to say about faith in Christ
> Jesus; but when he argued about morality, self-mastery, and the
> future judgement, Felix grew uneasy.   (*Acts*, XXIV. 24)

Nothing can stop him. On the way to Rome he warns the
captain that their ship will be wrecked, and when the voyage
grows dangerous it is he who comforts, advises and takes
charge of the situation. He acts as though those round him
were silly children, but when they grow troublesome, he is a
master at using whatever weapons come to hand. When he
does get to Rome, he has comfortable lodgings and a soldier
to 'guard' him – or serve him? – and settles down to more
evangelism:

> For two full years he remained in his private lodging, welcoming
> anyone who came to visit him; he preached the Reign of God and
> taught about the Lord Jesus Christ quite openly and unmolested.
>   (*Acts*, XXVIII. 30)

So he wins again.

St Paul's life in the service of Christianity is quite
amazing. He was a necessary link. The original simple yet
tremendous vision, or fact, or whatever we may call it, had
to be related to current affairs and contemporary thought.
Moreover, the Christian community had to be organized.

Before Paul's arrival on the scene, its chances were not impressive; martyrdom such as Stephen's was not enough; a practical force was needed and Paul aptly chosen. He was peculiarly fitted for the task: a Roman citizen, yet versed in Jewish theology; a man of great driving force – as was witnessed by his first vigorous persecution of the Christians – yet capable of infinite patience; arrogant and gentle by turns; one of the greatest visionaries the world has produced, yet with a most careful regard, as his letters show, to comparatively prosaic detail. By circumstance and nature he was uniquely equipped for his gigantic task.

II

In the Epistles he appears as an efficient organizer and as a powerful and intrepid thinker with a gift for ringing phrases. The first Epistle to the Corinthians illustrates his efficiency. He has heard certain unfavourable reports about them, but he begins gently, persuasively, urging them to leave their private quarrels. Having divided themselves into followers of Paul and Apollos, they have shown that they do not understand the first principles of Christianity. He gives them much general counsel, trying to help them in their difficulties, telling them to interpret what is spiritual in spirtual language; what the cynic foolishly rejects must be read with a spiritual eye if it is to be understood. True, he has not told them all this before: he had to address them as 'worldlings', as 'babes in Christ', and feed them with 'milk', not 'solid food'; and they are still not ready for 'solid food' (*1 Corinthians*, III. 1–2). He urges them to Christian commonsense. This is how he rounds off his exhortation:

> So you must not boast about men. For all belongs to you; Paul, Apollos, Cephas, the world, life, death, the present and the future – all belongs to you; and you belong to Christ, and Christ to God.
>
> (*1 Corinthians*, III. 21)

Notice his paternal gentleness and the terse comprehensiveness with which he sweeps away the impediments of foolishness. He aims to tell the blunt truth and preach the Gospel 'with no fine rhetoric, lest the cross of Christ should lose its power' (*1 Corinthians*, I. 17). 'Power': Paul is full of power. Gently he tells his pupils that he does not wish to make them feel ashamed; he is instructing them as loved children and is sending Timotheus to help them, and explain things. But let them not think his gentleness weakness:

> Certain individuals have got puffed up, have they, as if I were not coming myself? I will come to you before long, if the Lord wills, and then I will find out from these puffed up creatures not what their talk but what their power amounts to. For God's reign does not show itself in talk but in power. Which is it to be? Am I to come to you with a rod of discipline or with love and a spirit of gentleness? (*1 Corinthians*, IV. 18)

The personality that persecuted Christians has changed its direction without losing its 'power': Paul radiates power, in action and writing alike.

His thinking is powerful. Not that he sets great store by thinking: his philosophical passsages must be read in their very practical contexts. The main thing is Christ; intellectual reasoning he uses only to explain away difficulties. He elbows his way through the intellectual world in Johnsonian style:

> I demolish theories and any rampart thrown up to resist the knowledge of God, I take every project prisoner to make it obey Christ . . . (*2 Corinthians*, X. 5)[1]

What he tries to make clear is this: that the old order of good and evil is superseded and a new order has come to birth. The 'Law' is gone. The Law implants 'the consciousness of sin' (*Romans*, III. 20) and produces the 'wrath' of

[1] Here and sometimes elsewhere Moffatt prefers 'I' where other translators translate 'we'.

God (*Romans*, IV. 15). But under the new order of faith we are 'done with the Law' (*Romans*, VII. 6):

> Such a faith implies the presence of . . . a God who makes the dead live and calls into being what does not exist.
>
> (*Romans*, IV. 17)

In other words, he announces the royalty of creative life; and this, properly understood, involves the annihilation of death. A life-consciousness is to supersede the sin-consciousness, the death-consciousness: sin and death are interdependent. 'Sin's wage is death, but God's gift is life eternal' (*Romans*, VI. 23). Again:

> Thus, then, sin came into the world by one man, and death came in by sin; and so death spread to all men, inasmuch as all men sinned. (*Romans*, V. 12)

Now we are all to 'live and move in the new sphere of Life' (*Romans*, VI. 4). 'Life' is the key-word of the New Testament. And yet the Law is not equivalent to sin. Paul talks of 'the law of sin and death' (*Romans*, VIII. 2), but that is because the Law produces the sin-consciousness. That consciousness is good, in that it is dynamic, provided that we do not stay in it. Here our thinking gets paradoxical. Sin, apart from the Law which brings the sin-consciousness, is 'lifeless' (*Romans*, VII. 8). The Law urges toward goodness, which is life, yet by implanting sin in the mind it brings death:

> I lived at one time without law myself, but when the command came home to me, sin sprang to life and I died: the command that meant life proved death for me. (*Romans*, VII. 9)

Sin 'used' the Law to slay, but the Law itself is not sin (*Romans*, VII. 11–13). Nor is this 'death' final, for 'the law of the spirit brings the life which is in Christ Jesus, and that law has set me free from the law of sin and death' (*Romans*, VIII. 2). He who raised Christ will make our 'mortal bodies live by his indwelling Spirit' (*Romans*, VIII. 11). Paul

opposes 'life' to 'death', expecting a 'glorious freedom' which
will loose all creation from its 'thraldom to decay' (*Romans*,
VIII. 21), so that Jesus may become 'the first-born of a
great brotherhood' (*Romans*, VIII. 29). Within this resplendent intuition old rules of behaviour pale to insignifi-
cance. All Paul's reasoning, paradoxical and hurried, thrown
out with little care as to form, is secondary to the one
primary fact:

> For I am certain neither death nor life, neither angels nor princi-
> palities, neither the present nor the future, no powers of the Height
> or of the Depth, nor anything else in all creation will be able to
> part us from God's love in Christ Jesus our Lord.
>
> (*Romans*, VIII. 38)

Even angels are nothing to him. Nothing is anything to him
but the one immediate and blazing positive experience.

He writes much of the 'Law' explaining that it is superseded.
The Law is negative, without creative power. It involves sin
in that it is wholly dependent on the concept of sin and is
therefore parasitic on evil. The two are reciprocally interdependent, each causing the other; and this relation is a
reflection of a wider reciprocity. Sin and its correlative the
Law reflect the disorganized relation between man and
God. While there is sin the Law is necessary, but it is now
possible to attain a state where sin and the Law drop away,
meaningless and unwanted.[1] The unknown author of the
Epistle to the Hebrews tells us that Christ will come to save,
not 'to deal with sin' (*Hebrews*, IX. 28). The Law is abstract,
'a mere shadow of the bliss that is to be', and does not at all
represent 'the reality of that bliss' (*Hebrews*, X. 1). The

---

[1] St Paul is worrying at the heart of human psychology in its present
evolutionary stage, wherein delight and daring are sexually intrinsicate; as
expressed by the line 'How glowing guilt exalts the keen delight' in Pope's
Eloisa to Abelard. Compare my comment on Dryden's *Amphitryon* in *The
Golden Labyrinth*, VII. Paul, like Nietzsche, envisages a new, beyond-good-
and-evil, synthesis. [**1960**]

Law, being repressive and negative, cannot itself make for life, it has no creative power. Paul writes:

> Had there been any law which had the power of producing life, righteousness would really have been due to law . . .
>
> *(Galatians*, III. 21)

He asserts instead the splendour of the Christ newborn in man: all who are baptized into Christ take on his 'character' (*Galatians*, III. 27), all are now sons and heirs of God (*Galatians*, IV. 7), all now must let the peace of Christ be 'supreme' within their 'hearts' (*Colossians*, III. 15). Man has ceased to be at enmity with life. Therefore Paul strongly opposes all old rules and catalogues which cannot in their narrow compass contain the new birth.

In a powerful passage in his first Epistle to Timothy (I. 3–11) he attacks those who study old 'myths and interminable genealogies' and 'speculations' in place of the 'divine order'. 'Empty argument' he repudiates. Those who engage in it aspire to be 'doctors of the Law', but 'have no idea either of the meaning of the words they use or of the themes on which they harp'. Paul knows well enough that 'the Law is admirable, provided that one makes a lawful use of it', but he emphasizes that it exists not for honest people but for the lawless. We can recognize a general truth: those who make contact with a positive force in any field invariably throw off the laws on which they have been brought up, and invariably have to fight those to whom the law itself is a satisfying ideal. Since no 'law' has 'the power of producing life', it cannot produce righteousness (*Galatians*, III. 21); the commands of Moses were an 'administration of death' and the 'glory' of the Old Testament 'fades in Christ' (*2 Corinthians*, III. 7, 14). It was not easy to find words to express the new truth. Paul's thought tumbles out, vigorous and powerful, smashing old arguments, concise and splendid in conviction, but not always easy or coherent to a superficial judgement. All must be understood by seeing every argument and every image as a surface expression of the central experience: God is not to be associated with sin and the Law; rather He is Birth, Life and Immortality.

Paul opposes 'speculations' (p. 131 above). He can use them himself – no one better – but that is because he is talking to children. What he wants is for man to see the solid reality that is his. But is this reality physical or spiritual? What is the relation of Paul to D. H. Lawrence? Our answer depends on what exact meaning we attach to the concepts 'spirit' and 'spiritual'. As Paul uses them we must not regard them as denoting anything ghostlike: by derivation they suggest the 'breath' of life and breath is finally inconceivable without a body. Though Paul contrasts 'spirit' with 'flesh', spirit is not an abstract entity; it usually denotes a simple life-harmony. In so far as either the flesh or intellectual abstractions oppose such a harmony there is evil. 'Spirit' however remains vague and the antagonist to the Christian life may equally well be spiritual:

> For we have to struggle, not with blood and flesh but with the angelic Rulers, the angelic Authorities, the potentates of the dark present, the spirit-forces of evil in the heavenly sphere.
>
> (*Ephesians*, VI. 12)

This might have been spoken by Byron's Manfred: our understanding must be elastic.

The elements to be harmonized must not be confined to the individual; Paul envisages a larger harmony transcending any one person. Even supposing that we admit that his use of 'spirit' appears to emphasize the less physical element at the expense of others when referring to individual men, yet when he is referring to the community we shall find him insisting that it is a 'body'. He emphasizes the element in either that is most likely to be neglected, urging us to think of the 'spirit', or central life-principle, in ourselves, and of the metaphorical 'body' of the community: we are not to regard the community as abstract or remote. 'Body' and 'spirit' are both honoured. Besides, the body to Paul is not limited to the material; like spirit, it suggests a life-principle and organic harmony. 'Body' is generally, though not always, to be contrasted with 'flesh', and may like 'spirit' be related directly to 'life'. Paul draws us to a solid and interlocked marriage-harmony embracing flesh with mind and man with man, in Christ, which is Life.

He writes that his own 'flesh' is rebellious: 'I do what I detest' (*Romans*, VII. 15). Flesh fights against the harmony in which alone the true personality exists:

> That being so, it is not I who do the deed but sin that dwells within me. For in me (that is, in my flesh) no good dwells, I know; the wish is there, but not the power of doing what is right.
>
> (*Romans*, VII. 17)

This he emphasizes and repeats: 'I' is the true personality, 'me' the false one. The flesh alone has no 'good' or 'power' to do right.[1] Christians however are not 'in the flesh' at all but 'in the Spirit', since 'the spirit of God' dwells in them (*Romans*, VIII. 9): each is in the other. The flesh does not exist for them, as such; but he does not belittle the body. The organic harmony, which he calls either body or spirit, is an expression of sacred life. Physical vice is to him abhorrent for the very reason that the body is involved:

> Shun immorality! Any other sin that a man commits is outside the body, but the immoral man sins against his body. Do you not know your body is the temple of the holy Spirit within you — the

---

[1] We must not suppose that the 'sin' working through 'flesh' is limited to ordinary sexual desire. At *Galatians*, V. 13–26 the conflict of flesh with spirit involves a wide range of vices and virtues. Paul may himself have been intermittently troubled by some dangerous, sexually activated, psychological obsession. If so, this may have been the 'thorn in the flesh' or 'angel of Satan' (*2 Corinthians*, XII. 7) that preserved him from self-satisfaction. [1960]

Spirit you have received from God? You are not your own, you were bought for a price; then glorify God with your body.

(1 Corinthians, VI. 18)

Paul deprecates physical vice not because the body is unimportant, but because it is so excessively important, far more so than the 'Law', the 'speculations', the elaborate calendars and ceremonies, the 'genealogies' and intellectualities that raise his wrath. To join yourself with a harlot is to be 'one with her in body' (*1 Corinthians*, VI. 16): therefore it is no small act, but one of consequence.

He varies his remarks on the wider issue of marriage, considering it best in the rush and whirl of this new revelation that Christians avoid it if they can. This, he says, has suited himself, but he makes it clear that there is no 'sin' in marriage (*1 Corinthians*, VII. 28). He is full of a life that leaves him no time for marriages; it is merely a matter of expediency. Even so, marriage is important and both husband and wife must give each other their 'conjugal dues' (*1 Corinthians*, VII. 3). Again, 'Do not withhold sexual intercourse from one another' (*1 Corinthians*, VII. 5). He is sternly opposed to any loosing of the marriage knot, for marriage is divine; and yet again the unmarried are 'anxious about the Lord's affairs', whereas the married Christian has also to 'satisfy' his or her partner and is thus 'torn in two directions' (*1 Corinthians*, VII. 32–4). Paul wants his people to subordinate all to the immediate practical issue, and therefore counsels celibacy. This is his considered advice:

At the same time if any man considers he is not behaving properly to the maid who is his spiritual bride, if his passions are strong and if it must be so, then let him do what he wants – let them be married; it is no sin for him. But the man of firm purpose who has made up his mind, who instead of being forced against his will has determined to himself to keep his maid a spiritual bride – that man will be doing the right thing. Thus both are right alike in marrying

and in refraining from marriage, but he who does not marry will
be found to have done better.   (*1 Corinthians*, VII. 36)

The contrast of 'spiritual' with a specific physical action
in a specific context does not necessarily involve a contrast
with physical life in general. He is tentative, will not commit
himself finally, on marriage. A widow may remarry if she
likes: 'However', he adds, 'she is happier if she remains as
she is', concluding, very modestly for him, 'that is my
opinion' (*1 Corinthians*, VII. 40). He assumes that he is
writing to people who, like himself, are wholly dedicated to
the new revelation; and not only is this revelation not
necessarily opposed to marriage; it is itself a sort of marriage.
In a fine passage (*Ephesians*, V. 21–33) he compares marriage
to the relation between Christ and the Church. The husband
is the head of the wife as Christ is the head of the Christian
community. Christ is the divine Bridegroom. Husbands
must love their wives, for so Christ loves the Church and
would have her stand before him 'in all her glory, with never
a spot or wrinkle or any such flaw, but consecrated and
unblemished'. Husbands must love their wives, 'as their own
bodies'; a man's wife is 'himself', and no man hates his own
flesh but rather 'nourishes and cherishes it'. All of us are
'members' of Christ's 'body', and the old saying that a man
shall 'leave father and mother and cleave to his wife and the
pair shall be one flesh' is 'a profound symbol' concerning
Christ and his Church. Marriage-thought is integral to
Paul's teaching.

His imagery is strongly physical. The new community
is the body of Christ. The old order is the 'shadow', the
new the 'substance' (*Colossians*, II. 17). Abstract intellectualities are contrasted with Christian realism:

Let no one lay down rules for you as he pleases, with regard to
fasting and the cult of angels, presuming on his visions and inflated
by his sensuous notions, instead of keeping in touch with that Head

under whom the entire Body, supplied with joints and sinews and thus compacted, grows with growth divine.

(*Colossians*, II. 18)

Like the vast Eagle and Rose in Dante's *Paradiso* the physical metaphor suggests the organic nature of that greater super-personal life to which man aspires. Man may have to sacrifice his own bodily desires to serve this greater body. Nevertheless, those who 'get the name of wisdom' with their devotions, fasting, and 'rigorous discipline of the body' may be 'of no value', since 'they simply pamper the flesh' (*Colossians*, II. 23). Intellectualism is the concomitant of the sensuous, whereas Paul has his eye on a harmony unifying mind and flesh in what he calls either the 'spirit' or the 'body of Christ':

For He, Christ, is the head, and under him, as the entire Body is welded together and compacted by every joint with which it is supplied, the due activity of each part enables the Body to grow and build itself up in love.   (*Ephesians*, IV. 15)

Nor is this 'body' to be dissociated from Paul's worship of the individual's body:

The body is not meant for immorality but for the Lord, and the Lord is for the body; and the God who raised the Lord will also raise us by his power. Do you not know your bodies are members of Christ? Am I to take Christ's members and devote them to a harlot?   (*I Corinthians*, VI. 13)

The New Testament is the very poetry of incarnation superseding the 'elemental spirits' against which St Paul inveighs (*Colossians*, II. 8, 20).[1] We must not be led astray with words: often we must put 'life' for 'spirit'. The confusion reflects the experience of incarnation which is the message of Christianity; for body and spirit, man and God, are no

[1] These are however associated with traditions, formalities and rituals, and 'spirits' appears to be a doubtful translation. Compare *Galatians*, IV. 3, 9–10; and see p. 333 below. [1960]

longer properly distinct. Life-essences, life-processes, are everywhere suggested:

> I betrothed you as a chaste maiden to present you to your one
> husband Christ . . .   (2 *Corinthians*, XI. 2)

Those who would find evil in God's plenty are themselves evil. Paul attacks the false intellectualisms of teachers who see evil of their own making, men

> . . . who prohibit marriage and insist on abstinence from foods which
> God created for believing men, who understand the Truth, to par-
> take of with thanksgiving. Anything God has created is good, and
> nothing is to be tabooed — provided it is eaten with thanksgiving,
> for then it is consecrated by the prayer said over it.
>   (*1 Timothy*, IV. 3)

The New Testament presents the New Creation, or rather the old seen by eyes opened in a new sanity by men possessing a new life. So 'there is a new creation whenever a man comes to be in Christ; what is old is gone, the new has come' (2 *Corinthians*, V. 17).

To such there is no death. Paul unswervingly asserts immortality. This immortality is not ghostly: sometimes it seems 'spiritual', in the modern sense; sometimes 'bodily'. Whatever it be, it is real, super-physical perhaps but in no sense an abstraction. Here is the immortal life on earth:

> But we all mirror the glory of the Lord with face unveiled, and so
> we are being transformed into the same likeness as himself, passing
> from one glory to another . . .   (2 *Corinthians*, III. 18)

'The slight trouble of the passing hour' will result in a 'solid glory past all comparison' (2 *Corinthians*, IV. 17). Sometimes Paul is highly poetical and figurative, imagining how the Lord will descend from Heaven and the dead and living rise (*1 Thessalonians*, IV. 16–17). This he seems to expect during his own lifetime, but his words express a truth;

the truth that a union of Heaven and Earth was being accomplished day by day as Christianity upthrust itself into life.

In the great passage on immortality in his first Epistle to the Corinthians, he carefully elaborates his conviction, giving it coherent form. Christ's resurrection is a fact. He was 'reaped' (XV. 23) by the divine Harvester. Yet some will ask 'how do the dead rise?' And 'what kind of body have they when they come?' This is his answer:

> What you sow never comes to life unless it dies. And what you sow is not the body that is to be; it is a mere grain of wheat, for example, or some other seed. God gives it a body as he pleases, gives each kind of seed a body of its own. (XV. 36)

Animals differ, life-forms vary on earth and in the skies:

> There are heavenly bodies and also earthly bodies, but the splendour of the heavenly is one thing and the splendour of the earthly is another. There is a splendour of the sun and a splendour of the moon and a splendour of the stars – for one star differs from another in splendour. So with the resurrection of the dead:

> what is sown is mortal,
>   what rises is immortal;
> sown inglorious,
>   it rises in glory;
> sown in weakness,
>   it rises in power;
> sown an animate body,
>   it rises a spiritual body.
> (XV. 40)

And so on to his magnificent conclusion:

> Here is a secret truth for you: not all of us are to die, but all of us are to be changed – changed in a moment, in the twinkling of an eye, at the last trumpet-call. The trumpet will sound, the dead will rise imperishable, and we shall be changed. For this perishing body

must be invested with the imperishable, and this mortal body invested with immortality; and when this mortal body has been invested with immortality, then the saying of Scripture will be realized,

> Death is swallowed up in victory,
> O Death, where is your victory?
> O Death, where is your sting?
>   (XV. 51)

Typically, after this glorious rhapsody, he starts, 'With regard to the collection for the saints . . .' Never was there a more practical visionary. Notice his metaphors from sowing, the animal world, the sun, moon and stars; see how there are first two kinds of 'body', and then again how the immortal body is as an addition or vesture to the mortal, including, not rejecting, it.[1] All these are variable expressions of his one central conviction that Jesus Christ 'has put down death and brought life and immortality to light by the gospel' (2 Timothy, I. 10).

Death is not to Paul an unbodied, nakedly spectral, existence; the immortal life is not ghostly. This is clear from a less colourous, more contemplative passage:

> I know that if this earthly tent of mine is taken down, I get a home from God, made by no human hands, eternal in the heavens. It makes me sigh, indeed, this yearning to be under the cover of my heavenly habitation, since I am sure that once so covered I shall not be 'naked' at the hour of death. I do sigh within this tent of mine with heavy anxiety – not that I want to be stripped, no, but to be under the cover of the other, to have my mortal element absorbed by life.   (2 Corinthians, V. 1)

He craves not less, but more life. Exact questionings are vain. 'Body' and 'spirit' are both abstract concepts; it is

---

[1] But the Authorized Version is perhaps preferable: 'For this corruptible must put on incorruption, and this mortal must put on immortality.' [1960]

unwise to reason too insistently; and Paul bases his words on immediate experience. This is how he writes of his original vision:

> I know a man in Christ who fourteen years ago was caught up to the third heaven. In the body or out of the body? That I do not know: God knows. I simply know that in the body or out of the body (God knows which) this man was caught up to paradise and heard sacred secrets which no human lips can repeat.
>
> (*2 Corinthians*, XII. 2)

To Paul the body is anyway afire with spirit; he sees it with the erotic consciousness of a lover; it burns, flames, splendid with divine life. Through Christ we 'live and move in the new sphere of Life' (*Romans*, VI. 4); we have been 'brought from death to life' (*Romans*, VI. 13); and though 'the entire creation sighs and throbs with pain', we await and expect 'the redemption of the body that means our full sonship' (*Romans*, VIII. 22). The God of the New Testament is the wondrous God of Birth and Creation 'who makes the dead live and calls into being what does not exist' (*Romans*, IV. 17); and these two attributes are finally the same.

We must beware of trying to understand Paul's message on either life on earth or future immortality without giving primary attention to his symbols. He is a visionary; his imagery is exact, his thought chaotic and paradoxical. Christ has brought a death-vanquishing 'life' to men; this life is a marriage and man's body sacred. Ordinary marriage may be inexpedient because the life and immortality he preaches is itself a splendid marriage, and the two marriages are so similar that they may become rivals, the similarity being clearly apparent when we find him using the one as a 'symbol' (p. 135) for the other. He preaches a life which is love and a love which is immortality. He calls man to universal marriage and universal love in Christ: 'Above all you must be loving, for love is the link of the perfect life' (*Colossians*, III. 14).

St Paul is not aiming primarily at poetic power. He has a resplendent gift of phrase, but he does not set out to write poetry. His aim is to convince and convert, and next to organize the new forces whose future is in his charge. His theoretical arguments spring not from love of theory but from a burning desire to explain what to him is a patent fact: he is forced to fight theory with theory. Sometimes he is accused of falsely intellectualizing Christianity and taking us away from the purity of Jesus' teaching. Nothing could be more unjust: he writes hurriedly and anxiously, forced to oppose his pupils' pseudo-intellectualism by passionate reasoning; he is always practical, transfixing the heart of his subject and hurrying on without loss of time. There is nothing of the pedant in him: he writes from an imaginative centre and loathes the arbitrary rules which a theoretical religion or ethic imposes. All is subservient to his one burning faith in the living Christ.

III

Paul's writing makes slight concession to sobriety, and he is comparatively poor in the gentler naturalisms which we find in the Gospels. Eternal life is a harvest to which mortal existence is a 'seed' (p. 138 above); his missionary work is a 'planting' and God the power that makes the seed grow (*I Corinthians*, III. 6); and he has an extended passage comparing the Christian community to a wild olive tree (*Romans*, XI. 16–24). But these are widely scattered. The contrast between Paul and James is interesting. The Epistle of James, though brief, contains imagery of the 'surge of the sea', the 'flower of the grass', 'scorching wind', 'first-fruits', 'rank growth' (I. 6–21), bridles and horses, ships and their rudders, a forest lighted by a spark, 'beast and bird', 'creeping

animals and creatures marine', fresh and 'brackish' water,
the fig-tree, the vine (III. 3–12), mist (IV. 14), harvest, the
farmer, the autumn and spring rains (V. 4, 7). This reminds
us of the Gospels. Paul's characterizing effects are more
sumptuous:

> Wherever I go, thank God, he makes my life a constant pageant
> of triumph in Christ, diffusing the perfume of his knowledge every-
> where by me.   (2 Corinthians, II. 14)

'Pageant', 'triumph', 'perfume': a glorified language for
the glorious revelation, the 'vital fragrance', as he calls it,
'that makes for life' (2 Corinthians, II. 16). His vision is
radiant.

He is vividly humanistic. He sees primarily not nature
but man, and man transfigured, stepping free from death,
radiant, of divine stature, as in Shelley's *Prometheus Unbound*.
The finest passages in the Epistles burn with a white-gold
brilliance of light and glory, housed in solid imagery,
'dazzling' like his own vision (*Acts*, XXVI. 13), reiterating
his favourite words 'life', 'body', 'Christ', driving in the one
blinding intuition with phrase after hammering phrase. His
grandest statements, if gathered into an anthology, would
lack variety, subtlety, colour; he is no master of light and
shade. As he says himself, he preaches the Gospel 'with no
fine rhetoric, lest the cross of Christ should lose its power'
(*1 Corinthians*, I. 17). And yet the power of that Cross carves
out its own resplendent rhetoric: the Gospel so blazes in his
heart that it makes of his eloquence a golden trumpet, the
while his faith splashes the page with liquid flame. 'Power'
and 'glory' are favourite words, and the power and glory he
envisages are splendorously bright. It is the same with the
author of the Epistle to the Hebrews, whether Paul or
another: there Christ is imaged as 'reflecting God's bright
glory and stamped with God's own character' (*Hebrews*, I. 3).
All Christians, says Paul, must 'shine like stars in a dark

world' (*Philippians*, II. 15). But this glory-imagery is never loosed from concrete symbolism:

> For God who said, 'Light shall shine out of darkness', has shone within my heart to illuminate men with the knowledge of God's glory in the face of Christ.   (*2 Corinthians*, IV. 6)

'The face of Christ'; he is solidly humanistic. Now he sees darkly but soon he will see Christ 'face to face' (*1 Corinthians*, XIII. 12). He finely asserts that heritage of incarnation which from the start differentiates Christianity from other religions. In the Epistle to the Hebrews the Christ is superior to the angels (*Hebrews*, I. 1–14). Paul's vision may be limited to the one blazing fact of his 'Christ', and this he may reiterate in 'body' and 'glory' symbolism till we are a little tired, but the Christ-experience, however brilliant it may be, is yet vividly realized at every turn, the image solid and compact from line to line. He powerfully contrasts his own language with that of those who talk mystically 'of divine secrets in the spirit' (*1 Corinthians*, XIV. 1–19). His vision is proudly humanistic; he sees man invested with immortal strength. Here is his call to battle:

> Hold your ground, tighten the belt of truth about your loins, wear integrity as your coat of mail, and have your feet shod with the stability of the gospel of peace; above all, take faith as your shield, to enable you to quench all the fire-tipped darts flung by the evil one, put on salvation as your helmet, and take the Spirit as your sword . . .   (*Ephesians*, VI. 14)

The words ring with metallic clangour and glint like shining steel. But his militant rhetoric owes sole allegiance to imperial love:

> I may speak with the tongues of men and of angels, but if I have no love, I am a noisy gong or a clanging cymbal.
>   (*1 Corinthians*, XIII. 1)

From love his utterance gains its power.

Even his opponents admit that his letters are 'weighty and telling' (*2 Corinthians*, X. 10). Weighty indeed: at his best, his words are rounded and heavy, like ingots of gold. In splendid phrase he images the one absolute and eternal principle of Life:

> ... that blessed and only Sovereign, King of kings and Lord of lords, who alone has immortality, who dwells in light that none can approach, whom no man has ever seen or can see.
>
> (*1 Timothy*, VI. 15)

With such glory his pages abound. Had he so chosen he could have been a yet mightier poet than he was; instead he incarnated his poetic might in organizing the Body of Christ, in planting the immortal tree. Some of the grandest poetry the world has known is struck off, as it were by chance, to explain a difficulty, illuminate a doubt. Effortless, he writes only of what he knows, of what he has seen. Though his letters shadow in splendid speech a grandeur and a glory beyond words, his primary aim is to teach, not to write. Therein is his heart and purpose. For his pupils are to be his living poetry, 'written not with ink but with the spirit of the living God', not on 'tablets of stone' but graven on the more enduring tablets 'of the human heart' (*2 Corinthians*, III. 3). He works for one end only: he would have all men see and enter the radiance and the glory that awaits their birth in Christ. He would have them wake to their new-found heritage of life.

IX

THE PIONEER OF LIFE:
AN ESSAY ON THE GOSPELS

> We do it wrong, being so majestical,
> To offer it the show of violence;
> For it is, as the air, invulnerable,
> And our vain blows malicious mockery.
>
> (*Hamlet*, I. i. 143)

I

SINCE the fourth Gospel, known as 'the Gospel accord-ing to St John',[1] reads like an interpretation of the others, it will be a convenient point for our start. Paul's life and letters show us Christianity attaining a practical foothold. Though he is himself very practical, Paul's approach to Christ is mystical: 'Christ' is less a person to him than a condition; from his relation to Jesus is born anew the Christ, and wherever this marriage-union is consummated the Christ is risen in man. John is more strictly theological; he drama-tizes the mystic relation in objective terms; he is as much interested in the relation of Jesus to God as Paul in that of Jesus the Christ to man. In the first Epistle of John Jesus is the 'Logos of Life' (I. i) and John's Gospel starts:

> The Logos existed in the very beginning,
> the Logos was with God,
> the Logos was divine.

And

> . . . this life was the Light for men:
> amid the darkness the Light shone,
> but the darkness did not master it.
>
> (*John*, I. 1–5)

---

[1] For simplicity I shall refer to the author as 'John'. The authorship of the Fourth Gospel and of the First Epistle of John is discussed in my Epilogue.

Though John's narrative contains important incidents not found elsewhere, its most striking emphases are theological and interpretative. It has a peculiar way of making its hero self-explanatory: Jesus is always interpreting himself. This is a legitimate artistic process: Shakespeare's heroes may likewise be regarded as 'interpreting' themselves and John's Gospel is a necessary link in our understanding.

Jesus interprets his own imagery: 'I am the real Vine' he says, 'and my father is the vine-dresser' (*John*, XV. 1). The vine-image has less rights on its own: to John it is 'merely a metaphor'. When Jesus meets a Samaritan woman drawing water, he asks for a drink and says:

> If you knew what is the free gift of God and who is asking you for a drink, you would have asked him instead, and he would have given you 'living' water.   (*John*, IV. 10)

This he expands and explains:

> Anyone who drinks this water will be thirsty again, but anyone who drinks the water I shall give him will never thirst any more; the water I shall give him will turn into a spring of water welling up to eternal life.   (*John*, IV. 13)

Jesus translates his metaphors in terms of 'eternal life'. When the disciples ask him to eat he says that he has food of which they 'know nothing' (*John*, IV. 32). This food is the will of God. Then:

> Look round, I tell you; see, the fields are white for harvesting! The reaper is already getting his wages and harvesting for eternal life.   (*John*, IV. 35)

He counsels men to 'work for no perishing food, but for that lasting food which means eternal life'; God gives the heavenly 'bread' and 'life' and Jesus himself is the 'bread of life', dispelling hunger and thirst (*John*, VI. 27–35). Again:

> I am the living bread which has come down from heaven; if anyone eats of this bread, he will live for ever.   (*John*, VI. 51)

The interpretative method is maintained. Jesus compares himself to food, telling his followers that they must 'eat the flesh of the Son of Man and drink his blood' (*John*, VI. 53) if they are to have life. The author appears to be dramatizing his own reaction to Jesus' allusive speech and the tone is theological and abstract far beyond Jesus' words in the Synoptics. Life-symbols of the 'vine', 'harvest', 'water' and 'bread' are explicitly related to 'eternal life'.

It is the same with 'sight' and 'light'. When Jesus heals a blind man he draws a moral from the act:

> Then said Jesus, 'It is for judgement that I have come into this world, to make the sightless see, to make the seeing blind.' On hearing this the Pharisees who were beside him asked, 'And are we blind?' Jesus replied, 'If you were blind, you would not be guilty; but, as it is, you claim to have sight – and so your sin remains.'
>
> (*John*, IX. 39)

Physical sight symbolizes another 'sight' for which there is no exact name. There is much light-imagery, similarly interpreted. We have already quoted the opening passage where the Logos of God is equated with light. Jesus calls John the Baptist 'a burning and a shining lamp' (*John*, V. 35) and says of himself:

> I am the light of the world: he who follows me will not walk in darkness, he will enjoy the light of life.   (*John*, VIII. 12)

The image is emphatic:

> Then Jesus said to them, 'The Light will shine among you for a little longer yet; walk while you have the Light, that the darkness may not overtake you. He who walks in the dark does not know where he is going. While you have the Light believe in the Light, that you may be sons of the Light.'   (*John*, XII. 35)

Soon after he interprets:

I have come as light into the world, that no one who believes in me
may remain in the dark.   (*John*, XII. 46)

Light is vivid.

At great length Jesus explains his sonship to God, using
realistic terms about coming 'down from Heaven' (*John*, VI.
38). He is the 'good Shepherd' who is to give up his life
for his sheep (*John*, X. 14–15). He acts and speaks at every
turn with full consciousness of his mission and its implications. The result is a theological document, interpretative
rather than narrative, intellectual rather than pictorial.
Remembering the importance attached here to light, we may
again quote Blake's pregnant lines from *Auguries of Innocence*:

> God appears, and God is light,
> To those poor souls who dwell in night;
> But does a human form display
> To those who dwell in realms of day.

It seems that John writes from a consciousness nearer to the
intellectual darkness than Paul, who, glorious and shining
as his figurative language may be, is always richly humanistic. Paul presents a passionate experience of the mystic
Christ; John a meditative and theological interpretation of
Jesus as Son of God. Each sees a different facet of the central
reality. I have however emphasized only one peculiar quality
in the Gospel, and this does not do it justice.[1] Moreover this
interpretative quality is not a weakness; it is invaluable. Our
own interpretations of the Synoptics must always owe it a
debt: indeed, it directly points our course. For John is
especially receptive to the symbolic qualities of Jesus' talk
and actions; to these he calls our attention; and following
him we shall devote an especial care to the imaginative and
poetic colourings in the other Gospels.

[1] Other elements are handled in my Epilogue (pp. 302–15).

II

I shall use the Synoptics together, treating them as a single pattern and occasionally drawing again from the fourth Gospel.

The life of Jesus is told in narratives which are both convincingly factual and artistically significant. It pursues an unswerving tragic rhythm, showing an individual's clash with his environment. Generally in drama the tragic hero, though conceived on a grander scale than his community, can be said to fail partly at least through some fault. Here the protagonist is in every way a more perfect being than his world, the usual tragic relation being to this extent reversed. Jesus' life distils the quintessence of human reality: his story presents an absolute, finished and complete life in harmony with a supreme ethic; that is, with the innermost principle of life itself. It has accordingly a purpose and a direction which makes it clash with its environment; it is a life-force in a death-world.

A sublime imagination interlocks with our narratives. Single events possess significance in their own right leaving pictures printed lastingly on the mind's eye. They possess the curious quality of seeming to exist poetically independently of any verbal expression; the fact itself is poetical. Such are the Journey of the Magi, led by the Star of Bethlehem; the appearance of the Angel to the Shepherds, announcing the wondrous Birth; the Baby in the manger; the Massacre of the Innocents, with evil and tyrannic death opposing birth and creation, yet failing to destroy the Child who is to slay evil in the name of life. The description of the boy Jesus disputing with theologians has a peculiar fascination, while reminding us that all true originality in any field comes not to destroy but rather to fulfil the central tradition. There is a universal quality about the mission of John the Baptist as forerunner. It is the way things happen: great movements cast their shadows before them, they have their precursors, their voices crying in the wilderness (*Matthew*, III. 3). Jesus' fasting and temptation in the desert are likewise universal, all high endeavour being conditioned by a similar solitariness, a similar rejection of cheap splendours, a similar refusal to leave the pinnacle whose height is either a giddy fear or a lonely and loveless exaltation. The miracles, as when Jesus walks on the waters and stills the raging winds and seas, have symbolic overtones. His life is interthreaded with sublime experience; the Voice of God claims him as a Son at his Baptism, and when he is transfigured on the mountain the Voice again pronounces an assurance and an acknowledgement. The Last Supper is a deathless memory, the prayer in Gethsemane contains all that a tragic poet need learn, all disloyalty is summed in the thirty pieces of silver received by Judas, the Crucifixion encloses and transcends the furthest agony that mortal life may endure. After the Crucifixion there is an earthquake, the sun is blackened, the Temple's veil torn asunder. Symbolism is pregnant. The number three recurs. We have the three magicians who bring their gifts to the divine Child, the three temptations, the three disciples who witness the transfiguration, and their suggestion that three tabernacles be built for Jesus, Moses and Elijah. There are the three crowings of the cock, and the three crucifixions. Three women are named by Mark and John as attending the Crucifixion and three according to Luke find Jesus' grave deserted. Mountains are important: Jesus is tempted on a high mountain, he preaches on a mountain, he is transfigured on Mount Hermon and visits the Hill of Olives. The crucifixion is on a hill. The wondrous life is framed by a divine birth and a bodily resurrection.

These symbolic pictures are somehow staggeringly impressive without being sensational. Most are very quietly narrated and the colourings are subdued: some are dark with a dark beauty, others light with a beauteous light. But, whether happy or unhappy in suggestion, they are all magical; they are wondrously symbolic and wondrously real at once, like Keats' poetry, the more magical for its calm. We have no fiery excitations nor apocalyptic splendours, but the Star of Bethlehem shines in the frosty night; the streets of Jerusalem are strewn with foliage, as for a king's entry; and a young man, or what looks like a young man, stands beside an empty tomb.

Impressions of life and gentleness interthread a dark background. Nature-references are mostly pleasant. Jesus as a child is brought to make a ritual sacrifice of 'a pair of turtle doves or two young pigeons' (*Luke*, II. 24); doves are sold in the Temple (*Mark*, XI. 15); the Holy Spirit descends like a dove (*Luke*, III. 22). Gentleness is transmitted by pastoral impressions, for the flock is a unity, guarded, guided and fed by the shepherd. The Angel announces Jesus' birth to shepherds; Jesus is the 'good shepherd' and 'feed my sheep' a reiterated command (*John*, X. 14; XXI. 15–17). Fishes blend naturally with pastoral. Many of the disciples are fishermen; Jesus performs miracles with fishes both when he feeds the multitude and when he miraculously fills the nets that had been cast to no avail. Fishes, perhaps partly from Gospel associations, are impregnated with positive beauty in many poets. The paradisal connotations of still water are present when Jesus and his disciples walk by the shores of Galilee. Fruitful nature is a dominant colouring. When Jesus and his disciples are 'crossing the cornfields' the disciples 'pulled some ears of corn and ate them, rubbing them in their hands' (*Luke*, VI. 1). Zacchaeus climbs a sycamore tree to see Jesus (*Luke*, XIX. 4), and leaves are strewn before Jesus on his final entry into Jerusalem (*Mark*, XI. 8). He loves to retire to the Hill of Olives or 'the Olive orchard' (*Luke*, XIX. 29). According to John, he was buried in an 'orchard' (*John*, XIX. 41). Food is often mentioned. In the desert, Jesus suffers hunger and is tempted to turn stones

to bread; he performs miracles with food, there is the festival
of the Passover and his supper with his followers. He prays
in Gethsemane that the cup may pass from him, he is offered
'wine mixed with bitters' before the Crucifixion (*Matthew*,
XXVII. 34), and is later given a sponge 'soaked in vinegar'
(*Matthew*, XXVII. 48).

Beyond animal-life, nature-suggestion and food, we have
colourings drawn from human civilization. There are the
flash of coins, the thirty silver pieces received by Judas, the
coin with Caesar's impression, the money-changers in the
Temple, the woman who comes to anoint Jesus with perfume from an alabaster flask. Garments are vivid. Jesus is
robed with a scarlet mantle and crowned in mockery by the
Roman soldiers, who later draw lots for his raiment. Suffering and nakedness are often found together in poetry. Here
nakedness is associated with madness, clothes with sanity
(*Luke*, VIII. 27, 35). There is the young man who flies
naked at the arrest of Jesus (*Mark*, XIV. 52). Jesus is crucified in naked suffering; afterwards his body is wrapped in
'clean linen' (*Matthew*, XXVII. 59). The angel at Jesus'
tomb is radiantly clothed (*Matthew*, XXVIII. 3).

These are a few scattered examples. The Gospels are
poetical in word and incident. The events shine as though
from an inward lustre.

III

Jesus' parables may be read as poetry and before we draw
morals from them we shall do well to tune our minds to
their poetic quality. This is his teaching:

> Are not five sparrows sold for two farthings? Yet not one of them
> is forgotten by God. But the very hairs on your head are all num-
> bered; fear not, you are worth far more than sparrows.
>
> (*Luke*, XII. 6; also *Matthew*, X. 29–31)

Or again:

> Look at the crows! They neither sow nor reap, no storehouse nor
> granary have they, and yet God feeds them. How much more are
> you worth than birds?
> (*Luke*, XII. 24; and see *Matthew*, VI. 26)

Even so, he knows only too well the cruel severance of man
from the instinctive world:

> The foxes have their holes, the wild birds have their nests, but the
> Son of Man has nowhere to lay his head.
> (*Matthew*, VIII. 20; *Luke*, IX. 58)

Birds are love-images, they are gentle, peaceful creatures.
Filled by a univeral love, Jesus cries to the cities of the world:

> O Jerusalem, Jerusalem! slaying the prophets and stoning those
> who have been sent to you! How often I would fain have gathered
> your children as a fowl gathers her brood under her wings!
> (*Matthew*, XXIII. 37)

Jesus' thoughts are deeply tinged with natural and pastoral
imagery. Birds suggest nature's sweetness, happy flight and
nesting love; flocks of sheep suggest concord and a union
between the animal and human kingdoms. The scattering
of a flock may be an image of severe unrest:

> You will all be disconcerted, for it is written: I will strike at the
> shepherd and the sheep will be scattered.   (*Mark*, XIV. 27)

Luke gives us the full beauty of the image in all its delicacy:

> Fear not, you little flock, for your Father is delighted to give you
> the Realm.   (*Luke*, XII. 32)

The joy of Heaven over a sinner's repentance is similar to
that of a man who loses a sheep and leaves his whole flock to
search for the lost one. Finding it, 'he puts it on his shoulders
with joy', and when he gets home he calls his friends
together, and 'Rejoice with me', he says to them, 'for I have
found the sheep I lost' (*Luke*, XV. 4–6).

This is a typical parable: all that such pastoral imagery can do for us, it does. Before reasoning too closely on God and man we should think first about the owner and his sheep, his care and labour, his skill to know each of his flock, the one from the other; and the union and dependence which a flock denotes. Thinking like this we are to enjoy the parable and then, our minds filled, turn to the abstract application. Jesus' language is poetry: the poetry comes first, and this he elaborates, but the application he leaves vague, couched often in the most usual terms such as 'Heaven', 'God' and so on. He is a poet before being a theologian. Often he leaves his story uninterpreted. What is new in his teaching can be seen from this parable. He does not say merely that a repentant sinner is forgiven by God. Rather his statement is this: the universal love that beats at the heart of life is like a shepherd-love, and man to that wisdom is as a sheep in a vast flock, skill-less in his master's providence, easily and foolishly lost, and yet, if deepest care can do it, sought and found at the last. Poetry is not parasitic on the teaching; rather there is a teaching that flowers from the poetry. Jesus thinks naturally through pictorial and emotional associations. The Christian flock is to be compared with sheep or lambs; the disciples are to go out as 'lambs among wolves' (*Luke*, X. 3); Jesus pities the people, 'harassed and dejected', seeing them as 'sheep without a shepherd' (*Matthew*, IX. 36).

He is always thinking in terms of fertility. Even when he describes a selfish man, his tale may have a harvest richness: 'A rich man's estate bore heavy crops', so many that he had no room for the corn, but he builds a great granary and determines to 'eat, drink, and be merry', forgetting that death can cut short his joy (*Luke*, XII. 16–20). Such a man thinks crops are only to be possessed; instead he might have learnt from them and made his own life creative as the waving corn. Men are as a wondrous grass, earth-born, sun-ripened: if God clothes the grass 'which blooms to-day in the field, and is thrown to-morrow into the furnace', how much more will he regard the needs of man? (*Luke*, XII. 28–32). Man's life is a corn to ripen and store eternal granaries. The Lord of Creation is a farmer seeming to a wrong-headed servant to reap where he never sowed, gathering where he never winnowed (*Matthew*, XXV. 24). The words of divine wisdom are like seeds thrown on different soils by a sower, some dying as soon as sown, some maturing, and where the ground is good bringing forth richness an hundredfold (*Luke*, VIII. 5–8). Again:

> It is with the Realm of God as when a man has sown seed on earth; he sleeps at night and rises by day, and the seed sprouts and shoots up – he knows not how.   (*Mark*, IV. 26)

How simply and yet how masterfully the mystery of creative life is put before us. These images are not random illustrations; they are themselves more important than their application. Or rather they and their application are one; for laborious intellectual applications and interpretations, necessary though they may be, falsify the reality being expressed. The true good is like organic life; man must not be directed by laws only, by systems of ethic; these alone are powerless. Rather his deeds and thoughts must be themselves creative, so that he acts and thinks from the creative centre, the life-centre, the centre from which he lives, his words and deeds out-flowering from the great life which his very existence expresses:

> If you had faith the size of a grain of mustard-seed, you could say to this hill, 'Move from here to there', and remove it would; nothing would be impossible for you.
>   (*Matthew*, XVII. 20; and see *Luke*, XVII. 6)

Man must let his life create itself in thought and deed, as the life in the seed upthrusts and burgeons into bloom. The life that Jesus plants among men is to grow 'like a grain of mustard-seed' till it be a tree 'so large that the wild birds come and roost in its branches' (*Matthew*, XIII. 31–2). When the Realm of Heaven is grown to its full height, in that far summer angelic visitors may well find their pleasure in its sheltering leaves; and yet how much even that interpretation wrongs its context; for Jesus speaks not with any Pauline splendour, but with a poetry more sacred.

Man is as a tree known by its fruits:

> Either make the tree good and its fruit good, or make the tree rotten and its fruit rotten; for the tree is known by its fruit.
>
> (*Matthew*, XII. 33)

We do not gather grapes from thorns or figs from thistles (*Matthew*, VII. 16–20). A man who owns a fig-tree in his vineyard comes to gather fruit, but finding none he tells the vinedresser to have it cut down. He replies,

> Leave it for this year, sir, till I dig round about it and put in manure. Then it may bear fruit next year. If not, you can have it cut down.
>
> (*Luke*, XIII. 8)

This is a lovely parable: the fig-tree is so sympathetically drawn, so amazingly realized in so few words, its fate so strangely weighted with meaning. The parable is easily interpreted, but we shall do well to accept it first without interpretative associations, letting them next gather round it, or rather flower out from it, till the total meaning is born.

The vine or fig-tree may be human, or man may be the vineyard labourer:

> For the Realm of Heaven is like a householder who went out early in the morning to hire labourers for his vineyard . . .
>
> (*Matthew*, XX. 1)

Notice how curiously the comparison is made. The 'householder' here is 'God'. So either the Realm is itself God or the comparison applies rather to the whole story than to the householder alone. Both alternatives are ultimately the same, but the second is our best approach: often in these parables the 'realm' is like, not a person, but a drama, and many a story of other poets must be allowed to serve a similar purpose. Jesus preaches not only a poetic gospel, but also a gospel of poetry: the story-rhythm, the story-picture, presents a certain quality, union with which is our entrance to the Realm. The Realm is a state of love, of growth, of luxuriance, wherein we must take our part as labourers tending the vine of life, or as ourselves the vines unfurling to the sun, if we would bear fruit. The world is a vineyard whose master has two sons, one of whom promised to work in it and did not, while the other, first refusing, afterwards obeyed (*Matthew*, XXI. 28–31). This is followed by another vineyard parable:

> There was a householder who planted a vineyard, put a fence round it, dug a wine-vat inside it, and built a watch tower: then he leased it to vinedressers and went abroad . . .   (*Matthew*, XXI. 33)

The master sends messenger after messenger to his vineyard, and last his own son. All life is as a vine or fig-tree:

> Let the fig-tree teach you a parable. As soon as its branches turn soft and put out leaves, you know summer is at hand; so, whenever you see all this happen, you may be sure He is at hand, at the very door.   (*Matthew*, XXIV. 32)

We are directed to creative understanding, creative life, in language itself creative. These passages are never rhetorical, never resonant, never decorative:

> Look how the lilies neither spin nor weave; and yet, I tell you, even Solomon in all his grandeur was never robed like one of them.
> (*Luke*, XII. 27)

The very words live the gospel that they preach.

Though so often addressing us in naturalistic terms, Jesus' life-gospel does not exclude images from human civilization. There are many references to riches and raiment.

Jesus repudiates excessive desire for wealth. Money is relative, not absolute: a poor widow who offers a few farthings
at the temple shows more virtue than the wealthy who con-
tribute larger sums (*Mark*, XII. 41–4). When a master
engages labourers for his vineyard and pays them each a
shilling irrespective of the work they have done (*Matthew*,
XX. 1–16), the story has wide implications, since we cannot
rate anything worth having in figures. However, in a story
of less realistic suggestion two debtors, owing different
amounts, are forgiven equally, and he who owes the most is
the most grateful (*Luke*, VII. 41–3). Forgiveness of debts
is a favourite thought: a rich man forgives a debtor three
million pounds and that debtor next fails to forgive a brother-
servant owing him twenty (*Matthew*, XVIII. 21–35).
Avarice and lack of charity are evil: Dives is to be blamed
for letting Lazarus suffer (*Luke*, XVI. 19–31), and the rich
man who stores his garners, forgetting death, is a fool
(*Luke*, XII. 16–20). But the Good Samaritan pays two
shillings to help a complete stranger (*Luke*, X. 30–5). In
another parable a master gives his servants various sums of
gold, and praises and rewards those who increase the wealth
in their charge. The moral is:

> For to everyone who has shall more be given and richly given; but
> from him who has nothing, even what he has shall be taken.
>
> (*Matthew*, XXV. 29)

This is best understood in terms of growth: to one who has
in him the principle of growth and creation true wealth
comes unasked; without that principle, impoverishment must
ensue. These parables, though often superficially contra-
dictory, suggest nevertheless that while money may be a
means to life, the only true wealth is life itself, not mechanic-
ally but organically controlled. Debts, accounts, exact
amounts – these take us nowhere. Sun and rain are for the
just and the unjust alike (*Matthew*, V. 45). At the extreme,

we have a difficult parable where praise is accorded to the Factor who, about to be dismissed, makes friends for himself by falsifying the accounts of his master's clients (*Luke*, XVI. 1–9); with the conclusion that 'mammon' is to be used, even though the use of it seem evil, in order to make friends for us in 'the eternal abodes' (XVI. 9). The deeper life-realities come first, and all else is to be used in their service. Jesus' frequent use of money-illustrations itself gives money some poetic justification as a provisional expedient, though it must not be allowed autonomy. Let all be flexible, swaying to the needs of the hour and the breath of love.

In the young man who would be perfect yet fails when told to sell his possessions and give the proceeds to the poor (*Matthew*, XIX. 16–22), we have an example of the way in which riches may bar man from eternal life. 'Rich folk' are in danger (*Matthew*, XIX. 24; *Luke*, VI. 24); they may be forfeiting the 'riches of God' (*Luke*, XII. 21), the 'true riches' (*Luke*. XVI. 11). The symbol is developed:

> The Realm of Heaven is like treasure hidden in a field; the man who finds it hides it and in his delight goes and sells all he possesses and buys that field.
> Again, the Realm of Heaven is like a trader in search of fine pearls; when he finds a single pearl of high price, he is off to sell all he possesses and buy it. (*Matthew*, XIII. 44)

Money is desirable as a means to life, for life is what all desire, but since too often the means are confused with the end, money is to be the currency of little affairs, while the true search is for essential life. We are not to store up treasures on earth, for such are transient; moth and rust corrode, thieves break in and steal; rather should we store our treasure in eternal coffers (*Matthew*, VI. 19). 'Rich' is the 'reward in Heaven' blossoming from the true life (*Luke*, VI. 23, 35). Caesar's coin may be paid to Caesar; the Realm demands a more stable currency (*Mark*, XII. 17). When money is spilt out, however recklessly, by a pure devotion, the waste is blameless. Jesus will not reprove the woman who comes 'with an alabaster flask of pure nard perfume' to anoint him, even though it might have been sold for 'three hundred shillings' to give to the poor (*Mark*, XIV. 3–9).

Clothes, like money, are rooted in man's civilization. Dives in his worldly luxury wears 'purple and fine linen' (*Luke*, XVI. 19); the scribes 'like to walk about in long robes' (*Mark*, XII. 38); but men ought not to trouble so much about what they put on, for 'the body is something more than clothes' (*Luke*, XII. 23) and Solomon in his robes cannot match the vesture of the lily (*Matthew*, VI. 29; *Luke*, XII. 27). However, the Prodigal is given his father's 'best robe' (*Luke*, XV. 22) and a 'wedding-robe' is important in one of the parables (*Matthew*, XXII. 11–12). Clothes may be symbols of life:

> I was a stranger and you entertained me, I was unclothed and you clothed me.   (*Matthew*, XXV. 35)

Jesus uses the metaphor of a new patch and an old coat to illustrate his life-gospel (*Matthew*, IX. 16). As with money, we have two directions: as a means to life, our symbol is good, but when it ceases to be a symbol of life it becomes dangerous.

Jesus' richest poetry blends the human and the natural. We pass to the simplicities of human food and human marriage. We may remember that John imagines Jesus as saying that he is a 'living bread' or 'living water', and that he is come to satisfy a universal hunger (pp. 146–7.) These thoughts direct us to passages in the other Gospels where food is mentioned but left without explicit interpretation. Such an interpretation is implicit in Jesus' remarks to the Syrophoenician woman that 'it is not fair to take the children's bread and throw it to the dogs' (*Mark*, VII. 27) and in his remark about putting 'fresh wine into old wineskins' (*Mark*, II. 22). The Reign of God is 'like dough which a woman took and buried in three pecks of flour, till all of it was leavened' (*Luke*, XIII. 21). Observe the quiet homeliness of the illustration: it is suggested that true growth is less catastrophic than gradual. Jesus' followers are as 'the salt of the earth' which must not become 'insipid' (*Matthew*, V. 13) or 'tasteless' (*Mark*, IX. 50). A stone is contrasted with a loaf, a serpent with a fish, an egg with a scorpion, in a passage pointing God's care for man (*Luke*, XI. 11–13). Food is often mentioned by Jesus with varied symbolic or realistic content. We are to feed one another for his sake:

> Whoever gives you a cup of water because you belong to Christ, I tell you truly, he shall not miss his reward.
>
> (*Mark*, IX. 41)

Again,

> For I was hungry and you fed me, I was thirsty and you gave me drink.　　　　　(*Matthew*, XXV. 35)

Food is more important than ecclesiastical rules: David ate the loaves of the Presence when he was hungry (*Mark*, II. 26). When the Prodigal Son falls on evil times, he eats the food given to swine, but when he returns to his true home he is welcomed with music, dance and banqueting, the fatted calf being killed to celebrate his return (*Luke*, XV. 11–32). Jesus, the life-bringer, is one who comes 'eating and drinking' (*Luke*, VII. 34) and feeds the hungry by miracles. To these suggestions the more rigid interpretations of John may often be applied, provided that they enrich but are not allowed to impoverish the poetry. To John the interpretation is all-important; to Jesus it is part only of his statement.

Once when he is taking a meal Jesus talks about feasts to his host and other guests (*Luke*, XIV. 7–24). He says that a proud man may disgrace himself by sitting too high and enjoins his friends when they give a feast to invite not only the rich but the poor also. A fine remark comes from one of those present: 'Blessed is he who feasts in the Realm of God.' Then Jesus proceeds to make a parable in which a man invites his friends to a feast, but they make excuses, and the poor are invited instead. There is thought here of wide issues, the banquet is the heavenly kingdom. This whole conversation, starting from a real feast, shows how closely intermeshed in Jesus' mind is the image with the thought; either may blossom from the other. The two are never really distinct: the true life expresses itself by feeding the poor; but such a life is also itself a feast.

Jesus often talks about banquets, and it is usually a marriage-banquet. Marriages are often in his mind and we may say that all our life-symbols culminate in marriage festivity as the finest flower of the human and natural worlds. To these our other suggestions of nature's fertility and human life, animals and trees and harvests, raiment and riches and feasting, are all subsidiary. In the conversation just described one of the two banquets was a marriage-banquet. 'When anyone invites you to a marriage-banquet never lie down in the best place, in case a more distinguished guest than yourself has been invited' (*Luke*, XIV. 8). Of the other we have a variation in *Matthew*, where it is a marriage-banquet:

> Then Jesus again addressed them in parables. 'The Realm of Heaven', he said, 'may be compared to a king who gave a marriage-banquet in honour of his son. He sent his servants to summon the invited guests to the feast, but they would not come. Once more he sent some other servants, saying, 'Tell the invited guests, here is my supper all prepared, my oxen and fat cattle are killed, everything is ready, come to the marriage-banquet.'

Eventually,

> Then he said to his servants, 'The marriage-banquet is all ready, but the invited guests did not deserve it. So go to the byeways and

invite anyone you meet to the marriage-banquet.' And those servants went out on the roads and gathered all they met, bad and good
alike. Thus the marriage-banquet was supplied with guests.

This is the conclusion:

> Now when the king came in to view his guests, he saw a man there
> who was not dressed in a wedding-robe. So he said to him, 'My man,
> how did you get in here without a wedding-robe?' The man was
> speechless.   (*Matthew*, XXII. 1–14)

The man is cast into the darkness. Though the conclusion
appears perhaps illogical and certainly grim, the festal
hope is nevertheless beautifully bodied into this marriage-
symbol. The Realm of Heaven is compared (*Matthew*, XXV.
1–13) to ten maidens 'who took their lamps and went out
to meet the bridegroom and the bride'. Five however took
no spare oil and while waiting they go to sleep. Then 'at
midnight the cry arose, "Here is the bridegroom! Come out
to meet him!" ' As they trim their lamps the foolish maidens
find that they need more oil. They go to buy more:

> Now while they were away buying oil, the bridegroom arrived;
> those maidens who were ready accompanied him to the marriage-
> banquet, and the door was shut. Afterwards the rest of the maidens
> came and said, 'Oh sir, oh sir, open the door for us!' but he replied,
> 'I tell you frankly, I do not know you.'
>   (*Matthew*, XXV. 10)

Observe how unnecessary, in one sense, the tale is. The conclusion seems hardly to fit it and might have been expressed
more simply alone. But the conclusion is only part of what
the parable says: we are to regard the whole pattern, the ten
maidens, the lamps and the oil, the glimmering lights in the
dark, the weary waiting set against the coming joy, the
anxious watching for bride and bridegroom, the arrival and

the marriage-banquet. Jesus' parables are first poetry, second
teaching. Marriages are powerful in his thought:

> Keep your loins girt and your lamps lit, and be like men who are
> expecting their lord and master on his return from a marriage-
> banquet, so as to open the door for him at once when he comes
> and knocks.   (*Luke*, XII. 35)

In John's Gospel Jesus' first miracle is performed at a
marriage-banquet:

> Two days later a wedding took place at Cana in Galilee; the mother
> of Jesus was present, and Jesus and his disciples had also been
> invited to the wedding.   (*John*, II. 1)

Marriages are central.

It is sometimes thought that Jesus repudiates actual
marriage. This is wrong:

> Have you never read that He who created them male and female
> from the beginning said, 'Hence a man shall leave his father and
> mother, and cleave to his wife, and the pair shall be one flesh'? So
> they are no longer two, but one flesh. What God has joined, then,
> man must not separate.   (*Matthew*, XIX. 4)

True, some men may be eunuchs for the sake of the Realm
of Heaven: 'Let anyone practise it', he says, 'for whom it is
practicable' (*Matthew*, XIX. 12). The one marriage may be
neglected for the other, but both are good. In the perfect
state all the joy and union that marriage can bring is included:

> You go wrong because you understand neither the scriptures nor
> the power of God. At the resurrection people neither marry nor are
> married, they are like the angels of God in Heaven.
>   (*Matthew*, XXII. 29)

Marriage has a negative aspect; it is repressive, a law controlling desires; in the Realm, where desires are not unruly,
there can be no marriage as such. All life-suggestions have
both positive and negative aspects: though all point to life,
the partial may at any time be rejected to make way for the

absolute, and so it is better to get into life with the loss of an eye or a limb than that the whole 'body' or body-soul, be destroyed (*Matthew*, V. 29–30). Nothing is more powerful in Jesus' poetry than the marriage-symbol; his consciousness is never limited to men only. Paul is at heart a bachelor and can be irritated by women who usurp too much power; Jesus is rather a lover by nature, loving all that is creative, including human love.

Women and children are important in his story. To women he is gentle. He satisfies the Syrophoenician woman who begs him to cast a 'daemon' out of her daughter (*Mark*, VII. 25–30). He visits a woman called Martha, whose sister talks to him without doing her share of the work and so incurs Martha's reproach; whereupon he gently excuses her (*Luke*, X. 38–42). He can show a wide sympathy with a convicted adulteress (*John*, VIII. 3–11). Impurity is imputed by Luke to the woman who anoints him with rich perfume (*Luke*, VII. 37). Mary of Magdala, 'out of whom seven daemons have been driven' (*Luke*, VIII. 2), is his friend. He surprises his disciples by holding a lengthy conversation with a Samaritan woman (*John*, IV. 7, 27). The Crucifixion is attended by 'the women who had accompanied him from Galilee' (*Luke*, XXIII. 49). Mary of Magdala, Mary the Mother of James, and Salome bring spices to anoint his body after his death (*Mark*, XVI. 1). All three Gospels refer to women as 'following him' from Galilee, or 'waiting on him' (*Matthew*, XXVII. 55; *Mark*, XV. 41; *Luke*, XXIII. 49). He was clearly loved by them. They seem to honour him for his very independence of them, recognizing that although he himself has renounced marriage, yet that he is in some masterly way renouncing life-instincts in the name of life. Women love him in his loneliness, paying tribute to his manhood. His own mother overwatches his story, according to John being present at the crucifixion.

Children are loved by him and are given prominence in

his teaching: 'Their angels in Heaven always look on the face of my Father in Heaven' (*Matthew*, XVIII. 10). Again:

> Let the children alone, do not stop them from coming to me: the Realm of Heaven belongs to such as these.
>
> (*Matthew*, XIX. 14)

Those who wrong children incur a bitter condemnation (*Matthew*, XVIII. 6). To get into the Realm, one must become as a little child (*Matthew*, XVIII. 3). All that is natural and all that is human is loved by him, provided that it serves life. His words are life-words, creative words. He calls himself the Son of Man and sees himself as a bridegroom:

> Can friends at a wedding fast while the bridegroom is beside them? As long as they have the bridegroom beside them they cannot fast. A time will come when the bridegroom is taken from them; then they will fast, on that day. (*Mark*, II. 19)

The Son of Man and Bridegroom of the World.

As we contemplate this 'Pioneer of Life' (*Acts*, III. 15) we begin to see him as pure light in a dark world. The tendency is dangerous, unless controlled and directed: we must never see the light of this life as a pallid abstraction, a cold white ray. Light is here interfused with the physical, dependent on the body, not in itself a separate essence. Jesus' words on light are subdued, homely and realistic, as when in one of our parables a woman loses a coin, lights a lamp and 'scours the house' for it (*Luke*, XV. 8). Again:

> No one lights a lamp to put it in a cellar or under a bowl, but on a stand, so that those who come in can see the light. Your eye is the lamp of the body: when your eye is sound, then the whole of your body has light, but if your eye is diseased, then your body is darkened (Look! perhaps your very light is dark).
>
> So if your whole body has light, without any corner of it in darkness, it will be lit up entirely, as when a lamp lights you with its rays.
>
> (*Luke*, XI. 33; and see *Matthew*, VI. 22–3)

See how quietly realistic is this light-imagery, how far from intellectual subtleties; and yet to interpret its full meaning a book would have to be written. To Jesus sight illuminates the 'whole body', not the mind only, and this whole body he would have lit by a purified sight. What he asks is as simple and mysterious as light itself. The simplicity *is* the mystery, and we may begin to see new meanings in the parable of the ten maidens, their lamps and oil (p. 163). All this is very different from St John and St Paul, and the difference is that described by Blake: Jesus dwells 'in realms of day', not only his mind, but his body, full of light. To such reality is the only vision and 'nothing is hidden that shall not be disclosed, nothing concealed that shall not be known and revealed' (*Luke*, VIII. 17).

Light is only a part of life. The whole life is primary and any part whatsoever may be sacrificed in its cause:

> If your hand or foot is a hindrance to you, cut it off and throw it away; better be maimed or crippled and get into Life, than keep both feet or hands and be thrown into the everlasting fire.
>
> If your eye is a hindrance to you, tear it out and throw it away; better get into Life with one eye than keep your two eyes and be thrown into the fire of Gehenna.   (*Matthew*, XVIII. 8)

'Get into life'. There is no thought of 'souls' in our modern abstract sense; Jesus' mind does not work in terms of a body-soul dualism. His concrete intuition might be illustrated by our saying that he would sanction the statement that it is better to get into life with no 'soul', than to save your soul and be thrown into the fire of Gehenna. Life itself may be sacrificed for life's sake: 'whoever wants to save his life will lose it, and whoever loses his life for my sake, he will save it' (*Luke*, IX. 24). Of the whole life Jesus speaks. Concentration on any aspect, on wealth or on fine clothes, or on bodily pleasures – these may hinder life. So too may religious observance, intellectualization, spirituality. The

Scribes and Pharisees are blind guides 'filtering away the gnat and swallowing the camel', cleaning the outside of the cup and leaving the inside foul. Their piety secretes a death: they are as 'white-washed' tombs full of 'dead men's bones' (*Matthew*, XXIII. 24–7). The blind lead the blind, the dead prescribe to death. But 'the body is something more than clothes' (*Luke*, XII. 23); and life is more than the body, or the mind, or the soul. Just as the first creature to develop sight could only have explained that miracle in terms of smell, warmth and sound, so Jesus would explain his life-message in terms of other and lesser life-suggestions. All his life-imagery serves a greater life to which no one part must take precedence; and that life as far surpasses what we call life as the body surpasses its clothing. 'Do that', Jesus says to the lawyer who seeks his help, 'and you will live' (*Luke*, X. 28). Towards life – not only of the body, spirit or mind, but of all and more – the Gospels call us. Jesus himself is necessarily shown as independent of all but the true life: unmarried, fasting, without worldly wealth, his body nakedly crucified. His own life he finally throws down as the last challenge to death. There is then no death: 'He is not the God of dead people but of living. You are far wrong' (*Mark*, XII. 27).

IV

We have seen that Jesus' poetry is richly imaginative yet rarely flashes or scintillates. It has an assured mastery and quiet grace. It is homely, realistic and magical. Here I point especially to its life-quality. But Jesus moves in a dark world, and if we are to be true to his own realism we do wrong to see him only and always as an immaculate lord of peace. He drives from the Temple those who wrong its sacred stones. When blindness maddens him, he threatens eternal flames, the burnings of Gehenna; a generation of 'vipers' he condemns to weeping and gnashing of teeth (*Matthew*, XII. 34; XIII. 42, 50; XXIII. 33; XXIV. 51; XXV. 30; *Luke*, XIII. 28). Bitter woe he prophesies to all who love their own death, death to the dead, life to those who live. It is better to be drowned in the depths than wrong the child of life (*Matthew*, XVIII. 6). A dark anger burns from him. He images the apocalyptic end when one shall be taken and another left. Then:

> The sun will be darkened and the moon will not yield her light, the stars will drop from heaven, and the orbs of the heavens will be shaken.   (*Mark*, XIII. 24)

The Son of Man will appear 'like lightning that flashes from one side of the sky to the other' (*Luke*, XVII. 24); and the image is one of terror as well as beauty. An image of judgement. All these are reflections cast by the death-world on the Pioneer of Life, shadows thrown by the dark rocks and frowning fortress he invades. But his own natural words are life-words, in him there is no death, nor threat of death, save it comes from without; from impiety, from hypocrisy, from wilful blindness.

We see Jesus silhouetted against a world of formalized religion, hypocrisy, envy, evil and suffering. It is a world of death; of spiritual death and of bodily death. To this world he would bring life. His only gospel is life, and life put into words is poetry; and his only ethic is poetry, for poetry put into action is life. His words tell of the shepherd and his sheep, the harvest, and the vine; of food and of clothes, and of marriage. Life-words on his lips, himself a life-force, he feeds those who are hungry and saves those who are lost. All sorts of diseases he cures: leprosy, haemorrhage, palsy, paralysis, dropsy. Each withered limb he heals in turn, each sense in turn he restores, healing the blind, the deaf, the dumb. Spiritual torment he relieves, releasing those mastered by devil-possession, dark abysmal neurosis, the *Macbeth* evil, the *Macbeth* guilt. He cures madness, restoring the tameless maniac of the 'tombs' (*Mark*, V. 1–14). Sin he removes with a word and a look, sin and its correlative, death. The dead themselves rise at his command (*Matthew*, IX. 25; XI. 5; *Mark*, V. 42; *Luke*, VII. 15; VIII. 55; *John*, XI. 44). All partial death, all more absolute death, he cures, himself a force of life. But though all this he can do, though every disease and every mental evil he can cure for those who ask, though every physical sense he can restore, there may yet be lacking the one essential health, the final sense that sees without sight and hears where no word is spoken, the faith that moves mountains, the heart beating in unison with life. To him all are sick to death. This universal sickness too he would heal; by example, by miracle, by poem after poem, by reference to all life-forces and all senses in turn, by love and bitter anger, by his own life and bitter death, this one thing he would make clear to all men, a thing to him so simple, yet more hard to breathe into us than to feed five thousand with a few loaves and fishes or make the dead rise from their sleep. And yet this alone is life; the others, in this comparison, but shadows, parodies, ghostly unrealities.

So he speaks in parables, that men may not deceive themselves into a mockery of understanding. To those who have eyes and see not, he leaves his poetry without interpretation: better that they have the poetry without the teaching than think that they have the teaching before they see how it flowers from the poetry. But to his own disciples, whose understanding is tuned to his message, he will add the interpretation (*Mark*, IV. 10–20; *Luke*, VIII. 9–15). No symbol can be understood until the hearer is ready for understanding. Jesus would avoid an intellectual exploitation of his message; he leaves his theology and ethic vague and paradoxical; he does not think in intellectual categories at all. To him the body itself sees (p. 167). He talks about natural life, food, marriage; feasting, wine, rich perfumes are woven in his story; he cures by touching, or by being touched: the very 'tassel' of his 'robe' (*Matthew*, IX. 20) is magical to heal. He would not have men think so much as see, hear and speak. He would have them enter their inherited eternity of fullest life, he comes 'that they may have life and have it to the full' (*John*, X. 10). He speaks in poetry, for he is calling us to creative life, he tells us to blend our life with the life of harvest and tree and human marriage, to make metaphors and poetic symbols, true creations, of our thoughts and acts. We must live from the heart of creation, be one with the principle of creation, and thus possess our immortality. The Gospels are rich with tangible, physical, sensuous and super-sensuous life pitted against disease in mind and body, evil and death. That the New Testament should ever have been itself considered a message of death, of intangible spirituality, of pallid, lifeless and ghostly counsel, is one of the grand enigmas in this mysterious world.

Jesus' life is complementary to his words. By picture-language and by dramatic example his work is done. In word and act he is the 'pioneer of life'. This essential life of Life is both firmly realized and magically mysterious. Our symbols and events are solid, yet framed by a poetic aura. Jesus is human and real to us; we grow to know his natural-istic and humanistic poetry, his sympathy and endurance, his flashing wrath and prophetic ardour; but his personality, human though it be, is also symbolic, radiating a mysterious and mystic power. His life is framed by light, melting into the divine at either end; his birth is divine, he rises from the dead, and at choice moments he is vividly superhuman, as when the heavens open and God speaks at his baptism and at his transfiguration. Against these is the darkness of Gol-gotha, that stark suffering unrelieved, the black cross, the fifth act of death unlit by any limelight from the heavenly sphere, a silence broken by no assuring voice of God. All various colourings here, the vividly incandescent, the utterly

PART III

Prophecy

X

IMMORTALITY

SINCE life and death are the main subjects of poetry and prophetic writing, and since all such literature is labouring to reveal some paradise or essential life, it is necessary to give some attention to the concept 'immortality'.

There is a widespread feeling that man is immortal; and there is also a widespread knowledge that men die. In Christianity we have a bodily resurrection; in Renaissance and Romantic Poetry we find immortality expressed as an immediate experience, as in *Epipsychidion* where Shelley imagines love and death blended to create a deathless life; a thought found elsewhere, in *Antony and Cleopatra* and Keats. A poet may think of immortality in terms of birth rather than of life; Wordsworth, Shelley and Tennyson do this. Death is the end of life, yet man is immortal; immortality, they seem to say, may be approached through thought of the prenatal hinterland of earthly existence. Immortality often has something to do with love. Finally, there is the weighty consideration that life, not death, is our proper concern. Our understanding must take all such thoughts into account.

Our minds are clouded by false associations and illegitimate logic. We must concentrate on realities and refuse scrambling irrelevancies their desired entrance. The word 'immortality' signifies 'undeathliness', which in that it is less soiled by dangerous associations is perhaps a better term. Immortality means the opposite of death, which is life, yet it also suggests death. It means 'death negated'; it is an act rather than a static entity. We may call immortality 'life victorious over death'; and in reading poetry we must try to see life victorious, wherever it is so presented, as suggesting immortality, and conversely immortality as suggesting not a lengthy duration so much as victorious life. We must avoid thinking of immortality as a kind of ghostly continuance.

It is easy to argue not only that immortality can exist, but that it must exist. Death is parasitic on the life-concept and itself negative. Birth and death are a framework enclosing an individual human life; they are time-aspects from which we regard it. But an individual human life is an abstraction from the dramatic whole and so death is merely a negative aspect, as birth a positive aspect, of an abstraction. Clearly, death holds little reality: any bit of life, any positive and rounded whole, should be intellectually victorious over the wraithly line enclosing it. A line is scarcely real; it has length without breadth, as the geometry books say. This may appear a too easy proof of immortality. Where, then, lies our difficulty? By isolating an individual life I have simplified our problem, and the true difficulty is more complex. I shall now more closely enquire into what we mean by life and death.

'Life' may denote the working of the machinery which activates a physical organism. But there is psychic life as well as physical life and a man may be very much alive on his death-bed. Our consciousness has variations, some more vital than others; what we have called the imaginative or romantic consciousness pierces further than the lower or intellectual consciousness, which blindly feels the contours of realities that the other not only feels but sees and hears. The highest life-consciousness is not only mental; it will be physical too, permeating the body. We are seldom fully conscious of life. We sleep, we unrestfully dream, and the romantic sight is fitful for most of us. We may have degrees of psychical life, just as there are degrees of physical health. The most perfect state would presumably be one where the psychical and the physical were both in health and also in mutual harmony, a state rarely found since the one tends to prey upon the other. It may seem that neither would endure ill-health apart from such conflicts and that, as all our ills are to be related to this disharmony, we may expect our final good to depend on the corresponding harmony; for man is an organic whole transcending its constituent parts.

If there are degrees of life, there are necessarily also degrees of death. Death may be physical: we mean then that the body, whatever may have happened to the mind, is dead; dead, that is, as part of a human organism, though it is certainly part of the physical universe and must still be related to life. Our arguments are at every turn rendered hard by the fact that death is unreal: the body changes, but its constituents cannot die. With the psychic element things are much the same. Clearly there is much partial psychic death during life, an idea powerful in *Hamlet*, Wordsworth's ode on *Immortality* and Tennyson's *Maud*. But this death cannot be complete, any more than the other, since human thoughts interlace and a man's influence lives on. Absolute death is inconceivable. It would mean the utter extinction of the physical body and all psychic qualities; it would include the blotting out of a man's influence and works in time, his friends' memories and his enemies' dislike, as well as the chemical vanishment of his body. Then the universe might be as though that man had never been. This would be absolute death. It is true that, since man is a physical and mental organism, that whole as a whole is ended as soon as one part of it is gone or out of harmony with any other part; and that it might be objected that this alone constitutes an absolute death. That is arguable, but it is not what we usually mean, for in this sense we are absolutely dead when we have a tooth extracted or lose our tempers. Such death I prefer to call 'partial', and commonsense will support the term. So, though absolute life is sometimes achievable, absolute death appears inconceivable.

Moreover, if such a state of final extinction were possible, it would be desirable. It would be as a mysterious dream, super-natural; a vast, calm sea of unimaginable peace, an exquisite silent harmony with no clash or discord to mar its dark tranquillity. It is not undesirable, since the more we think of it the more it shapes itself into a symbol of universality, harmony and peace, without conflict or unrest. We could not object that to leave our dear ones would be an agony, since the very entrance of dear ones into the conception implies a connexion after death with things of this life, and that we have ruled out by definition. Similarly we cannot say, this would not matter to me if only my extinction were at stake, but I cannot bear to contemplate those I love so dissolved into nothingness; for if we remember them, they are not so dissolved. Therefore we may say that such a death is a philosophical abstraction; that it is inconceivable, except to flights of fancy, since death cannot so cut its moorings from the life of created things on which it depends; and that if it were possible to believe in it, then certainly, in this world where so much partial death, so much sin, sickness, pain, bereavement and misery, has to be endured, such a death would be no evil. Our values would be reversed. Life, so partial, so short, so readily giving place to an eternal nothingness, would be trivial compared with that overpowering infinitude. Though death were nothing, life would be recognized as a minus quantity, less than nothing. This is what happens in Shakespeare's *Timon of Athens*. Timon aspires to this eternity. He sees life as a world of partial death, burdened by the crimes and physical diseases that impregnate his curses with loathing. Therefore for him absolute death is an ideal:

> Come not to me again, but say to Athens,
> Timon hath made his everlasting mansion
> Upon the beached verge of the salt flood;
> Who once a day with his embossed froth
> The turbulent surge shall cover; thither come;
> And let my grave-stone be your oracle.
>
> (*Timon of Athens*, V. i. 219)

Timon wishes all men to die; the sun to go out; the world to end. Only by such a universal ending can any ultimate death be attained. This is Nirvana, and to Timon the highest good, since life has failed him. Shakespeare is, however, too excellent a poet to be able to express it, and the utter darkness, the vast emptiness and unending age he would suggest, are incarnated in a very lively symbol, the sea. This is Timon's utter death, and in so far as it is possible we respond to the grandeur of its everlasting and unsounded deeps of perpetuity.

It is not possible; and it is not this that troubles us. The varied melodies of absolute life are beautiful, and so to our imagination is the silent music of absolute death. It is only when the two conflict that we experience discord.[1] Of these two contestants, absolute life and absolute death, one is a reality, the other a dream; but the resulting discord is not a dream; and yet, being so closely bound to life, it is not an absolute negation either. If the word 'death' is to have its fullest hostile power it must be thought of as partial, or as a life-death relation. We can imagine a living body and psychic death, melancholia or, at an extreme, madness; or we can let our thoughts dwell on a dead body and a ghostly continuance of the spirit; or we may consider the material body seemingly half-dead, putrefying but still horribly human, skulls in graveyards. We can imagine the dislocation of a love-contact by death or separation, a dear one gone while lover, parent or son lives on; or murder by which a living force thrusts a life into death.

Death, to be horrible, must be parasitic on life; the emotions of life must be allowed to come into our discussion; death is a life-agony. Try to make it more powerful, a thing in itself, and it becomes pleasant. This is an intellectual equivalent to the well-known psychic rhythm described in

[1] For the application of this thought to the Hecate scenes in *Macbeth* see *The Shakespearian Tempest*, App. B.

William James' *The Varieties of Religious Experience*: awareness of partial death, submersion into absolute death, and a
recovery to awareness of the glory of life. The moment a
negation becomes absolute, it swiftly becomes positive, the
only permanent negative being in conflict, disharmony,
partial negation. That is why Shakespeare's work revolves
finally on the tempest-music opposition, and not on the life-
death conflict, which though important is not ultimate.

Death, like evil, is to be seen as an inharmonious relation,
not as a thing in itself: death and evil are almost synonymous
terms in the Bible and poetry. We must see death dramatically. It is an experience, and since it is an evil experience we
find our poets and prophets creating dramas of immortality
against it, for immortality will likewise be an experience, or
drama. In Shakespeare we find a powerful immortality vision
in *Antony and Cleopatra*, and his final plays dramatize the
same theme: a conquest of death by life. We return to our
former contention, that individual persons are unreal and
that reality is a relation or experience. It is dramatic. Death,
or what we usually mean by death, is an experience of disharmony, known from the emotional viewpoint of the sur-
vivor. In this sense the death-experience is only too real.

I proceed to make some diagrammatic illustrations. Here
is an individual's life cut short by death:

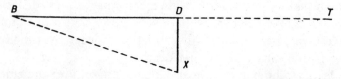

Born at B, he dies at D, and his plunge into nothingness is
represented by DX. This leaves us, his friends, with a sense
of disharmony. We are not regarding his death, or even his
life and death, in cold objectivity, but rather visualizing a
complex little drama, in which we, in life, have sense of our
companion's death. DB and DX are now two lines meaning-

lessly and cruelly divergent to us who live. We feel that he should be allowed to travel on immortal in time to T, because BDT is a straight line and therefore harmonious. It may be argued that BD is a complete and satisfying whole; that there is no plunge to X; and that D is just the limit of BD. But if we have any affection for him we shall think of his death as a big fact, and the diagram needs accordingly a death-line of its own; it is an emotion, our love, that forces the creation of DX; DX is an emotional line. To remedy our dualism, I join XB: this line restores harmony and unity by completing the triangle. Our disappointment might be removed could we clearly understand the line XB. It may represent reincarnation; or in that it remedies the mistake of DX, some higher state of consciousness in ourselves in which we give no reality to death; or an immortality in some way outside time; and it very clearly fits those poems which relate immortality to birth. Certainly it would appear that in the line XB rather than the time-stream DT the true immortality will exist. So the whole reality of the man who died begins to assume a triangular shape; it is an area rather than a line. This extra dimension is imparted to it by our emotional experience.

But we do not know how long to make our emotional line DX; and XB, depending on the position of X, is likewise uncertain. The length of DX will vary according to our sorrow, utter despair tending to make it infinitely long. If we imagine that the final truth of the life-death resolution should include all possible positions of X, we have next the accompanying figure. Though DX is unreal to the intellect, death being only a negation, our sorrow is clearly real; as an emotional line DX is no illusion. Our answers to these varied dualisms depend too on all the BX lines; if our sorrow is very great and the death correspondingly an infinite darkness, then BX can only meet DX at infinity and in this limiting case it will appear as BY, perpendicular to BD. We

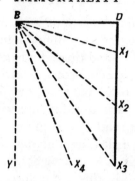

have now been filling up the area of a rectangle of infinite height, drawn on BD, and we may begin to see that the immortality of the life BD is not gained by stretching it out along BDT in time, but by completing a rectangle on the base BD. Eternal life is not a line at all; it is less tenuous, an area, an emotional field, of which the time-line BD is only one thin section.

This fits our facts. For if, in life or a Shakespearian play, we have sense of a time-sequence, we also have sense of an emotional field, what I have elsewhere called the spatial quality. This spatial quality may be regarded as vertical and the whole life thought of as lifted, generating a spatial area as it moves upward or downward, at right angles to the horizontal time-stream. This is a convenient way of showing ourselves how a single human life may be deathless, though it ends at death, its completed wholeness, rounded off by death and birth in time being bodily lifted up in the other dimension, where it has unlimited freedom. This other dimension represents the world not of time but of immediate experience, the mysterious drama in which we are always actors but which we never properly understand; the human drama which is also super-human, needing an experiencing subject and an experienced object. Our vertical immortality is dependent on an emotional experience: I am showing how a human life may be considered immortal by a surviving friend or lover, and how our experience of the deceased remains vital in eternity. We are here stumbling – no more – towards a definition in personal terms of a more than personal life greater than anything we can normally conceive; and this greater life over-arching us like the sky is an immortal life, the life of experience in which we are together actors from minute to minute, but which we cannot clearly focus. We are not to visualize single persons living on for ever in time, but rather our super-personal experience composed of them and of us and transcending both, our greater dramatic life itself, is deathless, upflowering in the other element of eternity. Life not only rises high; it also sinks deep. It is submerged in depths we never guess, like icebergs that meet each other in the ocean and never know that nine-tenths of themselves and their kind are always hidden, and that it is the force of currents on those nine-tenths that does more to direct their movements than any breeze blowing on their tops.

I have said that our super-personal experience of persons or things is continuous in eternity rather than in time. There is nothing distressing in this: time is a wraithly line, our rectangle a well-spread-out area. Time is a thread connecting rich pearls; those pearls are of value, the thread nothing. Our experiences on earth are valuable with a value we cannot always understand, and it is this value that is suggested by my vertical and emotional eternity. We have here an illustration fitting many facts. Those theosophical teachings which tell us that the soul dwells apart, corresponding to the bodily life but not exactly involved in it, are relevant. Plato's ideal forms of which things mundane are but shadows might also be adduced; and when Jesus says that the children's 'angels' always behold his Father (*Matthew*, XVIII. 10), he must mean something similar. This vertical eternity, corresponding to every event in the time-stream, is not abstract or unphysical; rather it is even more physical than our usual life; it is itself our usual life in all its physical and mental richness. The very physical love-consciousness opens our minds to it; Shelley's *Epipsychidion* is a vision of it; it makes D. H. Lawrence's intuition of a potential life far richer than that we enjoy. At any moment in life we may, if our minds and bodies are tuned to understanding, feel our experience developing vertically. Our time-stream is the pallid abstraction, one side only of the rectangle, with length but no breadth. And when Jesus tells us to see with our bodies (p. 166 above), he means that we should open our conscious life to the immortal existence that we live.

The true immortality is not immortality at all, a term only needed to counteract our death-thinking, but life itself, which is however not limited to the time-line and has an infinite and powerful expansion vertically. Immediate experience is our immortality, and whenever we see anything immediately with sense of its upward or downward reality, we know it, or rather our experience of it, to be immortal. This is what Browning means in *Abt Vogler* when he finely writes, 'There shall never be one lost good'. Such a vision Jesus pre-eminently possessed. This faculty is really the same as the space-time and forward-looking vision discussed in our first chapter; for, though it may not always think in terms of future time, the vertical understanding is creative in time as well as in eternity. The prophet at every moment feels life sinking its shaft to the rich centres below, and mines vertically before creating horizontally. Most of us live only on the surface. All such vision, revealing the true life at one point in the time-stream, inevitably affects that stream itself. Sight of the eternal world includes past, present and future. Beatrice at one point knows what Dante is about to enquire. She says:

> I speak, nor what thou wouldst enquire, demand;
> For I have marked it, where all time and place
> Are present.

> > > (*Paradise*, XXIX. 11)

The eternal world transcends time; time is merely an aspect.
Dante finely imagines this eternality:

> The celestial love, that spurns
> All envying in its bounty, in itself
> With such effulgence blazeth, as sends forth
> All beauteous things eternal. What distils
> Immediate thence, no end of being knows;
> Bearing its seal immutably impressed.
> Whatever thence immediate falls, is free,
> Free wholly, uncontrollable by power
> Of each thing new.
>
> *(Paradise, VII. 60)*

The immediately apprehended eternity cannot be controlled
by 'power of each thing new', that is, by time. And yet we
must regard the eternal world not as separate from the
temporal, but rather as enclosing it. An immediate experience of eternity raises us to a height overlooking time, not
turning our backs to it:

> Contingency, whose verge extendeth not
> Beyond the tablet of your mortal mould,
> Is all depictured in the eternal sight.
>
> *(Paradise, XVII. 37)*

Time is never finally distinct from eternity, and any time-
section has its vertical significance. Dante once imagines
time as a root, eternity being the leaves:

> The vase, wherein time's roots are plunged, thou seest:
> Look elsewhere for the leaves.
>
> *(Paradise, XXVII. 112)*

Which well suits our vertical diagram.

Such an understanding will illuminate our poets at every
turn. When a poet writes of immortality he may use the
conventional image of a life persisting in time after death,
which fits our minds well and is not to be ruled out as always

inadequate. But poetry quite as often sees immortality in terms of birth. There may be vague prenatal memories such as those of which Tennyson writes in *The Two Voices*:

> Moreover, something is or seems,
> That touches me with mystic gleams,
> Like glimpses of forgotten dreams.

These glimpses resemble the 'echoes' of an antenatal dream of Shelley's *Epipsychidion* (456). In his *Ode to the West Wind* Shelley regrets his divine childhood. Goethe makes his Faust recall child-memories when, on the verge of suicide, he hears the Easter songs and angelic choir. As a child, 'Heaven's love' floating down on him 'like a kiss', his soul was flushed 'with ecstasy':

> Then did a sweet, mysterious yearning
> Through field and woodland drive me ever on.
> Whilst in mine eyes the tears were burning,
> I felt a world within me dawn.
> My childhood's merry games proclaimed this music golden,
> Spring's free glad feast with it began;
> With childlike feelings now hath memory withholden
> Back from the last grim step, the man.
> Chime on, ye sweet angelic songs that thrall me!
> My tears well forth, to earth again ye call me.
>
> (23)

The 'Choir of Disciples' is heard chanting that the risen Christ is 'filled with birth-delight'. Childhood is a recurring theme of paradisal poetry.

Birth and childhood are immortality impressions called in to oppose death. Immortality is, as its name suggests, a death-opposer, and in dramatic action a child or child-thoughts may champion life against death with a semi-supernatural authority. Hence the child-symbolism throughout *Faust*, in *Macbeth* and Shakespeare's last plays. In *Macbeth* the conflict is a death-child conflict (p. 46 above). In

The Winter's Tale the oracle demands that the lost child be found as a condition of averting tragedy; both *The Winter's Tale* and *Pericles* present an opposition of evil, death and tempest on the one side and love, the child and music on the other. Birth-themes are often important. There is the divinely born Jesus, the death-force that would destroy the Holy Child and the resulting Massacre of the Innocents; and all this closely follows the story of Moses. Like Fleance in *Macbeth*, the protagonist-child escapes. Birth is mysterious. We have Macduff's mysterious birth and his accomplished revenge despite the prophecy that no man 'of woman born' (IV. i. 80) shall harm Macbeth. In Tennyson's Arthur we have suggestion both of divine birth and illegitimacy, a twofold direction shadowed also in the Gospels. All such symbols suggest birth to be a mysterious and powerful life-force; and when we have dramatically a life-force embattled victoriously against death, therein is explicated an active immortality.

Wordsworth's *Ode: Intimations of Immortality from Recollections of Early Childhood* does not aim at revealing a life after death, but rather contrasts child-memories and the eternal with the death which is the intellectual consciousness. The child-consciousness is supposed to have direct knowledge of eternality as opposed to the time-bound thinking to which we are subject later. The earth was then 'apparelled in celestial light', possessing 'the glory and the freshness of a dream'. But this 'glory' has now passed from the earth:

> Whither is fled the visionary gleam?
> Where is it now, the glory and the dream?

The child, 'trailing clouds of glory' from God, is for a while attuned to the divine and in this state sees earth itself as paradise. It is accordingly an apt symbol of immortality:

> Mighty Prophet! Seer blest!
> On whom those truths do rest,

> Which we are toiling all our lives to find,
> In darkness lost, the darkness of the grave;
> Thou over whom thy Immortality
> Broods like the Day, a Master o'er a Slave . . .

This is the centre of our ode. Wordsworth begins by regretting his lost paradisal child-joy; next he describes how the child is to be seen as fresh from paradise; finally he reaches his central invocation to the Child. Wordsworth sees immortality in terms of (i) the child and (ii) this earth transfigured by paradisal vision, the vision of childhood or of manhood in certain blessed moments. This is a poetic vision: Goethe's allegorical figure of poetry is a 'Boy-Charioteer' (p. 202 below), and we may remember that Jesus advises men 'to become like children' (*Matthew*, XVIII. 3; *Mark*, X. 15). Blake has many correspondences. Poetry is packed with this child-immortality.

In so far as the poet reaches back to a prenatal existence, he is doing little better than those who draw dream pictures of a future state; and descriptions of both states are best considered as creations from immediate experience. Wordsworth's Ode is great because of its imagery, its child-symbol, because it suggests that this earth might be a paradise were our minds awake, because what pre-existence it imagines is vividly depicted in a glorified earth-imagery. Immortality is an extension, or expansion, of life itself; there can be no other starting point in any profitable analysis. Remember how we saw it as the vertical flowerings of a life not limited to the horizontal time-line. Such an immortality is hard to understand, but so is everything. It is as easy to understand as life; it is life. It is no use when searching for immortality to start by trying to understand death in isolation from life; for, since such death is, if it is anything at all, then precisely and exactly nothing, there is nothing to understand.

And yet our death-line was emotionally real enough. After death, there is certainly a sense of loss, a shadow cast by the life we loved. This death-experience is attacked in Shakespeare's greater plays. In *Othello* the hero, through his own error, loses his wife and follows her to death. The Lear-Cordelia drama is similar. In *Timon of Athens*, the hero finds the objects of his love unworthy and seeks peace in death, following his homeless love into the eternal. In *Antony and Cleopatra* Cleopatra loses her lover; left alone, she sees him as one with the glorious universe; and triumphantly follows him. Here we receive an immediate immortality intuition beyond the ordinary tragic acceptance. Such tragic rhythms suggest that the love-experience is primary. The loved one lost, love is equated with death, the emotional death-line drawn, and the hero dies to restore harmony. Cleopatra seems to know that she is finding in death a universal love of which Antony is one aspect. Death is highly charged with positive meaning. No one person is being considered alone: a disorganized life-death conflict is resolved dramatically, needing at least two persons.

Among Shakespeare's final plays *Pericles* and *The Winter's Tale* develop similar situations to a different conclusion. The two heroes lose their wives and daughters, endure a period of deathly penitence, and finally receive again those they loved. Death is a disorganized relation, like evil: though Leontes knows that his own sin has brought about his suffering, Pericles, though blameless, endures a similar penitence. Both eternity and time appear to be involved. The dead wife is resurrected and the lost daughter found; the love-experience is deathless in eternity and its creation active in time; and that the child is born during the tragic conflict suggests that the conflict itself is mysteriously creative. We may observe that the hero suffers a partial death and that his loved wife is not exactly resurrected, but rather turns out never to have died. We may deduce: (i) that to be aware of death is itself a sin and a sort of death, a death-experience; and (ii) that death is not to be remedied by resurrection, but is rather a delusion. What seemed dead is, like Hermione, really alive; there is no death, there are no dead. These plays are plotted and woven to present a dramatic explication of the fact that the death-experience is not final and that life is harmonious. We conclude that it is eternal with an eternity which includes time.

My examples so far have needed a living subject. In Shakespeare's final plays the hero himself does not die or seem to die; it is his living experience of death that is attacked and conquered. But what of ourselves, as subjects? How are we to understand our own impending death? First, we can say that such death is a pure fancy. No one can experience dissolution, since experience needs a subject and an object, and if the subject is destroyed and there is no object there can be no experience. If it be replied that we shall all one day seem to others to disappear, we must agree; but this brings in the objective aspect already discussed. My thoughts of my own death are themselves merely drawn from awareness that others die, and that awareness once removed or vitally changed I shall have slight consciousness of my own approaching death: it will not be a significant reality. Death-thinking is always inbound with time-thinking, and that alone, being purely intellectual, becomes dangerous if intermixed with the wrong emotions. To let emotions overleap the present is evil: Macbeth's greedy desire for futurity is related to a death-consciousness ('nothing is but what is not', I. iii. 141) and results in death-activity. For me to fear my future death is wrong; there is however room for less emotional forethought. To plan taking the present into account is legitimate; to feel and think emotionally into the future through present facts is creative; but to fear is psychically unhealthy. Jesus counsels us both to take no thought for the future and to make plans carefully (*Matthew*,

VI. 34; *Luke*, XIV. 28–32). The well-ordered life will both think and feel into the future only through the present, and to fear death infringes this law.

People do nevertheless think emotionally about their own future deaths, making an illegitimate abstraction from the dramatic inter-relations of life-experience and regarding themselves as solitary adventuring units. They are fearing unrealities, but let us suppose them to be justified. I will try to explain what immortality would mean in their terms. It will be directly concerned, not with a future changed existence so much as the life they have already lived. They will find that that life is not finished as they thought, but is still going on in the eternity dimension. Many poets think like this, imagining immortality as union with the best that they have known in life: Wordsworth dreams of his happy childhood, Cleopatra dies to meet Antony. St Paul's desire to be 'absorbed by life' (p. 139 above) and certain thoughts in Shelley's *Adonais* are close parallels. Keats wishes in his *Ode to a Nightingale* to dissolve into the Nightingale's music, and imagines himself dying while enjoying a perfect love-union in his 'Bright Star' sonnet. A high life-experience may seem to find perpetuation most easily if synchronized with death, and such mystic dying seems to the onlooker, who is here also the subject, to round off and complete life at a perfect moment, so that its wholeness may be the more beautiful in eternity. Faust finds Gretchen in Heaven and Dante Beatrice. The eternal world is the life which we have already known, transfigured, at its best. Its best moments give hint of its future immortality, futurity coming into the discussion through our trying to see ourselves as solitary units adventuring into death. As Keats in his sonnet 'Why did I laugh tonight?' writes:

> Verse, Fame, and Beauty are intense indeed,
> But death intenser – Death is Life's high meed.

This is a death which is no negation but rather a consummation of life, a completing of it, the final sealing, stamping
and posting of the letter. Such an all-inclusive death we find
in Jesus' crucifixion; summing up and completing his life
and rendering it fit, as a whole, for its eternal existence.
Often death may be thus imagined. So much of our life in the
darkened consciousness seems derelict and lonely: in death
there is union. What was partial in life becomes richer in
death; the battered nickel currency of time is new-minted in
gold. Therefore the richest joys such as romantic love and
marriage are powerful in all high vision, in the poets and the
New Testament. Eternity thus known is not life's end nor
the beginning of an utterly new existence, but rather, as St
Paul continually suggests, and as Browning's *Abt Vogler* tells
us, the consummation and circumference of all earthly experience and desire. What seemed unrealized experience
becomes, in that completed whole, final: in the eternal marriage the blessed face and form is in our arms, our life lost in
union with its life.

An objection may be raised. I have shown how a life to an
onlooker may be considered as lifted into eternity, the whole
life being immortal. I have also said that if we think in personal terms of our own death we may expect to find mainly
our better and happier moments, whereas according to my
scheme we ought to be faced through eternity with our
sufferings and sins and many awkward incidents which we
had forgotten: a cheerless prospect. And yet, though the
whole life must first be considered to persist, both revela-
tory documents and commonsense demand that the good
conquer the evil. In temporal existence good is on the whole
victorious, and it seems unlikely that evil enjoys equal rights
with it in eternity. We must not think too rigidly in personal
terms. Dramatic experiences are the realities and these experiences have eternal growth; but harmonious experiences
must surely be allowed a richer development than those

which are evil, and we would prefer the worst to be utterly destroyed. Therefore we may say that Heaven is the crop and harvest of harmonious and creative experience, whereas evil experience is annihilated in Hell.

In Dante's Earthly Paradise there are two streams, Lethe and Eunoe, pouring down on two sides:

> On this, devolved with power to take away
> Remembrance of offence; on that, to bring
> Remembrance back of every good deed done.
>   (*Purgatory*, XXVIII. 134)

The taste of Eunoe exceeds 'all flavours else'.

The evil is forgotten, dissolved, as though not sinners, but sins, were to be condemned; and we may extend the thought to our reading of Dante's whole system, including Hell. In a play where he more closely than elsewhere analyses divine and human justice, Shakespeare has an interestingly analogous thought:

> I have a brother is condemn'd to die:
> I do beseech you, let it be his fault,
> And not my brother.
>   (*Measure for Measure*, II. ii. 34)

In this scene Isabella's arguments are all of the sort sanctioned by the play's Christian philosophy, and we may therefore diffidently relate this thought, through Shakespeare, to Jesus. All poetry works in terms of experience; everywhere we are most ill-advised to regard solitary persons as ultimate. Jesus' words about 'Gehenna' (*Matthew*, XXIII. 33), the word signifying a place of destruction, the destruction vision of the Book of Revelation, and Dante's Hell, all ultimately may be supposed to refer less to persons than to evil itself: evil is banished to outer darkness, all death-experience condemned to utter death. In those of Jesus' parables which are here most relevant the reference to actual persons is not explicit. Parables are always the more valuable in that their dramas remain generalized, so lending themselves to changing interpretations. Even when Jesus definitely threatens actual evil-doers with Gehenna we may accept the threat as the only image adequate to dramatize his experience of evil men. We must not finally regard even Jesus as a single oracular authority, but rather as the protagonist of a complex dramatic art-form. Incidentally, we may note that, though the Gospel of Matthew in particular certainly contains some powerful condemnations, the fires of Gehenna are not given a strong emphasis throughout the New Testament as a whole. The positive and negative forces are rather life and death, and an imaginative understanding will pay regard to such matters of emphasis.

Sin is not part of the real man at all; or we may say that he only attains reality through harmonious and creative experiences. Hence St Paul's statement that his 'sin' is not himself (p. 133 above). Sin is the enemy of man, not part of his immortality, like Hamlet's madness which the owner disclaims as his enemy and not part of his proper self (*Hamlet*, V. ii. 244–53). People in Dante's Hell sometimes seem to be there mainly through associations and experience, their own or Dante's, rather than through personal faults. It may even seem that some are there through past suffering only, for to suffer is to partake of evil and partial death. Dante might have met the same personalities in Hell, Purgatory and Heaven according to their various experiences, and we who watch see Dante himself in all three. His Hell is the reflection in eternity of evil experience; the persons are shown as recounting and reliving their earthly experiences, and it is these experiences that are being condemned to darkness. Only so can we today make any sense at all of Dante's statement (*Hell*, III. 6) that Hell is designed by the universal 'Love'. In this way it may be seen as the final signature of such a love. Certainly, if we think in terms of Heaven we must have a Hell too: rightly or wrongly we are conscious of evil and suffering, and somehow the negative forces must be slain. When John the Baptist talks of the threshing in eternity by which the true grain is saved and the chaff destroyed (*Luke*, III. 17), or when in the Book of Revelation the New Jerusalem is imagined in splendid triumph while all evil things are relegated to destruction (*Revelation* XX, XXI); whenever such pictures are offered to us, we must think in terms less of persons than of experiences.[1]

New Testament symbolism presents the complete life in a setting which negates causality and death. Jesus, says the Epistle to the Hebrews, may be called 'Melchizedek', that is 'King of Righteousness', and King of 'Salem', or Peace. Melchizedek 'has neither father nor mother nor genealogy, neither a beginning to his days nor an end of his life, but, resembling the Son of God, continues to be priest permanently' (*Hebrews*, VII. 3). Melchizedek and Christ have authority not through sacerdotal genealogy but through their intrinsic life: such a man is 'one of whom the witness is that "he lives" ' (*Hebrews*, VII. 8). The author goes on to argue that the priesthood and its rules cannot attain to perfection; there is a limit beyond which they are sterile (VII. 19); but at this point life itself, the creative principle, asserts its power. What he shows to be true of Melchizedek is even truer of the Christ:

> This becomes all the more plain when another priest emerges resembling Melchizedek, one who has become a priest by the power of an indissoluble Life and not by the Law of an external command.
>
> (*Hebrews*, VII. 15)

---

[1] There is some authority for such a reading at *Revelation*, XX. 13–15, where the emphasis falls on a wholesale destruction of Death, Hades, and all who are not 'enrolled in the book of Life'. The place of torment, Hades (*Luke*, XVI. 23), is itself destroyed, and this is called 'the second death' (Moffatt's rearrangement appears to be unnecessary). [1960]

This supreme life-authority is related to existence without 'beginning' or 'end', since life-power is to be seen as expressing an eternal reality not limited to our genealogies and surface causalities; as originating not from other life-manifestations but from the heart and centre of all life; and therefore as 'indissoluble'. Only so can we attain to a final understanding of any life, divine or human, or of any art-form expressive of the true life. Immortality is thus not of the past or of the future, but rather always at hand. St Paul tells us very clearly that we need not ascend to Heaven, nor go down to the abyss, to find Christ: the 'word' is in our own hearts (*Romans*, X. 8). Goethe, as we shall see, says the same (p. 255 below). Immortality is not necessarily eschatological, except in poetic creations, where it may sometimes nevertheless be best expressed in such terms. Jesus has a divine birth and bodily resurrection, and a short inspection of these symbols shows them to fall into line with my other statements.

We have already (p. 187) referred to Jesus' birth, comparing it with other birth-themes in literature: its divinity recalls the poetic attitude to birth as sparkling with the dews of paradise, divinely guarded and impelled. Jesus' bodily resurrection suggests, like so much of St Paul's imagery, that immortality flowers from physical life, in temporal terms repeating the substance of our vertical eternity. We have already seen Jesus' life as a powerful life-force; here we observe how it is completed at either end. Perfection in life is often to be seen as a blending of the spiritual and the physical. Now, whereas we too easily see birth in the false causal chain of the physical alone, we also tend, seeing the body decay in time after death, to imagine immortality as spiritual, since, the physical subtracted, it seems that there is little else that can be left. The divine birth and bodily resurrection oppose both faults: if we are to see this, as indeed any, life in its wholeness, its every moment must be known as an incarnation, a blending of spirit with the physical; its birth we do well to regard primarily as spiritual, its immortality as physical. Birth and death are falsified in our minds by erroneous abstractions: to see them aright, we must have them brought into line with immediate experience as concrete and solid realities blending the spiritual and the physical. The perfect life must be shown as possessing throughout, from start to finish, that positive interlocking with the mesh of all life which is too often lost when we abstract it from its dramatic context in the whole. Such reintegrations the Gospel story gives us. These are universal ideas. 'Whatever hath no beginning', writes Sir Thomas Browne, 'may be confident of no end' (p. 80 above). Conversely, to understand the origin of anything except in terms of the sacred principle of life is to know its death. Life itself has neither beginning nor end; it is only known by immediate experience. God is the eternal 'I am', or as translated by James Moffatt, 'I-will-be' (*Exodus*, III. 14). He is the God of the living, not of the dead, of the present and the future, not of the past. Life is a present-future dynamism, and the past only vital as an aspect of the present. Immediate life-knowledge is creative; creative in eternity and creative in that aspect of eternity we call time. As union in marriage is a surrender to life creative of life, so any union with our world is a marriage to which we are dedicated from moment to moment; and in that marriage we create our immortality.

Am I then in this essay denying personal immortality? Not properly. For what do we mean by 'personal'? Surely the word usually conveys only a quaint time-sequence abstracted from its varied dramatic contexts in life, a wraithly series, tenuous and fragile. Is this the real 'I'? Rather my proper self is the experiencing self, engaged from hour to hour in struggle, conflict, attainment or union, ever the more real for its loss in some wider engagement. Not less than personal, but more. If I am 'in love', I myself am lost in a

glorious surrender and know myself so lost while enjoying
the greater life with full consciousness: such is the super-
personal immortality. The succession of experiences that
make Shakespeare's work tell us not much of the personal
Shakespeare that Shakespeare himself would have recol-
lected in quiet thought after his retirement, but they are true
biographical documents of his immortal and experiencing
self, lost in immediate issues, passionately creative, dynamic
in either conflict or love-union. For to a final understanding
experience of disharmony is itself creative, has itself eternal
glory. Our minds in their darkness crave for the destruction
of destruction, and God in his kindness has promised them
the Hell they crave. While evil is real to us we must see it as
marked out for death. But Dante's Hell is also a noble
poetic creation, possessing its own grandeur and beauty, and
with awakened sight we may realize that there exists no
disharmony, nor ever did, nor any destruction nor death to
be destroyed. This also is the way of life. Our various paradoxes are summed and resolved in Shakespeare's line: 'And
death once dead there's no more dying then' (Sonnet 146).
Therefore all hell-visions, all death-visions are in great poetic
art themselves creative, and this potential positive within
evil is reflected in the beauty of the poetry. All evil is but an
aspect of good, all death but an element of life. Dante's
hatred of evil gives birth to his Hell; and that hatred, and
therefore that Hell, are in their degree good. All great poetry
mirrors our experiences, our immortality. Shakespeare's immortal self is like our own; the poet merely has the technical
gift of expressing in words his own and our own life-experiences. It is the same with Dante and Goethe: our greater
deathless selves are all alike. A poet's life-work is always a
record of his own and our own immortality, and this quality
is reflected in the fact that it has in the temporal sequence an
immortal persistence and appeal.

Additional Note, 1960

Subsequent discussions on poetry and immortality have appeared in *The Starlit Dome*, 1941, reissued with an Appendix, 'Spiritualism and Poetry', 1959; *Christ and Nietzsche*, 1948, IV. 147–8 and V. 187–93, on Nietzsche's 'Recurrence'; and *The Mutual Flame*, 1955, I. iv. See pp. 326–36 below; also, from a scientific standpoint, C. Conway Plumbe's *Release from Time*, 1950, and John N. East's *Eternal Quest*, 1960.

XI

EROS

IMMORTALITY cannot be understood except by a heightened consciousness. I have hinted that a state is attainable where good and evil are dissolved in beauty, and that poetry and prophecy flower from and direct us towards such a state. This is to emphasize no impossible or esoteric experience. We have all known these intuitions, since the experience of 'falling in love' is an awakening such as that to which our poetry points us. To the lover all dualisms within a limited field are resolved; a miracle happens wherein there is no tension or antagonism between the ideal and the actual. Suddenly the actual has become the ideal, the divine is incarnated in a human form. A whole universe separates such a sight from our normal clouded vision: it is so simple, there is nothing to explain; so profound, there can be nothing more to learn.

This is the purified consciousness, and from this consciousness, or one close to it, all poetry is written. The poet is necessarily a lover. When Dante in Purgatory is asked if he be the author of the poem beginning 'Ladies, ye that con the lore of love', he answers:

> Count of me but as one,
> Who am the scribe of love; that, when he breathes,
> Take up my pen, and, as he dictates, write.
> (*Purgatory*, XXIV. 52)

Shakespeare in *Love's Labour's Lost* is as decisive. Love is more than an emotion, it opens new floodgates, it explores new realms of life, of power, and of poetry:

> But Love, first learned in a lady's eyes,
> Lives not alone immured in the brain;

> But, with the motion of all elements,
> Courses as swift as thought in every power,
> And gives to every power a double power,
> Above their functions and their offices.
> It adds a precious seeing to the eye;
> A lover's eyes will gaze an eagle blind;
> A lover's ear will hear the lowest sound,
> When the suspicious head of theft is stopp'd;
> Love's feeling is more soft and sensible
> Than are the tender horns of cockled snails;
> Love's tongue proves dainty Bacchus gross in taste.
> For valour, is not Love a Hercules,
> Still climbing trees in the Hesperides?
> Subtle as Sphinx; as sweet and musical
> As bright Apollo's lute, strung with his hair;
> And, when Love speaks, the voice of all the gods
> Makes heaven drowsy with the harmony.
> Never durst poet touch a pen to write,
> Until his ink were temper'd with Love's sighs;
> O, then his lines would ravish savage ears,
> And plant in tyrants mild humility.
> From women's eyes this doctrine I derive:
> They sparkle still the right Promethean fire;
> They are the books, the arts, the academes,
> That show, contain and nourish all the world;
> Else none at all in aught proves excellent.
>
> (IV. iii. 327)

Love is Christian:

> It is religion to be thus forsworn;
> For charity itself fulfils the law:
> And who can sever love from charity?
>
> (IV. iii. 363)

Like poetry, the erotic vision pierces into life itself, its origin and fiery heart:

> Transparent Helena! Nature shows art
> That through thy bosom makes me see thy heart.
>
> (*A Midsummer Night's Dream*, II. ii. 104)

Goethe's allegorical Boy-Charioteer personifying Poetry is
described with erotic suggestion:

> One must avow
> Firstly, young and fair art thou,
> A half-grown stripling – yet the women's pleasure
> Would be to see thee grown to fullest measure.
> To me thou dost appear a future wooer,
> Frail woman's born and sworn undoer.
>
> *(Faust,* 207)

It is natural that poets should emphasize the relation of
poetry to love, for poetry is creative language and without a
love-union there is no creation.

The poet sees with the romantic vision. He does not
write while actually saturated in its fire, but recreates his
experiences in passivity. Poetry, like a human child, is born
from this union, this marriage joy. Either man or nature may
be involved. The poet sees not the clouded, muffled nature
we see in our uninspired moments; he sees nature in its
primal nakedness and paradisal grace, charged with eroticism and tingling with life. Dante's Earthly Paradise is
equated with the dreams of paganism:

> They, whose verse of yore
> The golden age recorded and its bliss,
> On the Parnassian mountain, of this place
> Perhaps had dreamed. Here was man guiltless; here
> Perpetual spring, and every fruit; and this
> The far-famed nectar.
>
> *(Purgatory,* XXVIII. 145)

Goethe's Boy-Charioteer calls himself 'profusion'; 'I am
Profusion, Poesy am I' (208). Nature seems, to use Wordsworth's phrase in his *Immortality* ode, 'apparelled in celestial
light' with 'the glory and the freshness of a dream'.

All paradisal visions are derived from sight of what Shelley
in *Adonais* (xxxi) calls 'Nature's naked loveliness'; the Earth-

Spirit of terrible beauty that strikes fear into Faust. This
nature is far from 'nature' as we usually think it; as different
as the lover's bride from all other women and not even expressed in the finest poetry without a certain loss and limitation. Thus the Earth-Spirit scorns Faust:

> Thou'rt like the Spirit thou graspest with thy mind,
> Thou'rt not like me!   (15)

There are two primary stages in reality: nature or man as
they appear to ordinary consciousness, and nature or man as
they appear to erotic perception. Between we have art and
religion drawing their content from the authentic sight,
themselves less than that primal wonder, though aiming to
lift us towards it. When Shakespeare compares 'art' and
'nature' we must realize that two natures, the lower and the
higher, may be involved. Thinking of her dream-Antony,
Cleopatra says:

> ... nature wants stuff
> To vie strange forms with fancy; yet to imagine
> An Antony were nature's piece 'gainst fancy,
> Condemning shadows quite.
> (*Antony and Cleopatra*, V. ii. 97)

'Fancy' is often more gorgeous than the actual, but the
actual illumined by love puts art to shame. Nature properly
understood includes art. In *The Winter's Tale* Perdita says
that she will not have 'streaked gillyvors' in her garden:

> POLIXENES: Wherefore, gentle maiden,
> Do you neglect them?
> PERDITA: For I have heard it said
> There is an art which in their piedness shares
> With great creating nature.
> POLIXENES: Say there be;
> Yet nature is made better by no mean
> But nature makes that mean: so, over that art

> Which you say adds to nature, is an art
> That nature makes. You see, sweet maid, we marry
> A gentler scion to the wildest stock,
> And make conceive a bark of baser kind
> By bud of nobler race: this is an art
> Which does mend nature, change it rather, but
> The art itself is nature.
>
> (*The Winter's Tale*, IV. iii. 85)

Throughout our thinking on art, religion or life we must remember this upward development: the lesser nature, poetry and religion, the greater nature. The greater nature is the divine: our categories represent really the natural, human and divine. This 'divine' is the life known temporarily to the lover. We do not understand our life: 'Though all men live it, few there be that know it' (*Faust*, 4). When in Dante human artistry is said to copy nature whereas nature imitates the Celestial Mind, nature is first, art second, in descent from God; and these two are, according to 'Creation's holy book', the 'right source of life to man' (*Hell*, XI. 100–13). This is the higher nature, divinely originated, the wondrous life of which we are part but which we do not understand. Poetry points us towards that nature, that life; and pointing us to life itself, speaks through the erotic vision.

This vision is more than mental. It is not an attitude to life; it is life itself. To the lower, mental consciousness the body of man may seem ugly and unclean, and nature drab and unpurposeful. This is because one small part cannot enclose the whole; the mind cannot know even its own body. The mental knows the mental, the physical the physical, but life only can know life. The fuller life circumferences both mind and body, its consciousness knows their true stature and strength. Such is the consciousness of love; and the union of lovers is an act of lightning beauty and resplendent power, for then the life of an individual drinks power from that fount and principle of all life to which our thinking

minds are but as sparkling pebbles to the sun. The union of
instincts in one human being creates a miraculous knowledge; and this is love and poetry and religion. The union of
human lovers creates a yet greater miracle than these: a
child. Life is greater and more miraculous than any mental
or imaginative dynamisms. Poetry, like religion, would
awake us to that life and immortality too close for our long-
sightedness to visualize: it speaks to awake the love-consciousness from which it is itself derived, and here the greater
Renaissance poets make a single statement.

Beatrice dominates Dante's *Divina Commedia*. Virgil
guides Dante through Hell and up the Mount of Purgatory
till, in the Earthly Paradise, he meets Beatrice. Henceforth
she is his guide. He is now lord of himself and there is no disharmony between his instincts and his will:

> To distrust thy sense
> Were henceforth error. I invest thee then
> With crown and mitre, sovereign o'er thyself.
> *(Purgatory*, XXVII. 141)

Poetry and religion lead us to the point where they may be
discarded: Beatrice, not Virgil, is the final guide. She it was
who originally sent Virgil to save Dante from the 'death' he
was enduring on earth (*Hell*, II. 108); she is both guide and
saviour; indeed, she all but replaces Christ. In the Earthly
Paradise she appears attended by figures symbolizing the
Old and New Testaments with a car drawn by the Gryphon,
symbolizing the union of the divine with the earthly, being
thus honoured as the culmination of Biblical revelation.
Even on earth she was marvellous:

> Never didst thou spy,
> In art or nature, aught so passing sweet
> As were the limbs that in their beauteous frame
> Enclosed me, and are scattered now in dust.
> *(Purgatory*, XXXI. 46)

Reflected and refracted in her eyes Dante contemplates the
ultimate mystery of dualisms transcended into unity, the
mystery of the Gryphon symbolizing Christ, in human terms
varying, but itself single:

> And then they led me to the Gryphon's breast,
> Where, turned towards us, Beatrice stood.
> 'Spare not thy vision. We have stationed thee
> Before the emeralds, whence love, erewhile,
> Hath drawn his weapons on thee'. As they spake,
> A thousand fervent wishes riveted
> Mine eyes upon her beaming eyes, that stood,
> Still fixed toward the Gryphon, motionless.
> As the sun strikes a mirror, even thus
> Within those orbs the twyfold being shone;
> For ever varying, in one figure now
> Reflected, now in other. Reader! muse
> How wondrous in my sight it seemed, to mark
> A thing, albeit steadfast in itself,
> Yet in its imaged semblance mutable.
>
> *(Purgatory*, XXXI. 113)

The *Paradiso* further glorifies Beatrice, her eyes, her smile,
her radiant light. Dante calls her 'the day-star of mine eyes'
(*Paradise*, XXX. 76). His whole Paradise circles round his
love for Beatrice. Nor is it any coldly abstract or intellectual
love. It is a divine flirtation:

> Then by the spirit, that doth never leave
> Its amorous dalliance with my lady's looks,
> Back with redoubled ardour were mine eyes
> Led unto her.
>
> *(Paradise*, XXVII. 83)

Richly he sees and depicts her smile, 'painted on her cheek',
her looks of love, her divine sweetness. Her 'laughing eyes'
are said to 'scatter' his 'collected mind' with their 'radiance'
(*Paradise*, X. 58). The erotic ideal is all but equated with the
divine; Beatrice all but identified with the Christ.

In Shakespeare love is described as harmonizing human faculties. Troilus describes his love:

> I take to-day a wife, and my election
> Is led on in the conduct of my will;
> My will enkindled by mine eyes and ears,
> Two traded pilots 'twixt the dangerous shores
> Of will and judgement.
>
> *(Troilus and Cressida,* II. ii. 61)

'Will' means 'passion': the instinctive passion is 'kindled' by the senses and the final harmony established under 'judgement'. Heroine after heroine witnesses to Shakespeare's ideal. The Sonnets see the Eros in terms both of a fair youth, who may be compared with Goethe's Boy-Charioteer, and – though very differently – a dark lady. His most wondrous single human figure is Cleopatra. From Juliet to Miranda and Queen Katharine his heroines are crowned and glorified beyond all other ideals but the divine. In Shakespeare love blends into the divine, as in Dante. The loved one is an 'angel' *(Romeo and Juliet,* II. ii. 26) and the state of love 'eternity':

> Eternity was in our lips and eyes,
> Bliss in our brows bent; none our parts so poor,
> But was a race of heaven.
>
> *(Antony and Cleopatra,* I. iii. 35)

Love is life's guiding star. It

> is an ever-fixed mark
> That looks on tempests and is never shaken;
> It is the star to every wandering bark,
> Whose worth's unknown, although his height be taken.
>
> (Sonnet 116)

Throughout love is associated with music and contrasted with disorders, conflicts, discords. Like Beatrice's eyes reflecting the mystic Gryphon, love in Shakespeare induces

unity and harmony in a chaotic world. Not only is it the
guiding star in life; it is also the gateway to immortal life-in-
death. This, the theme of *Antony and Cleopatra*, is compactly
expressed in *The Phoenix and the Turtle*:

> So they loved, as love in twain
> Had the essence but in one;
> Two distincts, division none:
> Number there in love was slain.

Shakespeare's world, wherein from the first the music of love
was a dream-sweetness, at the last finds love the stalwart
vanquisher of death. Even had the poet not written his last
play *Henry VIII*, we could say, watching the love-victories in
the final plays, that Shakespeare's love-intuition at the last
was close to, if not identical with, the Christian statement.
In both death is put down by a love; and this love is in both
an aspect of essential life.

It is the same with Goethe. Love, human, passionate,
romantic love, is the very opening of the immortal day-
stream, a deathless paradise, a conquering angel of life.
Gretchen asks Faust if he believes in God. He answers:

> Thou winsome angel-face, mishear me not!
> Who can name Him?
> Who thus proclaim Him:
> *I believe Him?*
> Who that hath feeling
> His bosom steeling,
> Can say: *I believe Him not?*
> The All-embracing,
> The All-sustaining,
> Clasps and sustains He not
> Thee, me, Himself?
> Springs not the vault of Heaven above us?
> Lieth not Earth firm-stablished 'neath our feet?
> And with a cheerful twinkling
> Climb not eternal stars the sky?

Eye into eye gaze I not upon thee?
Surgeth not all
To head and heart within thee?
And floats in endless mystery
Invisible visible around thee?
Great though it be, fill thou therefrom thine heart,
And when in the feeling wholly blest thou art,
Call it then what thou wilt!
Call it Bliss! Heart! Love! God!
I have no name for it!
Feeling is all in all!
Name is but sound and reek,
A mist round the glow of Heaven!

(*Faust*, 118)

Here, as in our quotation from *Love's Labour's Lost*
(p. 200), we watch the poet striving to encompass and
possess the greater life through experience of love. We are
close to the words of St Paul at the shrine of the 'unknown
God' (p. 125 above).

In *Faust* we meet the radiant Galatea in processional
royalty, like Beatrice. Her appearance is the culmination of
Homunculus' quest:

What glows
Round the shell and around Galatea's fair feet,
Now flares out resplendent, now lovely, now sweet,
As if by the pulses of love it were thrilled?

(305)

He shatters his life-fire, spilling his flame over his desire:

What fiery marvel transfigures the billows
That sparkling shatter them each on its fellows?
So shines it, so surges, sweeps onward in light,
The bodies they burn on their path through the night,
And all round about us in fire is embosomed.
To Eros the empire, whence all things first blossomed!

> Hail the Ocean! Hail the Surge!
> Girt with holy fire its verge.
> Hail the Water! Hail the Fire!
> Hail the chance that all admire!   (305)

Homunculus' fire is spilt over Galatea, sea-goddess gliding in a 'shell-chariot', her attendants on sea-beasts. Fire and water, Goethe's key-dualism, are blended in love union, and the paean is raised to Eros, lord of union, of marriage, of birth. The incident is followed by the union of Faust and Helen.

The poets one after the other present similar love-dreams and love-dramas. In Shelley's *Prometheus Unbound* the victory is consummated by the union of Prometheus with Asia whereby all discords are harmonized, nature glorified, and Man and Earth new-born. Asia corresponds to Beatrice. Like Dante, Shakespeare and Goethe, Shelley sees the divine in terms of reunion with a lost lover. Even Milton's Paradise in *Paradise Lost* is just like all other poetic paradises; there is a sweet and fruitful nature, an unblamed joy, a happy human love.

The statement of poetry on this erotic theme is compacted in Keats' *Ode to Psyche*, a poem directly supporting my main argument, for here the poet sees himself as offering to Psyche, the human soul loved by Eros, honours long-since due. Though it is too late for superstitious reverence, for 'antique vows' and 'the fond believing lyre', it is not too late for a profounder faith. This is our prophetic message:

> Yes, I will be thy priest, and build a fane
>   In some untrodden region of my mind,
> Where branched thoughts, new grown with pleasant pain,
>   Instead of pines shall murmur in the wind.

'Pleasant pain': in Keats the final beauty does not exclude the darker essences. This suffering joy brings 'branched thoughts' to luxuriant growth, honouring love, 'warm love' in his own phrase; no sainted ice-cold charity, but a warm, human love; rich, a dark rich wine, a dark rose, red with life.[1]

In his short poem *On Death*, Keats knows that the future doom of man is to 'awake'. He is the prophet of love and therefore the prophet of immortality. Perhaps the most beautiful love-song in our literature is also a death-song and a song of life:

> Bright Star, would I were steadfast as thou art –
>   Not in lone splendour hung aloft the night
> And watching, with eternal lids apart,
>   Like nature's patient, sleepless Eremite,
> The moving waters at their priestlike task
>   Of pure ablution round earth's human shores,
> Or gazing on the new soft-fallen mask
>   Of snow upon the mountains and the moors –
> No – yet still steadfast, still unchangeable,
>   Pillow'd upon my fair love's ripening breast,
> To feel for ever its soft fall and swell,
>   Awake for ever in a sweet unrest,
> Still, still to hear her tender-taken breath,
> And so live ever – or else swoon to death.

This is no tenuous creed of ghostly immortality; it celebrates rather a life in death which by including death and blending it with all life, shapes a present actuality, solid and warm and human, a love which is darker than death and more enduring bright than the eternal stars. Love, passionate love, is Keats' gospel at the last. On 13 October, 1819, he wrote to Fanny Brawne:

I have no limit now to my love – Your note came in just here – I cannot be happier away from you. 'Tis richer than an Argosy of Pearls. Do not threat me even in jest. I have been astonished that Men could die Martyrs for religion – I have shudder'd at it. I shudder no more – I could be martyr'd for my Religion – Love is

[1] The more subtle implications of this poem are discussed in *The Starlit Dome*, IV. 301–4; and see p. 276 below.

my religion – I could die for that. I could die for you. My Creed is Love and you are its only tenet. You have ravish'd me away by a Power I cannot resist . . .

'Love is my religion', a 'creed of love'. A pagan sentiment?

The divine books of our religion are poetic: they use symbols and imagery characteristic of poetry and crowning these we have the divine presented in human form, the Christ. Our poets, using similar effects, crown their visions with a human form given the insignia of divinity. The main statement of poetry is life and love, the erotic quest; the main statement in the New Testament is also life and love, universal love. The prophets of the modern world are the poets; they alone have streaked their pages with the sacred fire, they only transmit authentic, because original, statements of immortality; for Shelley's *Adonais* repeats no lesson learnt from books, but flowers direct from the origin of life. Today, despite all these convergent similarities, Shakespeare and the Bible, the prophets and poets, are on the one side; our established Christianity on the other.

The Bible is poetic. *The Song of Solomon* is a paean of praise to love and the little drama is accompanied by impressions of the child, the sun, harvest, flowers and glittering riches. This is typical:

> How neatly you trip it,
> O princess mine,
> your thighs are swaying like links of a chain
> that a master-hand has moulded;
> your waist is round as a goblet
> (ever be it filled!)
> your body a bundle of wheat
> encircled by lilies . . .

*   *   *   *   *   *

> You stand there straight as a palm,
> with breasts like clusters of fruit;

> methinks I will climb that palm,
>> taking hold of the boughs!
> O may your breasts be clusters of fruit,
>> and your breath sweet as an apple!
> May your kisses be exquisite wine
>> that slips so smoothly down,
>>> gliding over the lips and the teeth!

(VII. 1–9)

This is the poetical soil from which Christianity rose. The poet sees love as of transcendent power, potent as death:

> For love is strong as death itself,
>> and passion masters like the grave,
> its flashes burn like flame,
>> true lightning-flashes.
> No floods can ever quench this love,
>> no rivers drown it.
> If a man offered all he has for love,
>> he would be laughed aside.

(VIII. 6)

Love is itself life and it is the life-fire in such experience that makes man write his Bibles and creeds and systems of poetic fantasy. The argument as to whether the love in *The Song of Solomon* or the love and wine symbols in the work of Omar Khayyám are to be taken literally or symbolically is futile, since all love literature is to be taken both literally and symbolically. Until we understand that the terms are synonymous we do not understand poetry, for to receive a poetic effect with due surrender to its fullest content is to see it widening into universal meanings.

In the Old Testament Jehovah is the god of sun and stars, the seas and winds and gleaming clouds, the fruits of the earth, the birds and trees, god of the dove and the leviathan, the cedar and the vine. This is typical:

This is the word of the Eternal, who sets the sun to light the day and the moon and stars to light the night, who stirs the sea up till its waters roar (his name, the Lord of hosts).

(*Jeremiah*, XXXI. 35)

And again:

> When poor forlorn folk vainly seek for water,
>   with tongues that are parched by thirst,
> I the Eternal will answer them,
>   I Israel's God will not forsake them;
> on the bare heights I will open rivers,
>   and in the valleys fountains,
> I will make deserts into lakes,
>   and dry land into springs of water;
> I will plant cedars in the desert,
>   acacias, myrtles, olive-trees;
> I will put fir-trees in the wilderness,
>   and planes and cypresses;
> that men may see and understand,
>   consider and agree
> that the Eternal's hand has done it,
>   that Israel's Majesty has made it all.

(*Isaiah*, XLI. 17)

Jehovah is also a god of ethical fervour, exhorting his people to a righteousness demanded by the unswerving righteousness of the universe that surrounds them. He is active, dynamic and commanding. He includes not only nature but man with his aspirations and his world of good and evil. He is the god equally of the nesting birds and warring nations; of the ravenous tiger and human charity.

The finest visions of Hebraic prophecy may be couched in erotic imagery. Isaiah sees his nation as the bride of the Eternal:

> 'Forsaken' shall no longer be your name,
>   your land shall no more be called 'Desolate';
> you shall be 'my Delight',

      your land shall be 'my wedded wife',
   for the Eternal takes delight in you,
      and your land shall again be married.
   As a young man weds a maiden,
      so your Founder marries you,
   and as a bridegroom thrills to his bride,
      so shall your God thrill to you.
                              (*Isaiah*, LXII. 4)

Do we desire a more electric image? Or could we find a sweeter pathos and gentleness than this:

      The Eternal recalls you like a wife
         broken-hearted by neglect;
      'But a young wife' – your God asks –
      'how can she be thrown aside?'
                              (*Isaiah*, LIV. 6)

In the Book of Jeremiah the Lord speaks of Israel in erotic terms and concludes:

      But as a wife betrays her husband for her lover,
      so you have betrayed me,
      O house of Israel – says the Eternal.
                              (III. 20)

She is 'maiden Israel' (*Jeremiah*, XXXI. 4). No poet can write for long without such symbols.

    In the New Testament, as we have observed, Jesus continues the tradition, talking of the 'marriage-banquet' and calling himself a 'bridegroom'. The figure is carried on by St Paul. It is bright in the Book of Revelation. God 'has doomed the great Harlot who destroyed earth with her vice' (XIX. 2) and the true marriage begins:

      Hallelujah! now the Lord our God almighty reigns!
      Let us rejoice and triumph,
      let us give him the glory!
      For now comes the marriage of the Lamb;
      his bride has arrayed herself.   (XIX. 7)

Again:

> And I saw the holy City, the new Jerusalem,
> descending from God out of Heaven, all ready like
> a bride arrayed for her husband.

> (XXI. 2)

Prophet after prophet, poet after poet, asserts a divine betrothal. But there is little erotic suggestion in our organized
religion. Today, novels, theatres, cinemas are charged with
a passionate, dissolute, homeless but warmly human eroticism; while our religion, aloof, remains cold, chaste and
charitable.

The Old Testament presents human propagation as an
ideal. God tells man to 'be fruitful' and 'multiply' (*Genesis*,
I. 28). Creation is an end in itself, and what better thing to
create than human beings? But the prophets see another
creativeness apart from propagation, a love not limited to
sex. There are two ways of being thus creative: by art and
thought, and by action and religious fervour. The Greeks
chose the one, the Hebrews the other. Greek culture ran its
course to a conclusion, whereas the Hebraic power was less
easily exhausted. It made Christianity. So powerful a supersexual life-message could only come from a race with an
excessively developed life-instinct, and Christianity may be
regarded as the culmination of the Hebraic ideal of physical
propagation. The New Testament supersedes that ideal with
a new and different creativeness. It is not enough to have
children; the world is not yet fit for children. It is not enough
to love passionately; the world is not yet fit for passion.
Therefore the love-instinct, the passion-power, must create
this world. The New Testament does not repudiate sex as
evil; rather, like all poets, it gives human union high
imaginative honours. But we are urged primarily to a life
rich as any lover's, but unlimited; to a life passionately strong
and deathlessly loving. Sexual love is often as an April day,

uncertain and insecure, and its obverse, hate, is only too ready for entrance. The love-experience is to be channelled, developed, and allowed to irrigate the whole parched deserts of our lives from birth to death. Too often it is only a dangerous lightning in the midnight storm; rather it might burn as a star, a dawn-star, herald of a greater sun. We are never urged to be hostile to sex or unsexual but rather to be supersexual; to love universally, warmly and richly, yet with control; and, knowing the awakened life that comes to the lover, to possess it powerful, invariable and invincible.

If a conflict has arisen between sex and Christianity, this is not because the two are opposed but because they are so close. To two marriages we may be impelled, the one, as St Paul suggests, becoming a rival to the other. At the birth of Christianity, St Paul, though he uncompromisingly rejected teachings which denounced marriage as evil, yet counselled celibacy where practicable; so did Jesus, though not strongly (p. 164). This was necessary, if the new marriage was to gain any start in the human consciousness. Besides, the ascetic ideal at its best has accomplished great things and may be still often advisable, exerting a pressure on the passions, a thwarting and discipline, which may enrich and redirect those passions into high endeavour in art or service of one kind or another. But whether expressed in human marriage, social work or art, the erotic instinct is primary; it is the life-instinct. Calling us to life, Jesus is calling us to awaken the very Eros in ourselves which we too often think that he rejects as evil. It is a sorry mistake, though it may have been necessary, since for centuries man has had to control and direct passions elsewise curbless; the discipline was needed and asceticism was read into the Christian documents. And if the past attribution of too exclusive an ascetic ideal to Christianity proves its value as a temporary measure, then the clear sight we may have today that the New Testament stands for something more exciting than mere repression may argue that we have ceased to need this discipline. Today we should see in Christianity a message positive and assertive; physical as well as mental; exciting to action, exciting to life.[1]

The problem of sex is not answered for us directly in the New Testament; the book is remarkable in its baffling and ingenious indecisiveness. Enlisted for many years in the cause of ascetisism, today it might almost be used to support a theory of free love. It refuses to settle the question finally; had it done so, it would have grown out of date. As it is, concentrating on the essential life, it, like all poetry, is deathless. The Bible and the poets are one in using sexual symbolism to awake us to this life, and the life they would arouse, though it may include sexual action, is not conditioned by it. They rouse in us no instincts which they do not in the same instant satisfy: they awake us, and leave us pleased with our awakening.

D. H. Lawrence is accordingly a true prophet if properly understood, though we need to understand him more thoroughly than he understood Christianity. He was a poet of power standing at the threshold of an age that is about to see for the first time the relevance of poetry to life. His doctrine, in so far as it is poetry, holds nothing new; he follows the usual symbolisms. His insistence on primal passions, the deep origins of life, his cosmology that would make the sun a vital force, his sympathy with nature, all this is usual. In Shakespeare sun and moon take part in scenes of strong life-instincts; Goethe knows all about the primal life-passions; all poets sympathize with nature. Lawrence was original only in seeing that something new was to be done about it, though what exactly he did not understand. Seeing a divergence between orthodox Christianity and his

[1] The deeper implications of this paragraph are developed in my Epilogue. [1960]

poetic intuition, he reiterated his dislike of conventional doctrines. He is an example of the power exercised by associations; he cannot see Christianity straight because it was falsely inculcated or wrongly received in his youth. At the last, he falls back on the Book of Revelation to supply him with the symbols he wants. That is not strange, since his doctrines are Christian in essence. His twin ideals of love and power reflect the love and the power declared similarly by St Paul; his hatred of abstract intellectualities when allowed sovereignty is Pauline and repeats the attitude of Jesus; and his assertion of the physical is a modern reiteration of the Christian principle of incarnation. Moreover, in *Apropos of Lady Chatterley's Lover*, he counsels celibacy as a temporary measure in what he considers our present period of sex impoverishment. Many are 'happiest' if they stay apart, for 'ours is the day of realization rather than action'. Again: 'On the whole it would be better if modern people didn't marry.' Lawrence also makes here a special point of what he calls a 'blood-connection' binding all classes together, so recalling St Paul's use of physical imagery to denote the intermesh of life with life in the Christian community. To many Lawrence should be a direct step towards a proper understanding of St Paul.

His work is summed up in the short story, *The Escaped Cock* or *The Man Who Died*. What he takes to be the Christian ideal is set beside the pagan and the naturalistic. Jesus, alive after the crucifixion, realizes that he gave men only the ghost of love and surrenders to physical love-union with a priestess of Isis. And yet Lawrence here is directly Christian: in choosing such a theme, he is recognizing Jesus as the type and prince of idealistic heroism, and so doing is able to drive home his doctrine that such idealistic values are not enough. But these are our facts. Jesus asserts that in a world which often negates life-instincts, yet life may flower everywhere in all richness if we but touch the life-centre. Necessarily, himself he shows often as fasting, weary, loveless, without wife or home; in spite of this he takes pleasure in feasting, in human love and marriage, in domestic joy. All these are good. But man does not live by bread alone, nor marriage, nor even love; only by life; and even life may at the last be sacrificed in life's cause. To essential life he directs man and claiming the key to those rich coffers he shows his own life not dependent on any one subsidiary expression. Otherwise that life would have been invalid as an example and encouragement to the thousands who, suffering in a world of negation, have drawn peace from watching his conquest. Yet it is true that in so far as we see his life as shadowed by Calvary we tend to see too powerful a negation, and therefore we are told of his bodily resurrection; otherwise death would loom too large, and no negation must be allowed to shadow too darkly so positive a splendour. Jesus' life of sacrifice and final death is not the whole story, and Christian symbolism is one with Lawrence in asserting this. Whatever value we attach to a bodily resurrection it does not exclude the richest paradisal and physical actions. So Lawrence may be said to have expanded in realistic narrative the fact of the Resurrection, mythically outlining Jesus' personal immortality. His story is a valuable complement to the Gospel narrative.

This is no rash conclusion. The New Testament is poetry and being poetry is close to life itself, and in life there is nothing greater than sex and its law of creative union. Poetry flowers directly from the sex, that is the life, instinct. The Christian religion may likewise claim this honour. Poetry and Christianity, life-born, are life-creative; and since life itself is our final revelation and that revelation cannot exceed the primal splendour recognized by the lover, therefore poets write continually and necessarily of the Eros.

Love strikes the human consciousness as a risen sun lights the eye. Melting the opaque darkness, it banishes a thousand phantasmas of death and guilt to take refuge in their own unreality. The former consciousness seems then but a stark and barren land, a rock-strewn desert, greyly corpse-like as some unlitten moon whirling on its loveless track, unknowing, unknown, though aeons of purposeless flight. But the romantic vision dresses all things with the pigments of life. It holds the blue of sky and sea, the green which is the vesture to the earth, the earth's rich brown, the yellow of ripe corn. It is red with the life that mantles a human cheek. Love wears Caesarean purple. It is throned above all other knowledges that man's experience may know, bearing the crown and the sceptre to whose authority all human allegiance unhesitatingly bows. Love needs no tuition. It is the instinctive meeting and mating of life with life. It is life conscious of life, the highest pinnacle of life to which we come, and being itself life's richest flower holds the seeds of birth and of creation. In love man is more than human, or then only attains humanity. He is then a vessel charged with richest elixirs, and hence love's eyes are as jewels that sparkle with an unimagined joy. You must approach no philosopher nor theologian nor poet to learn the truth of this: question only one who loves, or one who, having loved, instates daily in his mind carven memorials to that vision, preserving their marbled integrity. But perhaps only one actually indwelling in that radiance and drinking of that deathless rose may speak with valid authority.

Yet, if a writer were to engage under the banner of imperial love in any warfare of words, he might expect an easy victory. He immediately enlists the deepest and most universal instincts and can advance a myriad facts to support his argument. Romance is daily afire in a thousand novels, a thousand plays, a thousand films. Those, you may say, are trash, whereas we of culture prefer less sentimental themes. But what of our poets; of Dante, Shakespeare, Goethe; of Pope, Browning, Bridges; of the Bible itself? Are not

Medieval and Renaissance literature alike dedicate to this
Eros? And were not also the ancients? Does it not vitalize
Oriental as well as Occidental myth and legend? You
cannot wisely play tricks with the instincts of a race, nor, as
Shakespeare puts it in *Measure for Measure*,

> . . . draw with idle spiders' strings
> Most ponderous and substantial things.
>
> (III. ii. 297)

Today eroticism is rampant, runs to waste, uncontrolled,
unrecognized, unblessed by our religion. Tigers of passion,
burning bright. A river dammed will surely overflow, and
we have dammed, and damned, the divinest fire coursing in
the human heart.

I have used the word 'divine' to express this ineffable
vision or fact. It is both fact and vision: in love the fact is
afire with visionary meaning, an apocalyptic vision miraculously interfused with fact. This is the marriage of Earth and
Heaven, this the eternal Virgin Birth striking a new wonder
and new glory and a rising life across our age-weary world
of death; the life-bringing stream from mountains invisible
come to irrigate our parched lands. The Christian dogma of
the Incarnation directly reflects the erotic and romantic
vision. The Christ himself may become to his chosen lover
alight with the plumed splendours of sunrise. Christian
mysticism, all mystic experience, is, like the lover's vision,
a flooding life, a wine of love; and wherever this Logos of
Life is newly incarnated, all theological intellectualisms, all
poetic systems, are but tinsel wrappings in that comparison.
In the New Jerusalem there is to be no temple. Religion is
less than life, a child greater than any creed: the Sabbath
was made for man. Yet again, we cannot, or do not, live for
ever so charged with vitality, nor would it be readily support-
able to us, death-weakened as we are. Love is unruly, un-
manageable often; and then again, like a fallen eagle, uneasy

in this darkened world, beating fractured wings in agony, soiled and ridiculous; wide wings that late outspread in massive span, to fan the azure steppes and climb with sun-fixed undazzled eye the shimmering paths that upsweep towards the burning zone. Yes, love-sight is an unrest, very often; un-at-home with us here in our twilit world, too tormentingly beautiful, too cruel in its grace. There is no Hell like a fleeting glimpse of Paradise.

And yet I refer not solely to the love of man, nor of God, but remember rather our finer phrase 'to be in love with' God, man, woman, or indeed anything whatsoever. That love, not its subject or object, is primary. It is 'to be in life with' someone or something; to be alive and know it and, knowing essential life, to know also immortality. It cannot be further expressed. Words wrong the fire and music of its majesty. If the genius of Dante, of Shakespeare, of Goethe were to combine all three to turn into glittering words one of the thousand romances that thread our country lanes and cinema halls tonight, those words would yet be as gilt paper beside the solid gold they imitate. No art, no religion, is to take precedence of life itself.

The great god Eros moves over us, shadowing our world with his wings, homeless awhile. A great God, searching for incarnation.

XII

THE ETERNAL TRIANGLE

REALITY is experience, and experience as we know it is the product of two or more factors, one at least of which is human; and what is human has an emotional element. Therefore no final statement about reality can be made by logic alone; either our logic must be presented in words impregnated with emotional power or paradox, in which case the logic is transcended, or an elaborate symbolism is needed. Jesus tells us that the Realm of Heaven is like, not a person, but rather a story: 'The Realm of Heaven is like a householder who went out early in the morning . . .' (*Matthew*, XX. 1). Only by making a story can he include those dynamic properties that he wishes to express. Reality to Jesus is dramatic rather than personal and so he uses miniature dramas to express the divine. Often in full-length dramas such as Shakespeare's symbols assist clarification. If we agree that in life as in literature reality is dramatic and that symbolisms may be needed to simplify complex relations or experiences, we may begin to understand the Christian Trinity as a kind of drama reflecting and simplifying a number of complex interactions. It may at first seem irrational; it may seem too elaborate and unrealistic; it may seem all sort of things. But reality is not simple: Browning chose to tell his tale in *The Ring and the Book* through many different persons in order to attain a richer statement than any single narrative, unless heavy with symbolic compensation, could be expected to compass. The Trinity might be called an arbitrary symbolism. Nevertheless, quite apart from the reference at *Matthew* XXVIII. 19 which is probably an interpolation, it is legitimately drawn from the New Testament and simplifies with amazing neatness our chaotic life.

Many earnest minds find no satisfaction in Christian

orthodoxy. The average thinking man of today stumbles at dogma and doctrine. His spokesman, the literary agnostic, from time to time sets forth a volume of religious enquiry and so far as may be formulates the beliefs of modern scepticism. These beliefs are not all negative: there is at least some faith left in most of us; failing all else, we still believe in values; but where a god or gods are concerned, we hesitate, since our current scepticism is not supernaturalistic. We also believe in nature. That is not by itself to be condemned; it depends on what we mean by nature. Do we mean the universal nature of paradisal poetry and the love-consciousness or the parochial nature drained of emotional significance and submitted to the dissecting and analytic intellect? If the first, we are right to say that nature is all-inclusive; if the latter, we blunder. That is where religion and poetic symbolism come in: addressing themselves to the lower, they aim to induce the higher, consciousness. They assert the universal in terms of the particular; and in so far as we understand this we shall begin to understand the Trinity.

Poetic symbolism does not aim to say: 'This is so'; rather it says, 'Look at this if you want to awake'; and how can a coldly intellectual treatise on the evolutionary process and the emergence of human values awake the imagination? But, you will say, is Christian symbolism true? We may say that it is. An intellectual statement is true in so far as it is in alignment with the laws of mental reasoning. The human mind, however, is one part only of a greater life and poetic symbolism is true in so far as it falls into alignment with that life; its truth lies in its creative power. Our thinking is hampered by our modern instinct to limit the word 'true' to one subsidiary meaning. Consider Wordsworth's lines in his poem *To a Skylark*:

Type of the wise who soar, but never roam;
True to the kindred points of Heaven and Home!

That is the sense in which we must read all greater 'truth', and it is finally an inclusive sense, since mental truth too has to produce creative results if it is to survive. But can our rationalist pseudo-philosophies thus qualify for life? Many things have been made the subject of worship in the past: animals, images, natural forces or human creations, the sun, the earth, heroes of history. It has been left to us to sink to the lowest of all superstitions and pay our adoration to a ghostly word such as 'values'.

Intellect and its systems change from generation to generation: the deeper things persist. Man still grieves in his bereavement just as his forefathers grieved; like them he falls in love; he endures their fear, their hopes, their disquiet, their passionate achievement. Facing the stars, dare we claim to have read their secret? We are all Chaldeans yet beneath the night skies. The tiger burning in the jungle is to us, as to Blake, a fearful being of mystic creation. These primal experiences endure and of them our poets and prophets speak. Suppose we offer a realistic interpretation today of the Garden of Eden myth in *Genesis*: will our interpretation be suggesting new meanings a thousand years hence? A paraphrase may be useful but it is not poetry. We may rationalize the New Testament; but is our thesis, like it, immortal? And if not, which holds the profounder truth? Nor is great poetry only emotional. Imagination circumferences both intellect and emotion; and to the imagination in man are addressed both poetry and Christian orthodoxy.

Suppose one of our modern prophets to be writing his treatise to replace Christianity. He rejects personal gods and writes about the evolutionary process, man, and his place in nature. 'Man' and 'nature' are presented unpoetically, quite unapparelled in celestial light, so that we are regarding the lower, not the higher, nature, and man as he appears to the ethnologist or barrister, not as he appears to the lover. But since this prosaic picture leaves out very much, leaves out the stars and all that we feel about them, leaves out love and ecstasy of any kind, indeed refuses to communicate the incommunicable, we have a sprinkling of words such as 'values', 'reality' and so on. These replace the symbolisms found in poetry and religion. This however does not at all dispense with symbolism, for these words are themselves ghostly symbols, antic shapes parodying the more vital and concrete creations they would replace and from which, if the truth were known, they have been abstracted. Science by its very nature refuses to formulate the inexpressible and the mysterious; it is a 'knowing', as its name implies. Intellect, as its name implies, is an 'understanding'. And yet there is much that cannot be known or understood because it is too large for our minds. Whereas intellect abstracts from experience only what it can understand, the mysterious and the ineffable are the proper territories of poetry and religious symbolism: our vague concepts are by them given local habitations and vital form. Poetry is creation. It explains the inexplicable mystery, life, not by a logical exposition but by itself creating: life can only be explained by life. A symbol is not a substitute for something more important; it is rather a dynamic and significant piece of imaginative life addressed as much to the emotions as to the intellect. Such life, created by poet, prophet, race, or divine being continues to exert power and suggest meanings, and when it ceases to exert power and suggest meanings it ceases to be an active symbol.

The Trinity is a symbolic art-form abstracted from the New Testament, and like all true art-forms it discloses new meanings as the centuries revolve. This is the interpretation for our time. God the Father, inscrutably existing in and beyond our world, is the creator of all things, good and evil, beautiful and obscene. He dwells in the enigmatic silences as a mountain crest beetles terrifyingly above the upturned faces of men, while simultaneously dropping his foundations into those black gorges whither man will not wittingly turn his gaze. In the heights and in the depths he strikes equal awe. God the Son is the friend of man. He champions man in this mysterious and unfriending universe; he teaches man life and love and suffers in his cause; he is Prometheus and Jesus the Christ. These two persons must yet, in some sense, correspond; in some sense the God beyond good and evil, beyond life and death, must be the God too of human good and human life; the God of nature's cruelty must be also the God of human love. The paradox is asserted, but we reject the dualistic irrationality. Consider the circle, how beautiful its completion and perfected rondure; or the triangle which, however unequally it be drawn, remains yet more graciously beautiful than the most symmetric quadrilateral. Odd numbers are more profoundly mystic than even numbers, each in its indivisibility holding the secret of unity; the three angles of a triangle reduce to the angle of straightness, and for straightness and unity the mazed soul searches, baffled by the dualisms of the even numbers dividedly arrayed against each other. We imagine time as a straight line and the immortality we desire is an infinite continuance which we find nevertheless cut short by the precipitous oblique of death; so that experience seems to present to us the two arms of an angle, one stretching back to birth in time and the other slanting into the unknown; and there is no peace in such two-legged incongruities. That is why we completed our immortality diagram by constructing a triangle; and that is why we have a Third Person to complete the Trinity. This Third Person is the Holy Spirit. What is this 'spirit', this unifier, this peace-maker? The spirit of life, perhaps, inspiring planet and star, earth and sea, the serpent and the butterfly, the trees and grass; and also man and his ideals, his civilization and art. The life-spirit infuses all things and all things are one as they are seen variously to manifest the one life that burns in creation. By power of this spirit, when filled with richest life, man ceases to know the dualism formerly so antagonistic, hearing rather the spheral harmony and knowing himself to be one with the universal. This life-spirit has strength to rend the veil of the good and the evil and expose the origin of life by love; by its visitation we are brought to recognition.

The Trinity dramatizes for us the experience of the race. It is not a statement, not a static picture, but rather cinematographic, a dynamic action, a multiplicity-becoming-unity. It is dramatic. All our thinking depends on conceptions of discord and harmony, diversity and unity. We have two sorts of experience: experience of unity, experience of separation; marriage and divorce experiences. Both must be included in a profound symbolism; both, and the dramatic interaction of the two, are found in this Trinity.

Dante's great poem is our supreme statement of harmony. His Hell, Purgatory and Paradise are circular. Movement is circular: we have spirallings, wheelings, rotations and revolutions of all sorts; and, being circular, motion tends to build a static, top-like stillness. The final vision, seen first in the circles of Beatrice's eyes, is at the last a circle of light. Dante's task is to fit his life experiences into this circular harmony. The ultimate mystery is seen as

> Three Persons in the Godhead, and in one
> Person that nature and the human joined.
> (*Paradise*, XIII. 23)

That is, the Trinity and the Incarnation. The mystery of the Gryphon is mirrored in Beatrice's eyes, where, though itself 'steadfast,' its twyfold nature, as from the human viewpoint, appears as 'varying' (*Purgatory*, XXXI. 117–27). Motion and stillness are blended, division is unity: through Beatrice's eyes Dante seeks his resolution.

This, the mystery of the Incarnation, is also the mystery of the Trinity. Here is Dante's creed:

> In three eternal Persons I believe;
> Essence threefold and one; mysterious league
> Of union absolute, which, many a time,
> The word of gospel lore upon my mind
> Imprints: and from this germ, this firstling spark,
> The lively flame dilates; and, like heaven's star,
> Doth glitter in me.
>
> (*Paradise*, XXIV. 138)

God to Dante is always this triune mystery and 'union absolute'. He avoids a rigid anthropomorphism, finding various titles for the supreme being: 'sovereign sire', 'primal mover', 'omnipotent sire', 'celestial mind', and so forth. The titles are vague. Any closer personification will only be necessary as a concession to human frailty:

> For no other cause
> The Scripture, condescending graciously
> To your perception, hands and feet to God
> Attributes, nor so means . . .
>
> (*Paradise*, IV. 43)

When Dante would be exact his God is the 'triune' love (*Paradise*, XIII. 53) and the ultimate reality given a geometric formulation:

> Here is the goal, whence motion on his race
> Starts: motionless the centre, and the rest
> All moved around. Except the soul divine,
> Place in this heaven is none . . .
>
> (*Paradise*, XXVII. 100)

In the final vision the divine circle is mystically harmonized with human experience. There is motion, an ever-changing wonder, yet no alteration nor variation in the heart of 'light' from which the motion comes:

> Not that the semblance of the living light
> Was changed (that ever as at first remained),
> But that my vision quickening, in that sole
> Appearance, still new miracles descried,
> And toiled me with the change. In that abyss
> Of radiance, clear and lofty, seemed, methought,
> Three orbs of triple hue, clipt in one bound;
> And, from another, one reflected seemed,
> As rainbow is from rainbow: and the third
> Seemed fire, breathed equally from both. O speech!
> How feeble and how faint art thou, to give
> Conception birth. Yet this to what I saw
> Is less than little. O eternal light!
> Sole in thyself that dwellest; and of thyself
> Sole understood, past, present, or to come;
> Thou smiledst, on that circling, which in thee
> Seemed as reflected splendour, while I mused;
> For I therein, methought, in its own hue
> Beheld our image painted: steadfastly
> I therefore pored upon the view. As one,
> Who versed in geometric lore, would fain
> Measure the circle; and, though pondering long
> And deeply, that beginning, which he needs,
> Finds not: e'en such was I, intent to scan
> The novel wonder, and trace out the form,
> How to the circle fitted, and therein
> How placed: but the flight was not for my wing;
> Had not a flash darted athwart my mind,
> And, in the spleen, unfolded what it sought.
>
> (*Paradise*, XXXIII. 103)

There is no easy, no intellectually formulated, solution: only a passing 'flash' reveals how the sharp antagonisms of human experience may be supposed constituents of the divine harmony; how the form of man is fitted to the circle.

Dante's poem creates an harmony within whose inclusive love all life has its existence. His harmony is primary, the circle given, and all else has to be fitted to it. Continually he reminds us that all reality radiates from the one heart and core; all the circles from Hell to Paradise must be supposed as somehow concentric, out-rippling like circles radiating in water. Though geometric these primary symbolisms are apprehended with poetic fire, the more so for being so closely associated with Beatrice. Not only is the mystery reflected in her eyes before the Paradisal ascent; through the guidance of her smile Dante reaches his final vision.

In contrast to Dante's circular harmony Goethe's *Faust* is a chaotic poem, an untrimmed natural growth, with what might be called an 'organic' harmony closer to the rough turbulences of actual experience. The poet in the Prologue speaks of his profession:

> When Nature on her spindle,
> Impassive ever, twists her endless thread,
> When all things clash discordant, and but kindle
> Displeasure in the jarring notes they spread –
> Who with the dull, monotonous flow doth mingle
> Life, and doth mark it off with rhythmic swing?
> Who to the Whole doth consecrate the Single,
> Blended in one sweet harmony to ring?
>
> (4)

Goethe approaches the same problem as Dante from the opposite direction.

Faust desires union. Dantesque universals do not satisfy him. He gazes on the sign of the Macrocosm:

> Into the Whole how all things weave,
> One in another work and live!
> What heavenly forces up and down are ranging,
> The golden buckets interchanging,
> With wafted benison winging,

From Heaven through the Earth are springing,
All through the All harmonious ringing! (13)

The sign of the Earth-Spirit appeals more to him: 'Thou,
Spirit of Earth, to me art nigher' (14). He cannot contemplate union with the vast whole and henceforth union with
earthly life is his aim. Gretchen is a symbol of such union,
and his life at Court, the raising of Helen, his allegorical
marriage with her, his warriorship, his selfless devotion to
service, all are earth-unions of the body or mind. The perfect
union is his union with Gretchen, not Helen, in Paradise,
Helen being too allegoric and spiritual a figure for Paradise. Paradise, to be Paradise, must hold all the warmth of
earthly life. In *Faust* union is attained through the Eros,
just as in Dante the mystery of the Gryphon is reflected in
Beatrice's eyes.

There is much turbulence on the way. The root dualism
in Goethe is that of fire and water, and both are turbulent
forces. In all systems we must find first a root dualism: Death
and Life in the New Testament, God the Father and God the
Son in Christian symbolism, the Circle and the Human Form
in Dante, Tempest and Music in Shakespeare. Here we have
Fire and Water. Both are natural forces, but the one at an
extreme is satanic, the other at an extreme creative. Most of
the poem balances them fairly equally since Goethe does not
recognize absolute negations. The poem is written around
these two symbols and at a high point of vision they are unified. Homunculus, fire-spirit of medieval aspiration, finishes
his water-quest, his search for incarnate life, at the approach
of Galatea the sea-queen, and spills out his life-fire over her.
The 'billows' are transfigured by a 'fiery marvel' and each
wave 'sparkling' shatters itself on its 'fellows'. All is shining
and 'sweeps onward in light':

The bodies they burn on their path through the night.
(305)

All is 'embosomed' in flame and a paean is raised to Water and Fire and the Eros that unifies them (305).

Goethe sees the union of fire and water as the highest good. Here is one of his Elysian paradises. It is a watery paradise:

> And in gentle wavelets gliding we endearingly will nestle
> To the far-resplendent placid mirror of these rocky walls.

> (355)

Again,

> Ever downwards, ever deeper, water we meandrous rolling,
> Now the meadow, now the pastures, then the garden round the house . . .

> (355)

In this paradise worship is given to 'the sun-god first of all', whose fire ripes the vine and raises all life. Air is too spiritual, earth too static, for Goethe; clearly, his dualism must have been the fire-water opposition. When he describes fertility he likes it liquid:

> So the pure-born juicy berries' sacred bounty insolently
> Underfoot is trod, and foaming, spirting, foully crushed and blent.

> (356)

This then is the Trinity of *Faust*: Fire, Water, Eros. Or we might regard Faust, or mankind in general, as central and set between the fire-principle and the water-principle, between Mephistopheles and goodness, as in the contrast between Faust's crime towards Philemon and Baucis, setting their home in flames, and his altruistic devotion to water-labour afterwards. The final reality will blend fire and water. As Faust ascends to immortal life, there are mountain-torrents and the dazzling light of Paradise: 'Still dazzles him the new-sprung day' (422). Gretchen, or the Eros, is again, as in Dante, the principle of union.

Shakespeare's dualism exists in terms of tempest and music. Since Goethe's fire and water are dynamic natural forces, these both correspond to Shakespeare's tempests which are usually sea-tempests and sometimes also fiery, as in *Julius Caesar* and *The Tempest*. Dante's Hell has tempests and his Paradise music. In *Faust* at high moments we have music. But though Dante and Goethe may both write in terms of Shakespeare's tempest-music opposition, it is not properly the root dualism of either. The one most strongly emphasizes harmony, even Hell being part of the circular scheme, whereas the other emphasizes turbulence. Dante concentrates on the divine and tries to fit man into the divine scheme and Goethe concentrates on nature and tries to fit man into the natural scheme. Shakespeare holds the balances. His tempests are associated with fierce beasts, both natural phenomena; whereas music is the least earthly of the arts and blends readily into the supernatural as 'the music of the spheres' (*Pericles*, V. i. 231). Shakespeare's world of men and women is set between the natural and the divine, between the world of Goethe and that of Dante.

In Shakespeare, as in Dante and Goethe, the Eros is the maker of harmony. Tempest accompanies tragedy and disunion, music accompanies love and union. This is a consistent symbolism throughout Shakespeare applying to plots political, comical, tragical and metaphysical: discord is set against concord, severance against union. In one poem, *The Phoenix and the Turtle*, this poetic philosophy is given a metaphysical expression. As in *Antony and Cleopatra*, two lovers blend in a dying wherein love and death are felt as aspects of life, or we may say that as in Keats' 'Bright Star' sonnet, love is the unifier, life and death the dualism:

> Here the anthem doth commence:
> Love and constancy is dead;
> Phoenix and the Turtle fled
> In a mutual flame from hence.

So they loved, as love in twain
Had the essence but in one;
Two distincts, division none:
Number there in love was slain.

Hearts remote, yet not asunder;
Distance, and no space was seen
'Twixt the Turtle and his queen;
But in them it were a wonder.

So between them love did shine,
That the Turtle saw his right
Flaming in the Phoenix' sight:
Either was the other's mine.

Property was thus appall'd,
That the self was not the same;
Single nature's double name
Neither two nor one was call'd.

Reason, in itself confounded,
Saw division grow together;
To themselves yet either neither,
Simple were so well compounded,

That it cried, 'How true a twain
Seemeth this concordant one!
Love hath reason, reason none,
If what parts can so remain'.[1]

'Number' is slain in 'love'. Neither duality nor unity, both being 'numbers', properly exist. We have not merely a transcending of duality: rather the duality-unity dualism is itself transcended. Division is now unity, unity division, the self no more the self and reason the only irrationality. Not

[1] A comparison of this poem with Trinitarian doctrine was made by Ranjee (Ranjee G. Shahani) in *Towards the Stars* (1930–1). A copy is lodged in the Brotherton Library, University of Leeds.

only does tempest become music; the tempest-music distinction is resolved.[1]

In *Antony and Cleopatra* tempests are stilled and music accompanies an apocalyptic love tragedy. *The Phoenix and the Turtle* and *Antony and Cleopatra* are outstanding examples of a general process. In Dante, Goethe and Shakespeare Eros is the principle of harmony.

Shelley's *Prometheus Unbound* evolves a theology in personal terms, thereby challenging a direct comparison with Christian symbolism. Prometheus is mankind, or mankind's champion, suffering under Jupiter, a god cruel, stupid, and evil. Prometheus corresponds to God the Son, and Jupiter to God the Father in so far, but only in so far, as he is in conflict with the Son. Faced by this dualism of the good Prometheus tormented by a stupid Jupiter, Prometheus' adherents, including his separated love Asia, go to Demogorgon to ask what and when the solution may be. Demogorgon is darkly mysterious but kindly, and corresponds to the human imagination (II. iii. 1–10). As Faust has to descend to the Mothers and get help from the learned Wagner before reaching Helen; as Dante has to go through Hell with Virgil before ascending Paradise with Beatrice; as all great poets have to burn through their satanic visions and intellectual agonies before creating their resplendent paradises; and as the intellectual reign of the Law and sin preceded the freer life announced by St Paul; so, before Prometheus and Asia are reunited in love, there is this descent to Demogorgon who symbolizes the consciousness of evil and foreknowledge of its reversal. He claims to know 'all things thou dar'st demand' (II. iv. 8). Questioned on various ills, he answers that they are caused by the one who 'reigns', that is Jupiter. Behind Jupiter however there is 'Almighty God' (II. iv. 28, 11). Although Demogorgon

---

[1] My more comprehensive discussion, and placing, of *The Phoenix and the Turtle* is given in *The Mutual Flame*, Part II.

cannot answer the problem of evil he can foretell the fall of
Jupiter. The time comes, Jupiter is thrown into the abyss.
Prometheus steps free and all nature joins in a paean of joy
as he wins his long-lost bride, Asia. She is transfigured
(p. 90 above), and music honours the reunion.

The marriage union of Asia and Prometheus is our Paradise. It is not properly eschatological, but rather a heaven
entwined with earth, an earth irradiated with the divine. It
depicts, like the Book of Revelation, the establishment of the
Kingdom of Heaven. Shelley's theology is close to Christian
symbolism. Prometheus is the Christ, or mankind at its
best; Jupiter corresponds to Satan or the Satanic attributes
of the Father; and 'Almighty God', who is allowed to be
ultimately responsible for Jupiter's evil, is God the Father.
Demogorgon only exists while Jupiter rules; he represents
the dark imaginations of man, probing evil, willing its end,
inspirer of satanic visions; he is explicitly related, like
Goethe's Mothers, to a stern and grim eternity; and *he goes
into the abyss with Jupiter* (III. i. 52–6). Though he returns
to speak an epilogue, it is spoken from the standpoint of
man's *present suffering* (IV. iv. 570–8). He may be equated
vaguely with Goethe's Wagner in his gloomy medieval room,
and more directly with Dante's Virgil. He is the Third
Person of the Trinity blackened by the dislocation of the
Father-Son harmony. When Jupiter gives place to 'Almighty
God' – who does not appear but must be allowed to cover
all things including the final paradise – Prometheus and the
universe are at peace; Demogorgon exists no more, vanished
into the abyss; and Asia, as Love, assumes new glory.

If we are to see the origin of evil in a single theological
person, it must be in the Father, since Satan is not personified in the Trinity. But a better solution may be found in
terms of the Father-Son relation. The Holy Spirit cannot
exist in its bright splendour when the Father-Son relation is
out-of-joint; it is then Demogorgon, a dark agony, a lonely

progress in the imaginative world. It is, however, always trying to assert unity; like all poetry it would unify the Father-Son dualism; and Demogorgon can foretell Jupiter's downfall. Jupiter is a false aspect of Almighty God as he appears while the God-Prometheus relation is disorganized. Asia represents the Holy Spirit, corresponding to Dante's Beatrice as Demogorgon to Dante's Virgil, incarnated in love; Beatrice, Cleopatra, Gretchen, Helen, Asia, all are unifiers; all correspond to the Holy Spirit, are incarnations of that spirit. The divine life is incarnated in these unions and in the elixir flooding and tingling through nature when union is accomplished. So the Trinity is a drama, like *Prometheus Unbound*, of disunion-becoming-union. Satan is no part of this ultimate reality since he only exists in so far as the Father-Son relation is out-of-joint, then seeming to usurp the place of either the Father or the Holy Spirit. We can say that the Holy Spirit is an aspect or condition of a Father-Son harmony, becoming the Evil Spirit when the Father and Son are in conflict: just as death is an inharmonious relation of life-elements, so evil is a dislocation of things good, having no individual strength. In poetic symbolism evil satanisms are usually to be related to a distorted and obscene sex-desecration, all harmony to a glorified sex-love. Evil is a homeless, unincarnated desire. The Holy Spirit, until incarnated in some union, is itself evil; only in incarnation is it 'Holy'. Today this 'Spirit' is far too wraithly, too 'spiritual', a reality; but the Eros we understand, we know its power, in poetry and in life. The Holy Spirit must accordingly be equated with the Eros.

In poetry evil is related to severance, loneliness and darkness; it is associated with some sexual desecration or some other unrestful and unruly aspiration. In the Bible sin originates from aspiration in close association with sex. Throughout the Old Testament the God-man relation is out-of-joint and the world darkened. The Hebrew prophets

and their nation endure a lonely quest. In the myth of Babel
(*Genesis*, XI. 1–9) man through unruly aspiration is divided
against man; there is error, misunderstanding and severance;
men speak henceforth in various tongues. As in the poets
misunderstandings, errors and all evils are resolved by a
paradisal union with a victory for the resplendent and fiery-
bright Eros, so in the New Testament the tragedy of Babel
is reversed. At the coming of the Divine Life-fire at Pentecost differences are levelled, man with man is unified,
difficulties of language and all barriers to communion
amazingly removed (*Acts*, II. 1–13). In poetry the Eros
corresponds to the Holy Spirit, or in better phrase suggesting
incarnation, the Sacred Life. When we see that our poets
ascend from life-impressions through the Eros to the divine,
whereas Christianity moves from the same life-impressions,
including erotic suggestion, to a more universal love, and
so on to divinity, the necessity of our equation becomes
patent.

This Eros will cover the whole domain of art. Art and
the Sacred Life are close. Goethe aptly shows his Boy-
Charioteer, an Eros-figure personifying poetry, as dis-
pensing Pentecostal flames to the chosen poets:

> A flamelet that my hand hath sped
> Glows upon this and yonder head,
> From one unto the other skips,
> Fastens on this, from that one slips;
> It flames up rarely like a plume
> And swiftly gleams in briefest bloom,
> Yet oft without acknowledgment
> It burns out sadly and is spent.
>
> (210)

Goethe writes of 'holy Poesy' (350), for both poetry and the
Eros are one with the Holy Spirit or Sacred Life. Nor will
this understanding be dangerous on ethical grounds. Art

and symbolism are not to be too rashly impugned by ethic or we risk crucifying every saviour in turn. The erotic instinct is both the gate to evil and the way to paradise, as when in the Book of Revelation (pp. 215–16) we have the Harlot set beside the Holy Bride. In failing to channel the erotic instinct Christian Orthodoxy lacks an essential understanding of its own symbolism. Vast areas of misery are to be related to our refusal to recognize the royalty due to this passionate God of Love.

A symbol is no slight thing. It is a sun whose attraction drinks the ocean on which it burns. In its passivity and mystery it draws adoration from thousands, centres their hearts on it so that those hearts find therein a serene freedom and joy, absolving and absorbing all guilt, channelling the passional instincts, purging, purifying, healing. We want this health-bringing life-symbol to oppose alike our shallow cynicisms and neurotic sanctities. The Eros in man is doubly portcullised in dark bondage and, crying for liberation, it finds no champion for its cause save in poetry and the arts. But were such a divine Eros, in beauty of eye and limb, to replace in our visionary thinking that third spectral figure in our Trinity, untold millions, their inmost souls hungering for a warm and human, not a ghostly, love, would have found release there, and happiness. It is no unknown spirit, no ghost however holy, that reconciles us to that tremendous dualism of the unknown God beyond good and evil and his children and their God of Love who strive for good alone. The dualism is resolved by the Eros in man, by this only. The sacred life of art, born from desire and love, has alone this visionary quality whereby we see the Good and the Evil slain together on the altar of Beauty; and the vision is always a life-bringing and creative experience leading not to evil but to good. This is, and must be, included in our understanding of the third Divine Person, since the Eros alone, in life or art, habitually resolves our dualism. This is our surest approach, following Renaissance poetry and the nature of man, to understanding of the Triune Godhead.

Many sincere Christians find their resolutions in Church teaching, and are satisfied; for all I urge is already implicit in Christianity. But it is not widely recognized nor are its implications followed in practice. It is still possible to think Shelley an unchristian poet; or Keats. It is still possible to think that the erotic theme of a cinematograph romance has nothing whatsoever to do with Christianity. I ask then that Christianity sanctify the Eros and all great art at least, allowing all this to be, at its best, included within the third Person of its Trinity. And I ask that we cease to betray the Christian law of Incarnation by continuing to refer to the 'Holy Spirit', or, worse still, the 'Holy Ghost'. 'Spirit' suggests a pallid spiritualism[1] rather than the warm breath of life; 'ghost' suggests not life but death, and therefore evil. Words are dynamic and mean what they mean, whether they should or not, the organic life of language caring no whit for derivations. Let us lay this ghost and incarnate this spirit. This is the New Incarnation. I ask that we recognize the Sacred Life alike in poetry, and Christianity, and human love.

Then once more we shall see the Triune Godhead reassume the blaze and grandeur it held for Dante. We do ill to wrong its majesty with our sorry understanding, for this is the noblest piece of symbolism that the race has produced. Our Church too often tries to defend its belief in a personal God; it does not however, or should not, believe in any such God, but in something far more complex: the Mystic Trinity. Nor is this to be unfaithful to Jesus' intuition; for it is for us to believe not directly in Jesus' God but rather in Jesus' belief in, and experience of, his God, and the Sacred Life which it

---

[1] The true 'Spiritualism' is far from 'pallid': see pp. 326–36. Even so, the movement has suffered in repute from the debasement that the word 'spirit' has undergone. [1960]

has created in St Paul and other Christians. God, Jesus, and the divine life-stream and love-stream welling from that fountain; this is our drama, our Trinity. The Trinity is a necessary complement to the New Testament, which alone would seem to our darkened minds to lack that philosophic and intellectual design possessed by our other poetic systems. The meanings of the Trinity are infinite. Call it a time-succession. God the Father is then the Creator God known vaguely to primitive peoples; the Son is Jesus the Christ, bringing in the Christian era; and the Divine Life of the Christian Renaissance I herald in this book. So we have the Creation, the Incarnation, the New Incarnation, or Re-naissance. In the Shakespearian system this sequence corresponds to Tempests, Mankind, and Music; the natural, human, and divine; Goethe, Shakespeare, Dante. It may likewise suggest the absolutes of the True, the Good, and the Beautiful: or we may reverse the order. But we can go on indefinitely finding new and ever new meanings.

This is more than a picture-language: it is dramatic. Reality only exists in experience and experience can best be expressed through drama. Not only is the Trinity a mystic drama of differentiation-becoming-unity, but all drama tends to create a mystic trinity: the hero, his desire, and some impeding force. So we have Faust, Gretchen, and Mephis-topheles; for Goethe's Devil cynically scorns the perfect love to which Faust aspires and at the last tries to drag Faust from union with that love. Or again, in Shakespeare: Hamlet, the good he loves, and the wicked world which denies his aspirations; Othello, Desdemona, and Iago; Leontes, Hermione, and Leontes' tortured guilt. And so on: hence our term, 'the eternal triangle'. Triangularity is eternal, and eternity is best imagined either, as Henry Vaughan imagined it in *The World*, in circular, or in triangu-lar form. Three is a divine and mystic number because it is rooted in the drama of our ordinary lives. There are three

persons in our grammar, myself, yourself, and the rest; and
Greek nouns had three numbers, singular, dual, and plural.
All drama attempts to build harmony from this triangular
scheme by either a happy ending or a tragic grandeur.

The Trinity is both one and three, three and one, asserting
the dynamic interaction of unity and multiplicity. Our experiences may be divided into those of union and those of
severance, into marriage and divorce experiences, and we
live in alternation from the one to the other. When we, the
sons of God, are severed from our Father and the sacred life,
there are three gods in the Trinity; but when we find union
and a new harmony, there is then a oneness. The Trinity is
accordingly creative, and the number three is the number of
creation, as when two elements are married to create a third.
So Jesus' experience of God's fatherhood, the Jesus-God
union, creates the Sacred Life of the Christian World.

This symbolism is universally valid. We are distraught by
the dualisms of experience. Within our horizon are rich
plains and sun-glittering peaks, towering eagle-flights and
melodies of air and water; yet also dark abysms, in whose
slimy depths serpents coil their inhuman hatefulness,
creatures whose existence is, it would appear, an obscenity
and disgrace to creation. From these our baffled gaze returns perplexed and searches inwardly for resolution. Though
banished for awhile by metaphysical argument, or love, or
faith, the good and the evil remorselessly return, plaguing us
with ambiguity; and the boa-constrictor drinks the same air
fanned by the royal eagle's wings. But love or mystic sight or
simple joy of any kind is the resolver; a spark leaping
antagonistic poles, ablaze in the dark; lightning that hovers
and is gone. When such dualistic pain and such resolution
cease to hold meaning, then the Trinity may appear an insubstantial dream and some other symbolism of East or West
dethrone the Triune Majesty. Till then this unfitting and
unnatural differing between what is or seems and what should

and must be, this consummate artistry entwined with so in-
scrutable an inconscience in creation, is more real, more
daily part of our experience, than any one person we know
or any sight we see. The Trinity is a sublime poetic abstraction from racial experience in the past and a sublime
foreshadowing of its futurity. Like all fine abstractions it has
a permanency denied to phenomena, but it also shares with
poetry the vesture and rounded completion of dramatic
symbol. Being dramatic, it is presented in human terms: for
we know no nobler nor any more significant shape than that
into which life has chiselled the mind and body of man.
Humanity alone can tap the deeps of humanity and that is
why Shakespeare is so transcendent a poet. And yet the
Christian Church does not believe in a 'personal God', save
for purposes of prayer, wherein nevertheless it rightly includes the name of the Christ. It believes in the New Testament, in Jesus' experience of God; or in the Trinity, in a
super-personal relation, complex, dramatic and dynamic.
The Trinity reflects the fact that drama is the only perfect
statement and that experience is the only reality.

The Trinity is the most sublime simplification of human
destiny ever imagined. Current agnostic speculation is
usually no more than a paraphrase of this eternal triangularity.
Who will prefer a paraphrase to poetry? All Western religious poetry is herein crystallized, the polytheistic symbolism of Hellenic religion blending with the monotheism of
the Jews. In the Trinity, the Three in One and One in
Three, the Olympian and Sinaitic hierarchies meet.

This Triune symbolism is a reflection cast by human
existence on to the heavens above that we may there observe
the eternal essence of that Life in whose drama we are actors;
uplifted as the Greek heroes are uplifted to blazon with
jewelled constellations the heroic arch of night. This is the
eternal drama of Good, Evil and Reconciliation; or Life,
Death and Resurrection; divinely and mysteriously set over

us, like some majestic Southern Cross athwart our darkened seas. By contemplation we are to understand the drama of our existence. Like all high dramatic art it tunes our minds to consciousness of the life we live and suggests an awakening while we sleep. But when, by its own activity, or by love, or any ecstatic experience, we indeed awake, the Trinity as formulated by intellect may cease to have meaning. There is a point where symbolism is known to be provisional only. The symbols of religion and poetry are not addressed to that consciousness which it is their aim to awaken but rather to the consciousness they would expel. When humanity in all its activities, in, and in despite of, sorrow and pain and fear, can yet preserve a radiant peace in knowledge and enjoyment of its own sacred life, then the Trinity will be dead, its dramatic persons dissolved in the one blaze they have created. There will be then no philosophy, no theology, no poetry. At the hour of that flaming apocalypse when the Kingdom of Heaven is established on Earth or Earth ascended into Heaven, neither will Heaven be Heaven, nor Earth, in that music, be any longer Earth.

XIII

THE SACRED BIRTH

THE final reality is Life and beyond it we may search no farther. 'Life', not 'God', or even 'love', is the keyword to the New Testament and to poetry. Though Jesus' God at the last forsook him, the great principle of Life, the living God of the New Testament, has ratified his sacrifice. Jesus' Mother was made pregnant by this sacred power, Jesus himself being the Son of Life. Life is the origin and purpose of its manifestations. We recognize many enemies to life: evil, fear, death. Against them are enlisted our sciences, philosophies and theologies, and all religious and poetic symbolism. They are all right and none wrong: or, all wrong and none right. Their values vary from age to age and place to place. Life is right and Death is wrong; all imaginative thought is mainly right, being fertile and creative, but no logical statement can be, by its logic alone, either right or wrong save at the cost of being both, its worth lying in its vitality. Intellectual formulation is useful provided that we do not expect the intellect to prove or to create. It may be powerful when serving the higher visions and only in such service will it be safe from its inherent contradictoriness. Though in this book there are many surface contradictions, they are not to be feared; for, since its statements are as lines radiating from one centre to a circumference, there can be no intersection and any contradiction could therefore be shown as apparent rather than final. Intellect is properly interpretative. It is a means to understanding, and never itself creative unless blended with emotion, instinct, vision, or whatever we choose to call those richer qualities that vitalize our literatures and religions.

Since important statements on these big matters must never fall further than is absolutely necessary below the higher realities of poetic creation, love and life, it will be clear that as many of our concepts as possible should suggest life-realities and life-processes. That is why we started by treating poetry as a 'marriage' of essences, as an 'incarnation' and therefore a 'creation', and proceeded to analyse its newness or 'virgin birth'. We have shown poetry to be closely related to the sex or romantic instinct; we have found it to be crammed with life-suggestions, creations splendid with created and creative imagery and symbols, the death-visions being the obverse of these. We have seen that the main themes in poetry are related to the erotic experience, the marriage-experience, and that reality exists only in some 'experience' or 'relation', a blending and marriage, or an antagonism and divorce, of two units. Never must we for too long regard individuals in lonely chastity: in the mental as in the physical world creation and life exist by continual unions. Our life on earth, whether physically married or single, is a succession of marriage and divorce experiences: interests and antagonisms, friendships and enmities, creation and destruction.

What is true of poetry applies also to the Bible. The New Testament asserts less any rule of behaviour than a radiant life. Poets and prophets are winged messengers from Paradise descending to fire our hearts with immortal possessions. Through imagery and symbol they announce a paradisal nature and a glorified humanity blending into other mysterious persons such as angels, seraphs and gods. The romantic perception of life is the heart alike of Christianity and of poetry.

The New Testament aims to enrich life with poetry. Jesus' ethic is paradoxical and his theology vague, but his imagery and symbolism are consistent. He is always making that transference from the poetic to the actual world which

D. H. Lawrence aimed to perform, so incarnating the divine Logos in human life. When his disciples ask him why he speaks in parables he answers that he aims to let those see who can, but does not even wish to be clear to those who have eyes but do not see (*Matthew*, XIII. 11–15). This is not only irritability; it is sound psychology, since it may be better for his hearers to remember the story without seeing the interpretation than to remember the interpretation while forgetting the story, poetry being more important than its paraphrase. Jesus preaches not merely a poetical doctrine but a doctrine of poetry, telling man to live in harmony with the birds, the vine, the harvest, the luxuriant growth of the seed and the gigantic powers of natural law. A mustard seed's faith can move mountains because it grows by the might of that same life which not only plants and overturns mountains, but sets the planets in their courses and makes the stars to flame.

The poet makes metaphors; the true Christian lives them, his thoughts and acts unfurling with the unhindered strength of spontaneous life. Drink, erotic fervour, art and religious mysticism, these in their different ways draw the curtain and display the life-drama in all its excellence, its colour, its song and music.[1] All are, in their degrees, difficult; some are usually inexpedient, all may become dangerous. Though life is what we desire we must beware how we grasp at it. An authentic experience may, in its transience and the consequent reaction, prove destructive. But poetry incarnates the life-instinct along more creative rhythms; and next poetry itself must be incarnated in action, out-flowering in the whole life; not limited to the sudden and short-lived blaze and lightning dangers that too often characterize the erotic experience, nor only an inward and meditative act unrelated to

---

[1] We might compare Aldous Huxley's fascinating account of the effects of mescalin in *The Doors of Perception* (1954); also *The Sacred Mushroom*, Andrija Puharich (1959; VIII. 121).

outward affairs. True art and true morality are like natural
growths. Shakespeare compares poetry to vegetable life:

> Our poesy is as a gum which oozes
> From whence 'tis nourish'd; the fire i' the flint
> Shows not till it be struck; our gentle flame
> Provokes itself, and like the current flies
> Each bound it chafes.
>
> (*Timon of Athens*, I. i. 21)

Poetry is nature-generated and inwardly prompted, awakened without external cause; not flashy but a 'gentle' flame; or
a 'current', like one of Goethe's cataracts, disciplined by its
banks though impatient of control. In his *Defence of Poetry*
Shelley compares poetry to 'the first acorn' which 'contained
all oaks potentially'; and Keats tells us that poetry should
come 'as naturally as the leaves to a tree' (to John Taylor,
27 February, 1818). Erotic experience in life is a sudden
blaze; but poetry, Christianity, and my assertion that the
Eros is to be equated with the Divine Life, all point not so
much to any riotous and blazing extravagance as to something more creative, a 'gentle flame', an organic growth.
Symbolism and poetry, dealing in essences so bright with
splendour that they may be dangerous when too rashly
expressed in action, are not themselves those actions; they
are our best safeguard against rash life-expressions, uni-
versalizing and directing what were else selfish and limited
satisfactions and reminding us that we only attain reality in
relation to the dramatic whole. Poetry and all high art induce harmony, they do not lead to immorality; they raise no
desires which they do not in the same act satisfy. The actions
which correspond to the rhythms of art are creative, not
rash; wise, not destructive; enduring and powerful and good.

Jesus speaks through a kind of poetry: 'He never spoke
to them except in a parable' (*Matthew*, XIII. 34). He plants
his teaching, leaving it to grow organically, not by man's

endeavour but by God's; and it has done so. The process is
explained:

> The Realm of Heaven, he said, is like a grain of mustard-seed
> which a man takes and sows in his field. It is less than any seed on
> earth, but when it grows up it is larger than any plant, it becomes
> a tree, so large that the wild birds come and roost in its branches.
> (*Matthew*, XIII. 31)

Again:

> It is with the Realm of God as when a man has sown seed on earth;
> he sleeps at night and rises by day, and the seed sprouts and shoots
> up – he knows not how.   (*Mark*, IV. 26)

The great God of Life makes the seed grow as He thinks
best, and all growth is miraculous. The growing of God's
Kingdom corresponds to the expansive growth which
Shelley attributed to the 'acorn' of poetry. Poetry and
Christianity can never be distinct, nor can the Realm of God
be considered to have flourished wholly or even mainly on
unpoetical soil. Our greater Renaissance poets, even though
they may not subscribe to Christian doctrine, are nevertheless
impregnated with Christian feeling and are, by virtue of this
and of their own intrinsic poetry, prophets of that greater
poetic Christianity to which the Church, with all its Christian
doctrine and symbolism, is likewise pointing us. This they
appear to recognize, their latest work being sometimes re-
markably Christian in surface detail: I am thinking of
Henry VIII, the conclusion to *Faust*, Shelley's *Prometheus
Unbound* and *Hellas* (*The Starlit Dome*, III. 206, 245–6) and
Wordsworth's alterations to *The Prelude*. Keats offers no
analogy, but his poetry is so spontaneously in the tradition
of Jesus' creative thinking that one would scarcely wish it
mixed with anything but its own perfection.

Poetic vision holds one of the two keys to the Realm of

Life; the Christian Church holds the other. This poetic Christianity, or Christian poetry, has grown organically, without pressure or effort, often thinking itself to be cut adrift from Christian teaching: Jesus' prophecy has been strangely fulfilled. We can see a Christian Renaissance rising in the near future; God has made the seed to grow after His own wisdom; and a mighty harvest awaits us. But no celestial avatar need be expected. The time for miracles is past: it always was. The Kingdom of Heaven is at hand: that too has been so before. Only our poetry awaits our understanding. The branches of the fig-tree are softening and putting out leaves and the summer is at hand.

Renaissance poetry is Christian on two separate counts. First it is Christian because it is poetry, and Christianity properly understood is not only a poetical religion but a religion whose central dogma, like the teachings of its central figure, is Poetry or Incarnation. Pre-Christian poets also are therefore complementary to our faith. The New Testament rises over former and subsequent visions, the heart of all poetry, its life pulsing equally in Hellenic and Renaissance literature; for we may imagine all literature laid out as an area, all contemporaneous, all supplementing and drawing life from the central origin and heart of life. While we isolate the New Testament, comparing it with no other poetry, we shall fail to understand its authority: all poetry is Christian. Secondly all literature of the Christian era is impregnated with Christian feeling. Its death-visions and life-visions follow the Biblical rhythms; poet after poet writes his Old and New Testaments. In both worlds death and evil are interdependent and their conquest related to love. Such has been the growth of the Realm of God.

But this rich poetic life has not been united with Christianity. The Provençal troubadours, blending the erotic ideal with a Christian sensibility, started a betrothal which has never been consummated. The Renaissance was well named.

A splendid rebirth, it vitalized our poetry with many Hellenic excellences but failed to integrate the new poetry with Christianity. That such an integration awaits us is no extravagant suggestion. Christianity was born from a marriage of East and West, Hebraism and Hellenism. Jesus was a Jew, of Judaic training; St Paul, by education and intellectual sympathy, partly at least, Greek; and the author of the theological passages in John's Gospel was a philosopher of Hellenic affinities. Jesus spoke in Aramaic, the New Testament was written in Greek. The stage of the first act was Judaea, at the meeting of the two worlds, Eastern and Western. For centuries of Christianity the Hebraic and ethical element preponderated over the Hellenic but at the Renaissance a new influx from Hellenic power-sources created a new life. There was a temporary inter-fusion, but no lasting union, and today poetry and religion are absurdly separated; two pursuits of the same kind, point-ing diversely and yet simultaneously honoured by our dis-traught and paradoxical civilization. If the Churches are failing, that is not through any intellectual and scientific advance, but because two gods, the Eros and the Christ, are contending in our hearts for sovereignty.

Our great prophet in this matter is Goethe. In Part I of his *Faust* he points the danger of the life-instinct allowed precipitate expression. In Part II he dramatizes Renaissance idealism. Starting with court entertainment introducing Hellenic and rustic personages, mythical and realistic, men and gods, he passes from entertainment, through Faust's fleeting vision of Helen and Paris to Faust's quest for Helen. He is helped by Wagner, the medieval student who is trying to create life. Homunculus is made, or all but made. He is still in his glass and not yet incarnated, not free from the laboratory, till he meets Galatea and spills out his flame in love-union with her. Goethe sees medieval science as on the brink of some new life and losing itself in a Renaissance it has helped to create, so leaving the stage free for Faust to unite with Helen.

Helen is told of the brave new world she is to enter. Here is the grand ceremony:

> Faust, after the pages and esquires have descended in a long train, appears above in the staircase in medieval knightly court-costume, and descends with stately dignity.

(328)

Faust addresses her in courtly and chivalric style. Helen, late in danger from Menelaus, is in a new world of chivalry: Greece did not know how to honour woman, but Christianity and romance literature stand between Menelaus and Faust. Faust reproaches Lynceus for not announcing Helen's arrival. Lynceus is

> the man
> With rarest eyebeam, from the lofty tower
> To gaze around appointed, Heaven's abyss
> And Earth's expanse keenly to overeye.

(329)

Is he the Christian Church? Yet his name is Greek. He stands for the Greek element within the medieval imagination which should have recognized her. He is now quickly subdued to the wondrous lady. Praise after praise he pours on her:

> We wandered from the Rising Sun,
> And straightway was the West undone!

(331)

Faust prepares for splendid life:

> Paradises
> That nothing lack of life but life prepare.

(333)

There is a pretty dialogue where Faust speaks in rhyme

unknown to ancient Greece, and Helen asks the secret of this novel speech:

> FAUST: 'Tis easy, so but from the heart it rise;
> And when the breast with yearning doth o'erflow,
> You look around and ask—
>
> HELEN: Who shares the glow?
>
> (334)

So the game goes on. This is no retrogression to a past age, but a dynamic and immediate union leading to new birth. Old legends are gone, the new is come:

> Hear ye tones most sweetly golden!
> Free yourselves from fables! Lo,
> Overworn the medley olden
> Of your gods is. Let them go!
>
> None your meaning recognises;
> Now we claim a higher toll!
> What from out the heart arises
> Can alone the heart control.
>
> (344)

Again:

> Quenchéd be the sun's high splendour,
> In the soul if day hath shined!
> What the whole world would not render,
> That in our own heart we find.
>
> (344)

'The Kingdom of Heaven is within you'.[1]

By this Hellenic and erotic Renaissance our Renaissance poets attain to Christian grace. Have Dante, Shakespeare, Goethe, been blundering in the dark? And is our Christianity, as preached today, all-sufficient? Goethe sees Euphorion,

---

[1] Moffat however translates 'the reign of God is now in your midst' (*Luke*, XVII. 21).

Byron or Shelley, the Romantic Age, born of Faust and Helen and therefore child of the Renaissance, failing through over-aspiration. So Shelley and Lawrence fail, in life, though not in art. Goethe presses on to a more tangible gospel of creative action and service to man and a Christian immortality. He creates the Hellenic splendour, and then returns to practical problems and his gospel of creative work. The sequel complements, but does not invalidate, the prophetic glory of the 'Helena'; just as the 'Helena' complements, but does not invalidate, the love-mysticism of Part I. All is finally unified when Gretchen, the primal love-force in the poem – since she has an actuality beyond Helen – receives Faust into a Christian Paradise.

The Renaissance is not yet over. It has not yet properly begun. From the first shock and kiss of that contact poetry and Christianity have reeled asunder, in amaze, embarrassment, fear. Today again they approach each other, and we are all weak in our fear and pale-spirited anxiety. Life's richness eludes us and no heaven compensates for our impoverishment on earth. But the poets sing to battle and a long succession of richest prophecy is ours. Though by our own wilfulness, or the will of God, it has been clasped in books sealed impenetrably to our understanding, those treasures are no longer closed to us and can now awake our unsettled dreams to a daylight sanity and Christian strength.

Our world is in a sorry case. On the one side, we have a weakened Christianity, irrelevantly defending itself against a science that has ceased to attack it; on the other, a chaotic art, in its popular expressions erotic to the point of immorality. Two joints of one limb are horribly dislocated and our civilization writhes in pain. While the churches lose power, dances, the radio, cinematographs, the revue stage, romantic novels, all draw men and women in multitudes, speaking directly to their hearts. Romance, actual or imagined, relieves the tension of a sterile existence, its restraint, mono-

tony and slow pain. In comparison our Christianity is dark
and threatening; or worse, pallid and fearful, diluting the
rich wine of its poetic heritage with the waters of scientific
rationalism. At its best it offers too much that is negative,
minatory and awe-inspiring, alienating rather than channelling the erotic instincts; it is not in any sense alluring. We
are still afraid of Israel's Jehovah, forgetting the Christ.

It is not possible to condemn eroticism as superficial,
since in the best literature as in the worst it remains powerful.
Distinctions of artistic merit can sometimes blur our sight
from universal significances. Just as it is fatal to make any
too rigid technical distinctions between one great poet and
another, so it is fatal to make any too final critical distinctions
between the powers beating within *Wuthering Heights* and *The
Rosary*. The popular novels of today, though not intellectually profound, are true enough to the main purpose of romantic narrative, the awaking and directing of the erotic
perceptions and the relation of these to the world-order of
frustration and death. It is the same with our cinemas. Is it
not right that masses, of varying culture, should take pleasure
in seeing youth, virtue, and beauty triumphant? Our sentimental films assert life's sovereignty over death. Youth and
love are universal ideals: we do not paint our angels on
crutches.

And all this is true, too, of the drama. Today the drama
endures an indecisive and baffling transition. We have a
realistic drama which aims at as much similarity to 'real life'
as possible; and yet such is not life at all but only the husk
or shell passing for reality to a hasty and unconsidering eye.
It is photographic and colourless, lacking those richer
qualities which the drama at its best includes; the surges of
emotion, rhythm in gesture, verbal melody, colour, grouping
and design. Photographic drama is a corpse whose life-
blood is drained. The richer elements are found elsewhere,
rioting in meaningless extravagance, without co-ordination

or control or any relevance to human life, and therefore dangerously divorced from ethic. We have violent and mechanical dances, drenching limelights of hectic colour, jazz-music unvaried and misapplied. Nakedness, by itself legitimate in service to the true Eros, is so employed as to raise sexual desire without any corresponding artistic satisfaction. Insubstantial emotions are jumbled together in a hashed medley of cheap vulgarity; and yet it is here, rather than in the intellectualized problem play, that we find those elements of gaiety and colour from which Dante builds his Paradise.

Our refusal as Christians to recognize and direct the erotic instinct is dangerous. Cut adrift from all issues but titillating amusement, the Eros is rightly vindicative. We have a popular drama awaking sex-instincts and leaving them undirected, while our Church concentrates on the anger or peace of God, preaching a message divorced from those instincts through which only it could be truly creative. Eros is a great god, powerful as Jehovah. Our cloistered palaces of devotion cast but a dim religious light across the stone floors of our minds, too sickly a pallor for a world so darkened by incertitude. How can this religion, concentrating on reproof, discipline and sacrifice, challenge with its ghostly canticles the lithe grace and laughing eyes of our as yet unrecognized Eros? But is this Christianity or merely the ghost of it? Is this the poetry of life, the freedom from the Law, experienced and announced by St Paul? Where is the living water promised by Jesus? Where today the resurrected and triumphant Christ? It is significant that Dante sees condemned souls as solemnly moving with a motion that suggests Church ritual:

> Earnest I looked
> Into the depth, that opened to my view,
> Moistened with tears of anguish, and beheld
> A tribe, that came along the hollow vale,

In silence weeping: such their step as walk
Choirs, chanting solemn litanies, on earth.
(*Hell*, XX. 4)

But Paradise is a place of 'laughter unblamed, and ever-new delight' (*Purgatory*, XXVIII. 98); of dance and song, smiles and laughing eyes, of 'amorous dalliance' (*Paradise*, XXVII. 84). Nor do we suggest that death-experience and that solemnity it creates be erased from divine ceremony. Ritual must take note of death without forgetting that its primary aim is to raise us to life. Today there is all too little life-splendour in the ecclesiastical imagination and paradisal hopes have deserted our pulpits. We prison the very Script of Life in solemn black and the priests of the living God are aptly uniformed in mourning.

Never in the world's history have poetry and religion, drama and divine worship, been so cruelly divorced, and until this separation gives way to union our pain must endure. Poetry and religion since the Renaissance have been as two coupled horses curveting and prancing aside from their direction, fighting the one against the other: one fiery and of sparkling eye, impatient of restraint; the other dignified but darkly suspicious of its companion, and angry that its unhurrying pace should be disturbed. The twin imaginative forces inspiring our Western civilization have been mutually hindered and the chariot they would lift onwards and upwards rumbles from its path, all but overturned, among boulders and watercourses and mud. We need today, as Christians, to face our Renaissance, our poetic heritage, accepting and ratifying this marriage union with all its implications and in all its splendour. Half-life is safe but life itself in its deathless naked beauty is a terror to us, squint-eyed and veiling our understanding from the sun. Nor when this marriage is consummated will Christianity be impoverished. As a man takes a wife and finds his self empowered by the other self he loves, its very difference a wonder and a liberation releasing an unguessed strength, so will our Christian revelation be found the more splendid for the new truth it encloses and transcends; its own dogmas most strangely revitalized; its own prophecies most miraculously fulfilled. Then our Church will cease to send missionaries to far countries: rather those countries will send their legates to us, as they have already in matters of scientific learning, searching in our Christianity for the secret of our life. But while the Church refuses to recognize its own children in inspiration, it denies the very life it cherishes.

Only a Christian Renaissance can fulfil the derelict purposes of the modern world. We may expect a newly Christianized literature and a newly poetic Christianity. Neither religion nor poetry as they are will survive. They will pass, they are already passing, towards the greater life of our newborn recognition. Dogma and symbol, though no longer strictures on our worship, will be known as the language of the ineffable and richest currency of truth. They will be seen to exist in order to extend and not to limit our understanding. A new poetry will arise and a new drama; and all our arts and our religion will alike recognize that each and all serve the one great purpose of their existence: the refraction of life, or immortality.

A new drama must accompany our revitalized theology. This dramatic art will respect the prompting instincts and diverse aspirations of man. It will distil the rich essences of human emotion, human desire and failure, life and death and that immortality enclosing both. The representation will appear as an idealized representation, since to express essentials we must employ poetry of speech and grace of movement, effects of colour and grouping and accompaniment, at times, of music. In this drama man will be transfigured by poetry, a creature of compelling life whether he be in the fiction criminal, lord or lover. Poetry has deserted our stage. But there will be a renaissance. The bastard forms may continue for awhile; the advent of the true cannot for long be delayed. The theatre is no place for trivialities. Its orchestration can and should release the varied harmonies of the life we live, revealing those extra dimensions of our psychic experience which we, our sight surface-bound, seldom observe. In great drama we know our life as it is, those deeper seas into which it sinks and which its movement cleaves, those sun-arrows glistening on its topmost peaks. Such profound knowledge reveals not sordid but noble qualities, riches of emotion, whether of tragedy or romance, vast forces of Christ-like good and Satanic evil, contesting powers of life and death. Every great drama is a branch on the Tree of Life. It crystallizes the meaning of our existence. It is dynamic and points towards futurity, since only by learning what we are do we simultaneously learn what we may become. Drama is creative of life. We are all alive but seldom know it. By knowing our life we expand and enrich it until, becoming one with Life, we attain our immortality. The drama, like the religious symbolism from which it has grown, awakes us to ourselves: addressing its meaning first to our unawakened consciousness, speaking in terms of disunion and disharmony, next, these antinomies resolved, it creates and recreates our life.

The advent of a new poetic drama will be one with the advent of a newly vitalized theology. In symbolism no rigid distinctions must be made between the human and the divine; the divine is symbolized in the human, is one with humanity. Poetic drama is throughout humanistic yet mystic, creating a greater humanity while revealing us to ourselves. Christianity likewise has been extravagantly humanistic, showing the brows of man ablaze with the fire-gold laurels of the divine; stating the fine hyperbole whereby, through the Incarnation, the splendours of poetry are inbound with a perfect human life in the present order of darkness and illusion. Our Christian Trinity is, as we have seen, a

simplification in human terms of all drama, the one dramatic
archetype and pattern to which all drama and all life, in
Dantesque metaphor, are as concentric circles out-radiating,
out-furling, out-flowering.

All this we shall not understand while we think a symbol
is a savage and idolatrous thing; nor while we fear its
mystery and resent attempts to exploit its meaning. Such
attitudes characterize only those to whom symbolic speech
is dead. But when once we recognize the fluidity and
elasticity of symbolic utterance, its height and depth, its
solid statement, its variation within unity, its modernity,
above all its creative power, we shall know symbolism to be
the very way to life. We shall then find truth in all high
prophecy, questioning less as to whether its reference to
future events be earthly or eschatological; usually we do well
to regard it as both, for both are projections into futurity of
an immediate experience. Unless so projected, such statements lose their creative power; they are creatively true and
to see their meaning we must first believe, their very truth
being conditional on our creative response. Symbolism is
alive, not dead; dynamic and creative, not repressive;
originating from the future to which it points and not to be
understood in relation to the past from which its face is
turned.

Though organized Christianity satisfies some, it repels
many others, leaving them anxious, unsatisfied and baffled;
because symbolism is dead to us and because the legitimate
and natural appeals are repressed, ignored or denounced. We
desire liberation and are loaded with fetters; we ask for life
and are reminded of death; we need to be awakened and are
given narcotics. Long past humanity ate of the Tree of the
Knowledge of Good and Evil: we have fed long on that
knowledge and the taste is bitter. We are still in the twilight
of good and evil and our eyes but fitfully focus the eternal
Beauty which is our star. In that Eden there was also the

Tree of Life, which had power to confer immortality and make gods of men, and its fruit is now swiftly ripening. Let but the Church recognize the inclusive splendours of her revelation. She is as a mother who, afraid that her child cannot preserve his own individuality, tries to hold him from contact with the world. Christianity has nothing to fear save fear itself. It holds greater treasures than any poet can create, and if all the pens that ever poets held were to unite to re-create the Christian drama, they would find one wonder at the least undigested in their art. But the poets and all that they stand for are necessary to us, just as Christianity is necessary to them. Through union only can there be a creative advance.

If it be asked how exactly this renascent life-force is to be brought to earth, one first condition may be stated. 'Spirit' in our theological metaphysic has been always, until incarnated, evil. The Holy Ghost or Spirit, in so far as it is not incarnated in our hearts, our lives, our actions or our art, is equivalent to Death, not Life. No ghost is good, but incarnate life is good. Therefore the New Incarnation and Christian Renaissance must see the embodiment in art, in ceremony, in our lives, of the Holy Eros and Sacred Life to which our Renaissance prophets direct us. This is the necessary fulfilment of our Trinity; this only, the relating of the third person of the Trinity to the erotic vision and the consequent recognition of all poetry's sacred life. From that all that we need will follow. Poetry alone can awake the Western world at the dawn of the white fire of Christ.

I must not conclude in a blaze of light. Both religion and poetry, as practised and understood today, will pass. They will pass, when the time is ripe, to bring to birth a greater than either, a new Life splendorously paling those twin candles that have stood before its altar. There is much talk today of a return to Christianity; rather must we advance towards it, grow up to it, measuring our understanding to its true stature. Throughout this book we have seen that the purest and richest visions are quiet, not extravagant; richly coloured but not dazzling. Jesus, Shakespeare and Keats are the great masters of the perfect speech. But our light-poets are necessary too, St John, Dante, Shelley, for we dwell mostly in realms of night; and yet we may remember how in Dante's final vision the triple Godhead was seen encircling a human form. Our religious literature, ceremonial and music, should awake us to life: there is all too much death already. We need a fiery star to glitter in our hearts and before our eyes, illumining our darkness; but human existence, richer often for sacrifice than for self-assertion, for sorrow than for joy, will continue as before. The eye alters all, and it is we who must first change, not our existence. We must create a finer life or rather let that life create itself in us. Already we have done so, and the world of men grows better hour by hour. Though the noblest wine may still be crushed from humanity by pain and thwarted longing, yet within the coarse texture of material things is woven a richer thread, a coloured pattern unexposed, foretold in dreams, in sleep, most exquisite and rich; no fevered flush, nor dazzling blaze, but a warmth, an embrace, a rich happiness. Our future poetry must see our city streets tipped with that pentecostal flame, but those cities will for long be areas heavy with suffering, with darkness, illusion and death. These themselves must pulse with life; through these we must burn our way, in spite of these know our freedom, because of these create our hope.

Nobly the Christian Church has worked and is yet working to alleviate this suffering. It is easy to blame it for all the thousand ills our mortal flesh inherits; to ignore both its leavening influence throughout the centuries and its activities today. It is all too easy to forget the arduous labours endured by the parish priest the while the poet spins his dreams. But again, our Church is itself the body given to a dream once lived in Judaea, and we neglect the vital power-sources at our peril. We have long obeyed and respected a father-god. Another desire is poignant today, craving not separation but union; not *agapé* only but also *eros* (p. 312 below). I ask that we receive the Holy Eros and divine comforter whose silent kiss and invisible embrace holds warmth and joy without which we starve. Though our days be darkly embroidered with suffering, our pain is not unheeded; and however grim the forces of death may seem to us, life is always marshalling new myriads to drive that death into the hell from which it first arose. Life, not death, has the victory; that is the message alike of poet and prophet. The poet is the prophet. We must henceforth see great poetry as prophetic, so that Shelley's words may be fulfilled in all their splendour:

> Poets are the hierophants of an unapprehended inspiration; the mirrors of the gigantic shadows which futurity casts upon the present; the words which express what they understand not; the trumpets which sing to battle and feel not what they inspire; the influence which is moved not, but moves. Poets are the unacknowledged legislators of the world.

And Jesus, as Carlyle tells us, is the greatest of all poets.

Epilogue (1960)

XIV

THE SERAPHIC INTUITION

I

THE argument of *The Christian Renaissance* appears to me still, in essence, both sound and important: somehow man's human instincts must be linked to Christ. Both D. H. Lawrence and Sean O'Casey have in our time laboured to show sexual love as a redeeming power. They remain, however, like my own first attempt, content with a primary emphasis on heterosexual engagements: Lawrence's homosexual interludes are not developed. My own study left loopholes only (pp. 207, 223, 241, 258). Its main limitations appear to derive from its failure to emphasize (i) the sadistic impulse; (ii) homosexual and bisexual tendencies; and (iii) Spiritualism. Of these three, the first is dark, but the second may aspire to light, and in so far as it achieves success may be touching what I now call 'the seraphic intuition', so blending into the third.

My later investigations have unearthed much relevant material. 'The Shakespearian Integrity' in *The Burning Oracle* (1939; reprinted in *The Sovereign Flower*, 1958) followed my early essay 'The Theme of Romantic Friendship in Shakespeare' (*The Holborn Review*; XX. new series; 1929) and some hints in *Principles of Shakespearian Production* (III; footnote on *Twelfth Night*) by noting more exactly the homosexual or bisexual elements in Shakespeare's Sonnets, *The Merchant of Venice*, *Twelfth Night* and *Timon of Athens*. *Christ and Nietzsche* (1948) concentrated on the sadistic instinct, treating the Christian Cross as a sublimating medium; on the bisexual integration; and on the comprehensive statement of Nietzsche's *Thus Spake Zarathustra*. In discussion of the sadistic I was helped by and used the work of two contemporary writers who have seen deeply into these dark clefts: the poetry of Robinson Jeffers and John Cowper Powys' *A Glastonbury Romance*. *The Dynasty of Stowe* (1945; III) developed a comparison of the Socratic *paederastia* with Jesus' relation to his disciples and the Christian Church. *The Mutual Flame* (1955) discussed Shakespeare's Sonnets and the bisexual Phoenix poems of *Love's Martyr*. The Sonnets were read as the experience of genius finding its objective ideal, like Plato's Socrates, in the presexual harmony of a loved youth of strength-with-grace regarded as his 'master-mistress' (Sonnet 20) and leading (Sonnets 113, 114) to an expansion of this experience into that harmonious ratification of humanity in general of which we are so strongly aware in the dramas. *Lord Byron: Christian Virtues* (1952) discussed Byron's love of children of both sexes and his semi-educational love of youth; and *Lord Byron's Marriage* (1957), supplemented by some important notes in *Essays in Criticism* (Oct., 1958), found in Byron's homosexual and bisexual proclivities the key to his extraordinary life. More recently *The Golden Labyrinth* (1962) has revealed the extent to which the bisexual or seraphic ideal merging into the spiritualistic impregnates British drama from medieval times to our own. I shall discuss these sexual matters first, before turning (p. 326) to Spiritualism.

The complexities are many. When Socrates in Plato's *Phaedrus* or *The Symposium* or Shakespeare in his Sonnets derives a mystical exaltation from love-sight we may suppose this exaltation to grow from: (i) the finding in a presexual form an objective equivalent to his own inward soul-harmony or aspiration; or (ii) the sight through an as yet uncontaminated body of the loved youth's real self, his spirit-self or spirit-body as opposed to its material veil, Shelley's 'vest' in a lyric already quoted (p. 91); or (iii) the vision through the bud-like form of either the creative essence and purpose in its original purity or (iv) hints of some seraphic order of which the earthly beauty is a reflection. To attempt exact decisions would be idle: we may remain content with supposing a seraphic experience without further definition.

Closely allied are our recurring literary themes of incest, with mother or sister in relation to high types of man: as in Sophocles' *Oedipus Tyrannus*; in Jacobean drama, especially Ford's *'Tis Pity She's a Whore*; in Byron's life and work; in Shelley's *Laon and Cythna* or *The Revolt of Islam*; in Wagner's *The Ring of the Nibelungs*. There are again implications, as in homosexuality, of a union not so much with an opposite as with a likeness or self-reflection. In the Bible we read of 'the friend who is your other self' (*Deuteronomy*, XIII. 6); and Jonathan loved David 'as himself' (*1 Samuel*, XVIII. 1, 3). In Plato's *Phaedrus* we are told that the loved one 'sees himself in his lover, as in a glass, without knowing who it is that he sees' (255). Sometimes we are aware of a narcissistic element, peculiarly strong in Byron's semi-autobiographical *The Deformed Transformed* and the many self-reflections of *Don Juan*; and also in Shelley, as in the line 'a pard-like Spirit, beautiful and swift' in *Adonais* (xxxii). In *Thus Spake Zarathustra* Nietzsche regards the self as our final goal: 'Not until he turneth from himself will he leap over his own shadow — lo! straight into his own sunshine!' Our deepest desire is 'the thirst of the ring' turning back on itself (35; 27).[1] The highly integrated personality searches for a self-reflecting love, which next tends to expand to a universal, Timon-like, benevolence — though *Timon of Athens* itself is the weaker for having no one *personal* love-pivot — so passing from unity through unity to unity.

[1] My quotations follow the Everyman translation by A. Tille and M. M. Bozman. My section numerals apply to the whole sequence apart from the Introductory Discourse, which I regard as unnumbered. (In *Christ and Nietzsche* a different system was used.)

Within the tradition of Western culture we have a succession of martyr-heroes who are associated with an unorthodox, either self-reflecting or universal, love. Prometheus, martyred for an impious love of man, is the first; Oedipus, rather differently, is another. Socrates' grand-scale and influential development of *paederastia* led to social opposition and condemnation.[1] Shakespeare's universal lover Timon, once called a 'Phoenix' (II. i. 32) and protagonist of a dramatic pattern wholly male except for Amazons and prostitutes, is forced from benevolence to denunciation. Marlowe (p. 304 below), Byron and Oscar Wilde are in trouble from homosexuality. The tradition becomes conscious in Nietzsche's opposition of the bisexual love-with-power (p. 315 below) to conventional ethics in *Thus Spake Zarathustra*.

Our heroes may be myths, fictions, prophets or men of letters, but in each there is some unconventional love forcing a conflict with the established order which is followed by a final recognition of spiritual and saving power, such as that so precisely dramatized in the wooing of the outcast hero by the erstwhile cruel community in the *Oedipus Coloneus* and *Timon of Athens*. These semi-supermen are to be distinguished, as Nietzsche distinguishes his Superman, from the more obvious power-bearers, the Caesars and Napoleons. Their power is more subtle, more spiritual, and more enduring. In them we sense a blend of male and female elements, of power and love, in a state intricately related to sexual abnormality. There is often a close mother-relationship, such as that dramatized and discussed throughout my *Atlantic Crossing* (1936; especially VII. iv. 203–9; IX. v. 291–9). The archetype is Oedipus, and it recurs in *Hamlet* and *Coriolanus*, and today in the lives of Oscar Wilde and

---

[1] In *The Birds* Aristophanes associates the school of Socrates with immorality, and in Plato's *Phaedo* Socrates appears to regard Aristophanes' attack as a part-cause of his condemnation.

D. H. Lawrence; and in *The Family Reunion*, and *The Ascent of F6*.

In so far as we admit Jesus' full humanity, we shall, following Robinson Jeffers' association of him with Oedipus in his *Meditation on Saviours* (p. 322 below), inevitably search for his humanity somewhere within, or near, this field.

I I

Genius has its hidden workshop, and it is unfair to accept its achievements while remaining blind to 'the cruelty of its hammer' (*Thus Spake Zarathustra*, 30). We may assume the presence of dangerous semi-sexual instincts hard to satisfy; these are turned inwards for self-conflict and a sublimation to be attained through religion, art or fantasy. Somehow the feared instincts must be not only accepted but loved, enjoyed and used, according to the doctrine of Pope's *Essay on Man* (*Laureate of Peace*; II, V). Since physical release through dream, being symptomatic of a split between consciousness and instinct, must be regarded as a second-best, a technique may be advisable whereby release is gained in waking contemplation. The process is shadowed in *Paradise Lost* where Sin and Death descend (p. 81 above) from Satan's head through a kind of self-incest; but what is there viewed as evil may be turned to a creative purpose. We have a glimpse of it in Mr Evans' 'orgasm of egocentric contemplation' in John Cowper Powys' *A Glastonbury Romance* (1933, XXV. 848; 1955, XXV. 812); and in his recent *All or Nothing* Powys has obliquely suggested that such mentally induced release 'is a much more important and creative act than ordinary or natural fornication or the raping, if we are male, of our feminine opposite' (XXVII. 192). Perhaps through a general acceptance and direction of such a technique large areas of human self-torment might be purified and a new age of enlightened behaviour succeed. Somewhere in this direction lies the self-making implied by Ibsen and more deliberately intended by Nietzsche, though his phraseology remains guarded. Ibsen's Third Empire will be inaugurated by the man who 'wills himself', who knows how to channel his whole self (*Emperor and Galilean*, 'The Emperor Julian', III. iv; and see his letter to George Brandes of 30 January, 1875). Nietzsche praises the moment when the 'body' is 'exalted and raised up' and 'its bliss ravisheth the spirit so that it becometh a creator and a valuer and a lover and a benefactor of all things'; and though Zarathustra would rather 'die' than confess the thoughts of his 'midnight heart', yet only he who has the 'courage' to say, 'Thus shall ye flow, ye great and small streams' will be 'lord of the earth' (*Thus Spake Zarathustra*, 22, 79). Powys has had that courage.

What fantasies are to be used, corresponding perhaps, and in part, to the private 'mythology' of Powys' *Wolf Solent*, will depend on (i) the nature of the dangerous instincts and (ii) the ideal striven for. In both *Thus Spake Zarathustra* (5, 17) and T. S. Eliot's *The Family Reunion* (II. ii) dark entities are transmuted into 'angels'. *The Family Reunion* is a dramatic hinge, as *Ash Wednesday* with its Dantesque presences is a poetic hinge, for the reversal from *The Waste Land* and *Sweeney Agonistes* into the martyrdom, already forecast by *Murder in the Cathedral*, of *The Cocktail Party*; the sexual-sadistic being reversed, through a new adoration, into the masochistic, to self-giving. In general sexual revulsions may often be said to give place to a recognition that they are merely the negative aspect, the backthrust, of a positive aim; and this positive aim is best figured in some form of presexual or bisexual unity and purity merging into the seraphic. Such a process is shadowed by the Dark Lady and the Fair Youth of Shakespeare's Sonnets, and examples of such seraphic figures occur throughout our dramatic tradition, one of the clearest coming in Mas-

singer's and Dekker's *The Virgin Martyr*, where Theophilus
the persecutor of Christians is transfixed by the beauty of the
page Angelo:

> It is, it is, some angel. Vanished again!
> Oh, come back, ravishing boy! Bright messenger!
> Thou hast, by these mine eyes fix'd on thy beauty,
> Illumined all my soul.
>
> (V. i)

These lines form a key to our argument; nowhere else is the
heart of it more lucidly and crisply given. Angelo turns out
to be a real angel. Theophilus is utterly transformed. The
new state will still be sexually impregnated, with the bliss and
rapture of self-giving, like the love-sacrifice in Browning's
The Ring and the Book wherein dying is 'to spurn the ground',
where death is 'the heart of life' and 'immolation' becomes
'bliss' with a 'thrill' in it to 'outthrob pain' (VI. 951-4;
972-3). Similar thoughts are found in *Thus Spake Zarathustra* (p. 323 below). The story of St Paul follows this
rhythm. From violence and persecution (*Acts*, VIII. 1-3; IX.
1) he is converted to a life of martyrdom. Shame and glory
are identified; instinct is still active; and every flower has its
root.

Our argument is covered by the Cross in Christianity.
The creative cruelties of nature have developed in human
consciousness into a sadistic evil. Condemned by the moral
law man attains self-reversal through enjoyment of the
Crucifix as an ambivalent symbol of both torture and love
(see *Christ and Nietzsche*, III).

These are dramatic and externalized examples of what is
normally an inward and perhaps half-understood process
leading towards what may be called 'integration' in a sense
near to that intended by Jung's *The Integration of the Personality*, and to a high state of being. The sadistic instinct need
not be strongly present; in Goethe, Byron, Nietzsche and

Wilde as persons there seems to have been little of it; there may be just a gradual flowering from the presexuality of youth to a mature bisexuality, without any apparent reversal. The final integration is a self-marriage. This is the state known transiently at the moment of artistic creation or athletic skill, and it is bisexual: the spirit of poetry comes in Nietzsche's *Zarathustra* as a blend of male and female (*Thus Spake Zarathustra*, 74; and see 39). The control of a love-story balancing the sexes and bringing them to union always presupposes a bisexual state in the writer. To maintain such a state enduringly and on every level is naturally harder.

Of this self-making we have strong poetic documents. One is the famous passage of Wordsworth already quoted (p. 93) where the spirit within nature replaces our seraphic ideal and union is felt as the 'creation' of a new personality fulfilling all myths and symbols of Paradise. Wordsworth's lines, which should be compared with the teaching of Powys' philosophic books, are discussed more fully in the chapter 'Eros and Psyche' in *Christ and Nietzsche*, and are there grouped with Keats' *Ode to Psyche*, wherein the ravishing by the unknown Eros, who must be equated with the erotic essence irrespective of what form, normal or abnormal, the fantasy may take, is associated with the 'branched thoughts new-grown with pleasant pain' (p. 210 above) of poetic creation. As we have seen (p. 26), the union of 'brain' as female and 'soul' as male described in *Richard II* is of a similarly creative order. *Thus Spake Zarathustra* dramatizes again and again this inward love-intercourse between the egocentric self and the various powers covered by the concept 'soul' (58) and other personifications. At the conclusion to Milton's *Comus* Cupid (= Eros) and Psyche are envisaged in bliss far above the sexual tragedy of Venus and Adonis. In the many Phoenix and Turtle poems studied in *The Mutual Flame* the Phoenix corresponds to Eros and the Turtle-Dove to Psyche. When Christ is symbolized by the

Phoenix we shall regard his Church as the Turtle (*The Mutual Flame*, II. v. 222). Phoenix is sexually indeterminate. Shakespeare's poem (p. 236) is our best definition of the reason-negating unity and purity towards which these various symbolisms are pointing us. The state indicated is that of the artistic moment, 'at war' as Shelley in his *Defence of Poetry* tells us, 'with every base desire'; wherein all desire, though included, has been dissolved into love. Love is to be distinguished from lust on the one side and sentimentality on the other: it is always bisexual.

Psyche, the feminine self, must provisionally accept the unknown Eros, in whatever guise he comes; and some of his disguises may be dark. But the more closely he approximates to Eros, as the seraphic winged youth depicted by the Greeks, the safer we shall be. In M. G. Lewis' Gothic novel *The Monk*, Lucifer, as the Devil, appears first to tempt Ambrosio as a winged youth of amazing beauty (VII; *The Golden Labyrinth*, IX), and when his grim task is over comes to claim his victim in hideous shape. This is the process which we must learn to reverse.

Our main authorities speak with a single voice, and it certainly appears to be right that, for us on this earth, what lures on the aspirant should generally be a male or semi-male youthful form, erotically impregnated but in essence a unity, blending strength-with-grace or power with love. In British drama from the sixteenth to the eighteenth centuries the more blessed figures may be either boys or girls provided that the girls assume male disguise; and up to the Restoration all feminine parts were played by boys. In Dante we have a girl, Beatrice, but she is a figure of presexual unity and significantly associated by Powys with the bisexually conceived Tegolin, in *Owen Glendower* (XIX. 722).

In the Platonic intuition sexual feelings are fused with intellect, and male forms best meet its requirements in that they are the less suggestive of the biological process and sexual or other distinctions and desires. The love is an attunement to beauty bringing wisdom; we may call it 'love-wisdom'. The very term 'Hermaphrodite' signifies this union, as is specifically stated in Francis Beaumont's poem, adapted from Ovid, called *Salmacis and Hermaphroditus*, wherein the river-nymph Salmacis, with the river suggesting the sexual centres, loves the beautiful but unresponsive youth Hermaphroditus, son of Mercury (= Hermes) as god of wisdom and Venus (= Aphrodite) as goddess of love. The gods in pity make the nymph and youth into one person, and it is said that whoever henceforth bathes in the waters where the miracle was performed will enjoy a corresponding integration.

Byron to his contemporaries appeared strangely bisexual and his Don Juan, when in uniform like 'Love turned a lieutenant of artillery' (*Don Juan*, IX. 44), is throughout conceived as a self-reflection of bisexual grace (*Lord Byron: Christian Virtues*, II. 81, 95; *Lord Byron's Marriage*, VII. 256). Coleridge in *The Pang more Sharp than All* laments the passing of a semi-magical 'bright Boy' who has left re-membrances of himself of 'either sex' behind; and in *The Destiny of Nations* (426–39) we find a seemingly hermaphro-ditic figure of stronger sort. Shelley's *The Witch of Atlas* has an Hermaphrodite to guide the boat of poetry or vision; and in the Fragments related to the aptly named '*Epipsychidion*' he associates a sexually ambiguous love suggested to be of Socratic and Shakespearian affinities with the birth of a 'naked seraph', so regarding it as creative in another than the biological order (*The Starlit Dome*; for Coleridge, II. 120–1, 141–2; for Shelley, III. 228, 241–2; *Christ and Nietzsche*, IV. 149–50). In our day bisexuality is written firmly into the dramas of Bernard Shaw and T. S. Eliot's *The Waste Land* (*The Golden Labyrinth*, XV, XVI).

Goethe's *Faust* has more to offer than was surveyed in my earlier pages. Not only have we the Boy-Charioteer of the

Masque personifying poetry and described in erotic and semi-feminine terms, but still more important are Homunculus and Euphorion. Homunculus is both beautiful and 'hermaphroditical' (297–8). Euphorion symbolizes poetry with especial reference to Byron. He is first 'naked' and 'a wingless genius, faun-like yet in no wise bestial' (341), leaping always upwards. Next

> Raiment wrought with trailing flowers
> He hath donned majestical.
> On his arms are tassels waving, ribbons flutter round his bosom,
> In his hand the golden lyre, wholly like a little Phoebus,
> Blithely trips he to the margin, to the beetling brink. We marvel,
> And his parents fall enraptured each upon the other's heart.
> For about his head, what splendour! Hard to tell were what there gleameth,
> Is it gaud of gold or is it flame of intellect supreme?
> Thus he moves with graceful gesture, even as boy himself proclaiming
> Future master of all beauty, every limb athrill and trembling
> With the melodies eternal; even so ye too shall hear him,
> Even so ye too shall see him, with a most unique amaze.
>
> (342)

The 'gold' is one with 'intellect', glory with truth.

At the vast poem's conclusion, we are among the seraphic hosts. Mephistopheles regards their singing as a 'boyish-girlish botchwork' (410), but that is his loss. In significant contrast to the Chorus of Penitent Women there is a chorus of Blessed Boys, who had died before sin and now, as the chorus of 'Younger Angels' announce, are to function as the agents of Faust's purifying:

> Wreathing the rocky height
> A little distance,
> Mist-like, there meets my sight
> Spirit-existence.
> Now grow the cloudlets clear,

> Blest boys I see appear,
> A stirring legion,
> Freed from the stress of earth,
> Ranged in a ring
> In the Upper Region
> Revelling in the birth
> Of its new spring.
> Let him first yoked with these
> Work out by due degrees
> His perfecting.

(418)

They circle round Faust, and Faust's Beatrice, Gretchen, comes close. Together they raise him towards the Virgin Mother: 'Still dazzles him the new-sprung day' (422).

Wagner's *Parsifal* follows *Faust* with its various youths or boys as servitors and songsters of the Grail, the boys having the higher place; and with as its hero Parsifal, a youth of purity and beauty who survives the machinations of a wizard and the sexual advances of female allurement to fulfil his appointed task. *Parsifal* may be defined as a grand expansion of the 'seraphic'.

These higher intuitions of love-wisdom are drawn from direct human experience. To Tennyson the idealized Arthur Henry Hallam was remembered in *In Memoriam* for his

> Seraphic intellect and force
>   To seize and throw the doubts of man;
>   Impassion'd logic, which outran
> The hearer in its fiery course.

(CIX)

In him Tennyson was aware of 'manhood fused with female grace', recalling Shakespeare's thought of his Fair Youth as 'the master-mistress of my passion' (Sonnet 20).

What the Platonic lover sees in male youth is the compacted essence, like a bud, of human creation more true to the divine intention than the divided and care-worn beings of

maturity. But unlike female beauty, the loved essence, as
Shakespeare's Sonnets so poignantly remember, passes; the
insight is, in any one instance, brief, and to this extent tragic.
That is why so many of our finest expressions of it occur
when the death of the loved one allows the experience to
flower in tragic terms. So, in descent from the old ritual
lamentations over Adonis we have the Greek and Roman
elegies of the ancient world; Ben Jonson's lyric on the boy-
actor Salathiel Pavy; Milton's *Lycidas*, Byron's *Thyrza*
poems, Shelley's *Adonais*, Arnold's *Thyrsis*, Tennyson's *In
Memoriam*, and the more suffused sense of tragic youth in
Gray's *Elegy in a Country Churchyard* and Housman's *A
Shropshire Lad*. The tone is set by the two lyrics of Plato on
his pupil 'Aster', the name meaning 'star', quoted by
K. J. Freeman in *Schools of Hellas* (1907, 1922; I. vi. 202).
One, in Freeman's translation, goes:

> Star of my soul, thou gazest
> Upon the starry skies;
> I envy Heaven, that watches
> Thy face with countless eyes.

The other, as translated by Shelley, was written after the
boy's death:

> Thou wert the morning Star among the living,
> Ere thy fair light had fled:
> Now, being dead, thou art as Hesperus, giving
> New splendour to the dead.

The inmost melody of this experience was never more surely
captured than by Byron in *Thou art Dead, as Young and Fair*,
one of the 'Thyrza' poems addressed to John Edleston:[1]

> The flower in ripen'd bloom unmatch'd
> Must fall the earliest prey;
> Though by no hand untimely snatch'd,
> The leaves must drop away:

[1] For the 'Thyrza' poems see *Lord Byron's Marriage*, I. 30–8.

And yet it were a greater grief
To watch it withering, leaf by leaf,
    Than see it pluck'd to-day;
Since earthly eye but ill can bear
To trace the change to foul from fair.

I know not if I could have borne
    To see thy beauties fade;
The night that follow'd such a morn
    Had worn a deeper shade.
Thy day without a cloud hath pass'd,
And thou wert lovely to the last;
    Extinguish'd, not decay'd;
As stars that shoot along the sky
Shine brightest as they fall from high.

The note sounds across the centuries. Today we recognize it in Francis Berry's *Malta Elegy*:

Child, Musician, Genius, Quest,
Whom I looked for, found, now lost;
In you sublime, my youth, my past;
That better self is now a ghost.

The great archetype of all our tragic elegies is David's lament over Jonathan:

O Jonathan, my brother!
You were my dear delight,
your love for me was a wonder, far
beyond a woman's love.
                    (*2 Samuel*, I. 26)

It is within such tragic contexts that these experiences attain their fullness. Though peculiarly subject to time, they are shadowed by the eternal; at once transient and transcendent.

The Platonic and Shakespearian intuition lies at the heart of Western culture; it is the fountain-spring of centuries of education, expanding, as Plato explains, to the understanding of all high concerns. As Hugh Ross Williamson puts it in *The Arrow and the Sword* (1947, 1955): 'The "biological" protest against Uranianism is inevitable if the race is to continue on the plane of procreation; the safeguarding of Uranianism is vital if civilization is to continue on any other plane' (V. 81). Based on the *paederastia* of ancient Greece, itself an educational relationship as described in K. J. Freeman's *Schools of Hellas* (1907, 1922) and G. Lowes Dickinson's *The Greek View of Life* (1896, 1907), the Platonic intuition has persisted in poetry and drama, independent of social convention. To write it off as sinful is to regard our culture as poisoned at its source.

Renaissance drama has a long succession of boys playing the parts of girls who disguise themselves as boys, always as redeeming powers. Massinger's page Angelo (p. 275 above) turns out to be a real angel, but in Nathaniel Lee's *Caesar Borgia* a dramatically idealized boy bears the name 'Seraphino': to the Renaissance dramatic imagination there is no real distinction. Shakespeare's angels are regularly imagined as youths (*The Wheel of Fire*, enlarged, App. B) and his friend of the Sonnets is his 'better angel' (144). The boy of Coleridge's *The Pang more Sharp than All*, after being compared to an 'Elphin Knight', is said to be left as a 'sylph' in the poet's 'heart':

> Ah! he is gone, and yet will not depart! –
> Is with me still, yet I from him exiled!
> For still there lives within my secret heart
> The magic image of the magic Child . . .

This 'faery Boy' is Love, or Eros. Byron saw the boys who so attracted him on his first visit to Greece as 'sylphs' (*Correspondence* etc., ed. Murray, to J. C. Hobhouse, 23 Aug., 1810); and the loved chorister, John Edleston, was, in another of the 'Thyrza' poems, as 'a dream of Heaven' (*If*

Sometimes in the Haunts of Men). Many of Byron's friendships were protective, and some of them semi-educational,
in tone (*Lord Byron: Christian Virtues*, II); Loukas on his
last adventure in Greece he called 'not the Evangelist but a
disciple of mine' (*Letters and Journals*, to Hancock, 5 Feb.,
1824). It is the office of such intuitions to keep our spirit-
senses awake.

And what of our religion? In Plato's *Phaedrus* the love
there honoured is the condition of the soul's ascent and the
way to supernal insight. In *The Symposium* Eros, depicted by
the Greeks as a winged youth, is defined as a '*daimon*', or
spirit-link, a being 'of an intermediate nature' whose office
it is 'to interpret and carry messages' between men and gods
(202). He is, for Plato, what I insisted in my original study
that he must again become (p. 239 above), the Holy Spirit.

III

We shall not deny that there are dangers. The human plight
will not be resolved by reiterations of the loveliness of youth
or the beauty of love. The balances are delicate; the highest
and the lowest are in all such matters blood-brethren in joint
alliance against the middle ways of respectability or convention; and aspiration and crucifixion are natural
correlatives.

We are not here concerned with morality. As usually
understood, as a rough-and-ready way of dealing with chaos,
it is a matter for the sociologist. In more religious terms,
true righteousness can never be defined by writing down
certain actions as always good and others as always bad,
since everything, even murder, depends on the context and
the individual. So much admitted, we can say that the moral
issue has been provisionally settled by Plato in the *Phaedrus*.
Three types of lover are described: (i) those prompted by
sheer lust; (ii) genuine lovers who succumb to temptation;

and (iii) those who maintain their aspiring course. The first group is condemned and the last honoured; the second is allowed, though their progress will be retarded. It is here assumed that even the higher aspirants will, as did David and Jonathan (*1 Samuel*, XX. 41), engage in kisses and caresses (255). In *The Symposium* there is a more especially *creative* emphasis, as we shall see (p. 292); in the *Republic* and the *Laws* and in the report of Socrates' teaching in Xenophon's *Symposium* moral strictures are stronger. It must be remembered that we are here concerned with the semi-educational love for a boy or youth as accepted within the convention of *paederastia*, and not with a wholly adult relationship. We are urged to engage in 'the *right* kind' of *paederastia* (*The Symposium*, 211).

The horror aroused by sodomy throughout the ages raises problems too dark for our present discussion. That there may be some attendant mystique involved may be realized from the close association asserted by John Cowper Powys of the physical areas in question with both sexuality and the Grail.[1] The important statements, which I have already discussed in *Lord Byron's Marriage* (VII. 261–2), occur in the preface to the 1955 edition of *A Glastonbury Romance* and in the main body of the book at the following pages: edition of 1933 at XXVIII. 981–2, 991; edition of 1955 at Preface xv–xvi and XXVIII. 938–9, 948. During Holy Sam's mystical experience there is a sense of penetration from below and memory of it afterwards fuses with a medical experience of physical disgust to create 'a strange second sight, an inkling, as to some incredible secret, whereby the whole massed weight of the world's tormented flesh was labouring towards some release' (XXVIII. 991 or 948). In his preface (1955; xvi) Powys refers to Rabelais, and relevant passages on

[1] Ritual sodomy was apparently among the pagan rites that in ancient times invaded the Temple at Jerusalem (Robert Graves and Joshua Podro, *The Nazarene Gospel Restored*, 1953; Part II, 283).

physical disgust and taboo occur in the concluding chapters to his *Rabelais* (1948); and also, from a Freudian standpoint, and with especial reference to Swift, in Norman O. Brown's recent *Life against Death* (1959). The disgust is a biological reaction to biological poisons, like the disgust aroused by death in Jacobean drama. Though the particular sexual practice at issue may occur in both heterosexual[1] and homosexual relationships, and though it may be far from frequent among homosexuals, there is little doubt that this fear has its part in the distaste aroused by homosexual propensities of all, even comparatively innocent, varieties. It may accordingly be worth while to suggest that even within the worst there may be a mystique which Powys' passages go some way towards illuminating, and which would make sense of the semi-mystical homosexuality during the Middle Ages studied in Hugh Ross Williamson's *The Arrow and the Sword*. For we are involved in a union of life-forces with areas of death: the act is a tragic act.

A usual process is this. The genius on his lonely approach to a full integration, is tormented, not by his partiality but by his own bisexual abundance; there is an overflow and the tormented desire for human contact. This torment is written into Shakespeare's sonnets, where he, over-full of 'sweetness', 'sick of welfare' and 'rank' with very 'goodness', turns to 'bitter sauces' and 'poison' for remedy (Sonnet 118). Byron's line in *Manfred* 'I plung'd amidst mankind' (II. ii) may be applied to his subsequent self-engagement with the lowest types of sexual or homosexual practice in Venice (*Lord Byron: Christian Virtues*, V. 256). Nietzsche records a similar soul-state, his Zarathustra in superabundance of 'virtue' hungering for wickedness to 'touch' the human 'souls' of others (*Thus Spake Zarathustra*, 31). Within these engagements is still a love; an ecstasy in loving even the lowest,

[1] See my article 'Lawrence, Joyce and Powys', *Essays in Criticism*, XI. iv; Oct., 1961.

fusing, as in Powys' description of Holy Sam's experiences in *A Glastonbury Romance*, the highest with the lowest, mystical ecstasy with the repellent. Of his life in Venice Byron himself said that he 'disapproves' but 'endures' (P. B. Shelley to T. L. Peacock, 22 Dec., 1818). Degradation was a kind of duty. We who live normal and respectable lives must accord to such men our sympathy. If they are diseased they are at least diseased with a disease that proves more vital than health, leading to lives and works which the race will not willingly let die.

We have been preparing a context for some notes on Oscar Wilde. I do not claim to know the exact degree of Wilde's legal guilt. He himself said that 'while there was much amongst the definite charges that was quite untrue' his life had certainly 'been full of perverse pleasures' (*De Profundis, The Works of Oscar Wilde*, ed. G. F. Maine, 1948 etc.; 883). The nature of his relationship to his mother is said to have left him with what psychologists call a 'mother fixation' (Frank Brennand, *Oscar Wilde*, 1960; I. 15); the association recalls Byron's, though Byron's was less happy. His mother dressed him as a girl until he was nine (Brennand, I. 15). Like Byron, Wilde was a lover of children (*Lord Byron: Christian Virtues*, II. 75–83; Hesketh Pearson, *The Life of Oscar Wilde*, Penguin 1960 edn., XI. 187; XVII. 334), and both exerted a strong fascination over women. Both often appeared effeminate, and yet both were capable, when challenged, of disconcerting feats of male strength. Wilde's love of flowers and interest in both male and female dress – he started his literary career as editor of a woman's periodical – were allied with a robust physique, physical courage, intellectual brilliance and a devastating wit to give him a position of artistic and social dominance that proved intoxicating both to others and to himself. From youth onwards he maintained, like Byron, a boyish immaturity often difficult to distinguish from the integration of a seer.

Within was a strong idealism and a rich mine of human sympathy. His first play *Vera or the Nihilists* sets a justified revolution against a tyrannic aristocracy and touches solution under the crown – 'this little fiery-coloured world' (IV) – an enlightened sovereign, and love; through these, unified and expanded, is glimpsed a solution to human misery. *Vera* is of a higher order than his subsequent dramas; it failed; but its key-thoughts continued to impregnate Wilde's serious writing. *The Soul of Man under Socialism* demonstrates the necessity of preserving the individual's freedom or soul-worth within our planning; seeing the royal, or aristocratic, valuations *as they exist in each one of us*, as sacred. The symbol of this soul-worth may be the crown; or more often riches, and especially jewels. Jewels and other rich solids constitute Wilde's central symbolism; for him the City of God is 'like a perfect pearl' and 'the pearl of my soul' a natural phrase (*De Profundis*; *Works*; 865, 866).

Throughout literature rich metals are used ambivalently.[1] They may hold connotations of material greed or may be symbols of the transcendent. Jewels normally exert positive radiations. The Kingdom of Heaven is a 'pearl' and the New Jerusalem made of precious stones (*Matthew*, XIII. 46; *Revelation*, XXI. 18–21). Dante's *Divina Commedia* sparkles, and Milton's *Paradise Lost* is loaded, with rich stones. We have Shakespeare's 'mine eternal jewel' for the soul in *Macbeth* (III. i. 68), Othello's 'pearl' as a love-symbol (V. ii. 346) and the jewel-imagery in *Pericles* (III. ii. 102; and see *The Shakespearian Tempest*, V. 222–3; also II. 65–9); Byron's contrast of 'seraph'-eyed Aurora and Haidée in terms respectively of a jewel-like transcendence and flowery nature in *Don Juan* (XV. 45, 47, 58; XVI. 48); Yeats' metal-imagery and Gold Birds in *Sailing to Byzantium*; and the spiritualized gems at the conclusion of Sir Herbert

[1] This ambivalence is discussed in my article '*Timon of Athens* and its Dramatic Descendants', *The Review of English Literature*, II. iii; Oct., 1961.

Read's *The Green Child*. We may compare Charles Doughty's beautiful passage on gems in his *Travels in Arabia Deserta* (edn. of 1926; XI 315): 'Those indestructible elect bodies, as stars, shining to us out of the dim mass of matter, are comfortable to our fluxuous feeble souls and bodies; in this sense all gems are cordial and of an influence religious. These elemental flowering lights almost persuade us of a serene eternity.' 'Flowering'; and yet rich metals contrast with flowers in point of solidity. In them spirituality is solid and beauty permanent: even a miser's lust has a transcendental aspect.

Rich metals are apt correlatives to transcendence housed in male beauty. In the love-duologue of the *Song of Solomon* the female receives her best adulation in imagery of fertility (p. 212), the male in imagery of rich stones. His fingers are like 'golden tapers' tipped with 'topaz', his body 'ivory' veined with 'sapphire' and his limbs of 'marble' and 'gold' (V. 10–15). This supposedly physical description blends readily with a vision of the seraphic, as recorded by Daniel:

> ... I saw a man standing, robed in linen, with a girdle of fine gold from Ophir round his waist, his body gleaming like a topaz, his face like lightning, his eyes like lamps of fire, his arms and legs like the colour of burnished bronze, and the sound of his words like the noise of a crowd!   (*Daniel*, X. 5)

Such elaborated metallic associations would not be quite so suitable for a woman. We are reminded of the Oriental phrase 'diamond body' (Norman O. Brown, noting Rilke's poetic quest for the hermaphroditic, *Life against Death*, 1959; XVI. 313), used to designate the etheric, or astral, body which interpenetrates and survives the physical.

Wilde as aesthete knew both the fascination and the danger of the transcendent housed in the material. Through young male beauty he saw an eternal, jewel-like, perfection. But his experience of it, as of rich stones too, was ambivalent,

balanced between eye-lust and transcendence. Almost lust
was transcendence; or rather the lust aroused was *a lust for
the transcendent*. This was Wilde's star; it, like the Crown in
Vera, should somehow, if joined to love, be the heart of a
great good: a Christian good. The complexities are handled
in his parables.

In *The Young King* a prince before his coronation dreams
of those who suffer to make his luxury and state, and accordingly rejects his coronation finery for a beggar's clothes.
Standing before the image of Christ he prays and is
transfigured:

> And lo! through the painted windows came the sunlight streaming
> upon him, and the sunbeams wove round him a tissued robe that
> was fairer than the robe that had been fashioned for his pleasure.
> The dead staff blossomed, and bare lilies that were whiter than
> pearls. The dry thorn blossomed, and bare roses that were redder
> than rubies. Whiter than fine pearls were the lilies, and their stems
> were of bright silver. Redder than male rubies were the roses, and
> their leaves were of beaten gold.

The flowering metals point a merging of nature into the
transcendent. The 'Glory of God' fills the church and as the
Young King comes from the altar 'no man dared look upon
his face, for it was like the face of an angel'.

Variations are played on the central theme. Our next hero,
in *The Fisherman and his Soul*, gives up his soul, which henceforth exists without a 'heart', for love of a Mermaid, the
Soul returning to tempt him to crime with lures of gold and
luxury. Here natural love and nature, with water and flowers
as fertility symbols, are on the one side and the soul, crime,
and riches are on the other. Riches, even when evil, are to
be aligned with the 'soul' – a key-concept in Wilde – here
functioning as tempter. Easier alignments occur in *The Star-
Child*, where a star-born child becomes a boy of beauty and
Narcissistic pride, scorning poverty and ugliness and engag-

ing in deliberate cruelty. Punished by the loss of his beauty and now himself an outcast, from the depths of his suffering he takes pity on a diseased beggar; so winning back his beauty and being finally crowned as a king.

Wilde is trying to relate his central intuition of youthful beauty to love and good works. That a kind of love-wisdom rather than any normal love is his true centre can be seen indirectly from the contrast of a natural and flower-like love with the soul in *The Fisherman and his Soul*. Wilde senses a dangerous co-presence of selfishness and spirituality, an all-too-solid presence of a transcendency directly associated with the 'soul', and yet seemingly as *infertile as rich gems*; and as dangerous. How, then, may the 'soul' and its jewelled and seemingly infertile Eros be related to love and Christian values? Young royal figures help most, since their human beauty lives and acts within the temporal order under the Crown whose rich stones symbolize the eternal.

In *The Happy Prince* the aim is clearer: the parable expresses the potential sovereignty of youth-beauty or love-wisdom even though, in our era, it is constricted. The Happy Prince is a gilded city-statue with sapphires for eyes and a ruby on his sword-hilt, much admired for his beauty and like an 'angel'. He is a royal Eros. A Swallow, symbolizing the human self, leaves his lady, a Reed, because of her feminine ways, and rests beneath the statue, which is weeping for human misery. Being himself fixed, the Prince needs the Swallow for three missions, and sends him bearing his ruby and two sapphires in turn to a destitute mother and her fever-struck little boy; to a young author cold and starving; and to a little girl, seller of matches, in dire need. Finally he gets the Swallow to strip the gold-leaf from his body piece by piece to relieve the destitute within the city. The Happy Prince symbolizes *that within the erotic vision which is not being used*; recalling to our minds those stores of 'hidden kindness and power' in man of which Nietzsche speaks

(*Thus Spake Zarathustra*, 55). Though set on high where he can *see* 'all the ugliness' and 'all the misery' of mankind, yet he himself 'cannot move'; but though his heart is of 'lead', his beauty has the needed wealth; and after he is melted down and only his leaden heart survives with the dead Swallow, God in his good time will welcome both to his 'garden of Paradise' and 'city of gold'. Every phrase is loaded. It is a consummate and final statement, even to the heart of lead. Though the emotion may be, or seem, worthless, it survives the fires of mortality.

The essence of love-wisdom is creativity. Plato's final doctrine in *The Symposium* defines it as the desire to 'beget upon the thing of beauty' (206); having glimpsed the transcendent and creative essence within the youth-bud more excelling than maturity, to make from this sight fine works in art or action (209). In two sonnets (113, 114; *The Mutual Flame*, I. v. 119–20) Shakespeare tells how the harmony seen in his Fair Youth is next seen everywhere, in all that is most deformed and ugly; Nietzsche speaks of 'the creative friend that hath ever a perfect world in his gift' (*Thus Spake Zarathustra*, 16); and Robert Bridges of 'our happiest earthly companionships' as holding a foretaste of (i) 'salvation' and (ii) some 'super-humanity' to be (*The Testament of Beauty*, IV. 1408–11). So too Christian love may be defined as the love 'for the ideal of man in each individual' and to generate this love the admiration of *one* individual may be enough (Sir J. R. Seeley, *Ecce Homo*, 1865; XIV). Such is the doctrine within *The Happy Prince*: Eros, weeping for sympathy with human misery, wants the human soul to spend his wealth.

Difficulties remain. The beauty, unlike female beauty, is, as Shakespeare's Sonnets drive home (e.g. Sonnet 104), though a window into the eternal, yet in earthly terms transient; and so is the purity, or virtue, which it appears, for a while, to express. In *The Picture of Dorian Gray* the young

hero of amazing beauty becomes, like the Star-Child, cruel
and vicious, and though he remains outwardly young and
perfect his advancing age and crimes are horribly objectified
in the ever-changing and damning portrait, which recalls the
externalized evil of *The Fisherman and his Soul*. What is
the relation of human beauty to worth? Do we admire form
and colour only, or do we in the act of adoration see through
to the soul, as Spenser in his *Hymn in Honour of Beauty* (120–
140) and *Epithalamion* (186) thought? Is human beauty
simply in Byron's phrase 'the precious porcelain of human
clay'? Or shall we, looking inwards, compare it to 'a lighted
alabaster vase'? (*Don Juan*, IV. 11; VIII. 96). May not the
soul-flame, when tested, prove ugly? Is there nothing both
exquisite and permanent, except jewels, which are anyway
infertile unless on a crowned king? *Dorian Gray* contains
one of Wilde's finest passages on jewels (XI); and it is surely
the subtlest critique of the Platonic Eros ever penned.
Throughout Wilde's thought-adventures there is this analysis of the interrelationship of soul, beauty and Christian
goodness. Somehow there must be a harmony and a per-
manence and a creative result. But how? Perhaps the truth
can only be tragically defined; and perhaps, from the depths,
he realized this.

Not only was Wilde's a quest of a high order, but it had
strong Christ-like affinities. The New Testament wavelength and Biblical style of the Parables is obvious; and from
his youth onwards Wilde was deeply attracted, and in his
works again and again engaged, by the Christian religion.
In *Salome* a decadent and bejewelled paganism in a sul-
phurous atmosphere of beauty and blood-lust asserts itself
statically and repetitively against the equally repetitive de-
nunciations of Jokanaan, or John the Baptist, whom Salome
desires. Always in Wilde the two worlds want to meet.
Here they coexist in unhealthy opposition: the atmosphere
is like pressure before thunder.

We must see Wilde's homosexual engagements in the context of these works. They were prompted by his innate love of all youth from children upwards and also by his own state of male-female, and often seemingly boy-like, integration. The drama of his relationship to Lord Alfred Douglas, with its see-saw of idealisms and angers, repeats the story of those Sonnets of Shakespeare of which Wilde has himself left us a study in *The Portrait of Mr W. H.*, relating the Fair Youth to the boy-girl actors of Shakespeare's stage. Wilde's less idealistic engagements were prompted by (i) the instinct, as felt by Shakespeare, Byron and Nietzsche, to plunge low when the disparity between the near-integrated self and the community becomes unbearable (p. 286 above), so that we find him writing, 'Tired of being on the heights, I deliberately went to the depths in the search for new sensation' (*De Profundis*; *Works*, 857); and (ii) by a genuine liking for the lower orders of society; not any deep and lasting love for any one person, but a lightning contact with thrill in the very disparity and sexual ratification of human unity. He once said that he found the young men of the underworld as dangerously fascinating as 'panthers' (*De Profundis*; *Works*, 882).

And because there is an exhibitionist compulsion on such men to reveal themselves, Wilde could not remain content with his social mask. Though he was genuinely fascinated by the glitter of high society which was, like his jewels, a symbol of his aim, he also saw through the superficiality, making his terms with it, like Hamlet and Byron, by wit. That could not last; his scornful speech of congratulation to his first-night audience for admiring one of his comedies was in part genuine, the more so since he must have known that the play was inadequate. So, as though compelled by an instinct for self-revelation, he half-willingly exposed his life to society's revulsion. He played with fire, 'with that tiger, Life' (Pearson, XIV. 255), in deadly earnest, and when he might have done so refused, again and again, to escape the conflagration. 'That', he said, 'would be a backward step' (Pearson, XV. 276). This does not mean that he did not suffer, but simply that he was impelled from the depths to put in train and abide by a sequence of events which would lead to suffering. As Lewis Broad puts it, 'the vision of St Sebastian, "the youngest of the martyrs", had vividly impressed him, years before' (*The Truth about Oscar Wilde*; 1957 edn.; XV. 175). Such men may appear to embrace their martyrdom – 'I had to pass on' (*De Profundis*; *Works*, 866) – but it remains a martyrdom, a crucifixion, a self-exhibition in agony and shame. The shame may be of the essence; at the least it shatters all the pseudo-dignities and masks of our lying civilization.

At his trial Wilde also lied in answer, though he might have done better to speak out. And yet he did, on the important issue, speak firmly. The famous letter of his to Lord Alfred Douglas containing the phrase 'your slim-gilt soul that walks between passion and poetry' may appear over-decorative, but the words are precise. 'Slim-gilt', if we remember *The Happy Prince*, Wilde's jewel-symbolism and the term 'diamond body' for the etheric or spirit body interpenetrating the physical (p. 289), is an exact term for the seraphic intuition. 'Between passion and poetry' matches the blend of instinct and intellect within the Platonic Eros. Of this blend Lord Alfred Douglas had been the symbol, the living truth. Faced with this letter and the words in Lord Alfred's sonnet on 'the love that dare not speak its name', Wilde replied:

> The 'love that dare not speak its name' in this century is such a great affection of an elder for a younger man as there was between David and Jonathan, such as Plato made the very basis of his philosophy, and such as you find in the sonnets of Michelangelo and Shakespeare.

He continued by asserting its 'spiritual' nature and its

relation to 'works of art'; its worth as 'the noblest form of affection'; its natural quality and its intellectual status. According to Lewis Broad this defence has been called 'the finest speech of an accused man since that of Paul before Agrippa' (Broad, XIV. 167; *Acts*, XXVI).

Wilde's *De Profundis*, written from prison, is a commentary, from a Nietzschean standpoint, on his tragic experience. Sorrow and suffering are now experienced as revelations of the creative purpose; the wholeness of his own drama is accepted and ratified; the deep insights of his parables, which he recalls, are lived. There is no repentance, no morality in any usual sense, but there is a lengthy and profound concentration on Christ. From the start Christian sympathies had run concurrently with his Hellenic and aesthetic passions. Now Christ is his central interest. He is seen as, above all, the supreme artist; more, as the first and greatest romantic, behind the romances of medievalism, of Shakespeare, and of more modern times. He notes his respect, so like Wilde's own – as indeed he himself says (*De Profundis*; *Works*; 875) – for children as exemplars for us all; and his insistence on wholeness, recalling how he himself had written in *The Soul of Man under Socialism* 'that he who would lead a Christ-like life must be entirely and absolutely himself' (*Works*, 867). Christ had a strange sympathy with sinners:

> The world had always loved the saint as being the nearest possible approach to the perfection of God. Christ, through some divine instinct in him, seems to have always loved the sinner as being the nearest possible approach to the perfection of man . . . To turn an interesting thief into a tedious honest man was not his aim . . . The conversion of a publican into a Pharisee would not have seemed to him a great achievement. But in a manner not yet understood of the world he regarded sin and suffering as being in themselves beautiful holy things and modes of perfection.
>
> (*Works*, 877)

Wilde admits the danger, and also agrees on the need for some kind of repentance, viewed in Shakespearian wise (*The Sovereign Flower*, V. 249) simply as *recognition*, in order to harmonize and ratify the whole (877–8). He is trying to see life-as-art, with tragic form. More precisely, he is asserting, in the manner of Browning's *The Statue and the Bust*, that within the criminal there may exist certain elements of fire and courage necessary to perfection but too often absent from morality. He is thinking less of any sin of his own – he himself regrets nothing (866) – than of the fascination exerted on him by the young 'panthers' and 'gilded snakes', whose 'poison was part of their perfection' (882), of the underworld. His main emphasis on Christ's repudiation of legality and hypocrisy is valid, and his relation of Christ's Judaea to his own Britain (876) reasonable. The essay is written from a Nietzschean standpoint recognizing that 'between the famous and the infamous there is but one step, if as much as one' (862).

Christ is a key to Wilde's life. I quote again from Hesketh Pearson. Wilde was 'drawn to the personality of Jesus Christ' (XI. 188) and his interest 'increased every year until at length he almost identified himself with Christ and often spoke in parables' (X. 141). 'Both thought and taught in stories, and both had a strong intuition of their tragic destiny' (XIII. 218). One of his parables, *The Doer of Good*, was on Christ (XIII. 218; *Works*, 843). 'He saw himself in the role of Christ, the shouts of his first-night audiences being his hosannas', with Calvary to follow (XV. 282). He felt that his life needed a tragic completion (XV. 282) and wooed disaster 'under the influence of a mystical concept' (XV. 284). While there was still time to flee, 'He has re-solved', said his brother, 'to stay, to face it out, to stand the music like Christ' (XV. 301). Finally 'his own condemna-tion and sufferings had completed the parallel with Jesus which for many years he had instinctively drawn' (XVI.

323); and 'in his last years the two figures whom Wilde was readiest to talk about were Napoleon and Jesus Christ' (XVIII. 358).

Those who knew Wilde personally recognized a stature impossible to recapture from reported epigram and printed essay. Beerbohm Tree's comment is typical: 'Oscar was the greatest man I have ever known – and the greatest gentleman' (Pearson, XIV. 232). His record of lived virtue recalls Byron's, though he lacked Byron's thrust and range of purpose. The softer intuitions of both were on the wavelength of Christ's. Resemblances to Christ are clear in Wilde's Byronic love of children, his egotism blended with humility, his repartee, his utter lack of malice, his forgiveness and Timon-like generosity (e.g. Pearson, XVII. 335); his magnanimity, his refusal to save himself, and patient endurance of shame. His record of kindly actions is as high as Byron's (e.g. Pearson, V. 65; VI. 73); his fight for removing the hideous wrongs of children in prison alone (*Letter to the Daily Chronicle*, *Works*; 897–903), when set against the system, leaves no question as to Wilde's moral superiority over the society that condemned him. Long before his own fall, he had like Christ a natural sympathy with all outcasts (Pearson, VII. 93–4). His natural friendliness for the rough and low from his American tour onwards is recorded again and again. Active criminals were rapidly deflected by his courteous and kindly reception (Pearson, XV. 273; XVIII. 367) and what he wrote of Christ was true of himself: 'He does not really teach one anything, but by being brought into his presence one becomes something' (*De Profundis*; *Works*, 878). Naturally, he made friends in prison. A warder, named Martin, at Reading gaol wrote of him: 'What that poet was before he went to prison I care not. What he may have been after he left prison I know not. One thing I know, however, that while in prison he lived the life of a saint, or as near that holy state as poor mortal can ever hope to attain' (Broad, XVII. 193). Vincent O'Sullivan received the same impression: 'If terrible sufferings courageously borne, the enduring of dire injustice and reviling without complaint, be matter of saintliness, then Wilde was a saint' (Pearson, XVIII. 358).

How far the analogy to Christ is valid we cannot say without a much deeper knowledge of the forces in play than we at present possess; and it would be wise to suspend judgement. Honesty at least will not deny that it would have been our loss had Wilde's life been other than it was. This is not to say that his actions were right, but rather that to us his actions together with their consequences are extraordinarily valuable; they are at least tragically justified.[1] His story dramatizes much that lies close to the essence of art. His statement that 'the artist must live the complete life, must accept it as it comes and stands like an angel before him, with its drawn and two-edged sword' (Pearson, XVIII. 357) – 'angel' to match the homosexual-seraphic and 'two-edged' to cover tragedy – is *not* true of the artist; but it may be true of those who attempt the yet higher and far more difficult quest of living their art. Wilde's most famous works were written for money, and are of the second order only; and his paradoxes, on paper, pall. His genius went into his life, his living talk; into his spoken or written parables; and into *Dorian Gray*, itself an extended parable. He was by instinct a teacher. When his last days are called 'unproductive', Hesketh Pearson justly comments, 'Yet no one has ever called Christ or Socrates unproductive because each of these spoke his thoughts instead of writing them down' (XVIII. 366); and each, like Wilde, uncomplainingly paid the penalty demanded by civilization for their impact.

Wilde's life is a drama, and seen in all its excess, its brilliance, its degradation and its tragedy, it has the form

[1] This is perhaps a place to pay a tribute to the fine film based on John Furnell's vivid dramatization of Wilde's life, *The Stringed Lute*.

needed to correspond to the matters contained. His flamboyance, exhibitionism and heady enjoyment of success, these must be admitted; and also his shocking inability – Timon-like in this as in his generosity – to handle money (Pearson XVIII. 363), his dishonest misleading of his legal helpers, and his unjust attack on Lord Alfred Douglas written from prison. But all must be judged in relation to the difficulties inherent in his life's central, Blakean, aim: to make of the senses elements of a new spirituality, to cure the soul by the senses and the senses by the soul (*The Picture of Dorian Gray*, II: *Works*, 29, 31). This aim he carried through with a daring consistency; it motivated alike his aestheticism, his anti-social acts and his perception of Christ. About his lowest engagements there was an element of the sacramental. Of cruelty he knew as little as he knew of caution; his instincts were of a childlike, positive and embracing kind. In these terms he lived and acted in allegiance to the royalty of the crowned and diamonded Eros. His sin was total self-expression acted out in spontaneity 'not wisely but too well'; and he took tragedy uncomplainingly in his stride.

His influence for good, though it was an influence that cold print cannot record, was empowered by a Falstaffian and Byronic humour (e.g. Pearson, quoting Douglas, XVIII. 359; also 367). According to *Thus Spake Zarathustra* our new, Renaissance, way beyond religion must include humour, without which 'truth' is suspect (56), for 'all good things laugh' (73). 'I have hallowed laughter' (73) means the hallowing of much before which religion veils its eyes. Powys in *Rabelais* (1948; Part IV) explains this new life-wisdom. Wilde went far to incarnate it.

IV

In his classic study *Ecce Homo* (1865) Sir J. R. Seeley explains that Jesus saw himself pre-eminently as a King, as

God's vice-regent and founder of His new realm in succession to Moses and David, great men elected by God for their genius (II; III; IV). Jesus' royal status and coronation as Messiah or Christ have been vigorously asserted by Robert Graves and Joshua Podro in *The Nazarene Gospel Restored* (1953; see Part II, 102–24, 492, 564–71, 713; Part III, 843–9, 946–8, 951, 970, etc. Different types of Messianic expectation are listed at Introduction, 15–17). The words 'king' and 'genius' possess today a lustre lacking to the more strictly theological terms: without loss of magic they yet suggest what is human, real and splendid. Here is Seeley's comment on Jesus' response to Zacchaeus (*Luke*, XIX. 1–10):

> Adopting the royal style which was familiar to him, and which commends the loyalty of a vassal in the most delicate manner by freely exacting his services, he informed Zacchaeus of his intention to visit him, and signified his pleasure that a banquet be instantly prepared.   (*Ecce Homo*, XX)

Despite a slight embellishment of the original account, that comes closer to the living Jesus than many a paragraph of theologizing. Jesus' disciples, says Ernest Renan, surrounded him 'with a kind of rustic pomp' (*The Life of Jesus*, XI). Today such thoughts may appear alien, far back or far ahead; but even though Jesus' sovereignty remains clouded, we can respond to his imaginative powers; and we shall now enquire how far what we know of him may be placed within the psychology of human genius.

Not only is Jesus not married, but he is so presented to us that it would seem utterly wrong if he were. 'Christ', writes Seeley, 'never entered the realm of sexual love' (XX); and in trying to give him a mate (p. 219) D. H. Lawrence simultaneously defined a discrepancy, pointed a false direction, and underlined the necessity of a better. Jesus' closest associates – I am thinking of tradition and dogma as

well as the Gospels – are (i) his Mother and (ii) his male
disciples.

The symbolic emphasis Christianity has placed on Jesus'
Mother may be regarded as a grand-scale symbolization of
what lies behind the Freudian stress on the 'Oedipus' processes of human psychology. This, which I had noted in
Lord Byron's Marriage (VII. 281), I have since found suggested in passing by Norman O. Brown in *Life against Death*
(IV. 51), writing from a Freudian standpoint: probably it is
a well-known thought to Freudians. In the York Cycle of
Miracle plays the relation is developed romantically with a
reiterated emphasis on Jesus' reunion with his Mother to
enjoy bliss beyond all marriage joys as King and Queen in
Heaven (*The Golden Labyrinth*, II). Whatever were the
historic facts, this romantic relationship was highly honoured
during the ages of faith. A careful exposition of the orthodox
doctrine is given in the chapter 'The Veneration of Our
Lady' in Sergius Bulgakov's *The Wisdom of God* (1937).

Jesus' more intimate friends are male. Women are most
important in the Gospels; Seeley asserts that the female sex,
so slighted in the ancient world, 'was understood for the
first time by Christ' (*Ecce Homo*, XX); but even so we are
mainly aware of their devotion to him in excess of his to
them, on the distant yet valid analogies of Shakespeare's
Venus and Adonis and Beaumont's *Salmacis and Hermaphroditus* and the nearer analogies of Pope's *Eloisa to Abelard*,
where Abelard is all but equated with Christ, and of the life-
stories of Swift, Byron and Wilde. To males Jesus' response
is more explicitly emotional, as when, looking on the rich
man who sought his counsel, it is recorded simply that Jesus
'loved him' (*Mark*, X. 21); and his greatest miracle, the
raising of Lazarus, was empowered by a love (*John*, XI. 36).
What is needed, however, to establish Jesus' humanity is
some record of an affection more dramatically central, and
this we have in the 'Beloved Disciple' of John's Gospel,

traditionally regarded, with reason, to be John the son of Zebedee. Tradition also asserts that John's authority lies behind the composition of the Gospel. It was written later than the others.[1]

Scripture and tradition indicate that Jesus' most intimate personal relationships concerned (i) his Mother and (ii) the Beloved Disciple, so conforming to the pattern we have noted in other exemplars; and he had an especial love of children like that of Byron and Wilde. The result is a tension with society leading to a tragic conclusion. A great deal is accordingly covered by the presence of the Mother and John, alone of the disciples, at the Crucifixion and by Jesus' handing over of his Mother to John's care (*John*, XIX. 26–7); and by the many paintings showing these three figures. This grouping has been observed by Hugh Ross Williamson in *The Arrow and the Sword* (1947, 1955): 'The characteristic symbol which first meets the eye in any Catholic Church – the Rood, with the Crucified between the

---

[1] The authority of John, son of Zebedee, has been powerfully defended by H. P. V. Nunn throughout *The Authorship of the Fourth Gospel*, 1952, especially at II. iii. 124–32, and is accepted by E. V. Rieu, *The Four Gospels*, 1952, xxvi–xxvii. The omission of the disciple's name from the Gospel though all the other leading persons appear under their names as in the Synoptics is itself evidence for his identification with the Beloved (Nunn, II. iii. 132). C. H. Dodd, *The Interpretation of the Fourth Gospel*, 1953, App. 449, does not deny the possibility of John's authority, and Sir Edwyn Hoskyns in *The Fourth Gospel*, 1940, II. 670, remains simultaneously sympathetic and dubious. C. K. Barrett in *The Gospel According to St John*, 1955, accepts John on balance of probability as the Beloved, but is not convinced regarding authorship and authority; I. 97–101; 112 (for early evidence, I. 83–8). Some scholars, while agreeing that the Beloved's authority is present, think that he was 'a young Jerusalemite disciple, outside the number of the Twelve' (F. C. Grant in *The Gospels: their Origin and their Growth*, 1959, XII. 176; quoting G. H. C. Macgregor). Such a disciple was not very likely to play a central part at the Last Supper (p. 304 below), and this difficulty is not obviated by regarding him as 'a mere boy' (Nunn, I. ii. 12; v. 65). The most convincing discussion of the various problems at issue appears to be that of Charles E. Raven in *Jesus and the Gospel of Love*, 1931, VII and VIII, favouring the tradition.

Beloved and the Mother – has a significance which is not always understood' (V. 86).

Jesus knew the will-to-power. As Seeley explains, the Temptations must be supposed to record a genuine experience (*Ecce Homo*, II); and, though the impulse to political power is resisted, Jesus' later words and actions certainly witness a terrifying spiritual power accompanied by what, in any other man, we should regard as the egotism of genius. But this power, like Byron's, is interpenetrated by, and enlisted in the cause of, love; and that love has a personal centre. Let us see what we are told of the Beloved Disciple.

We shall assume John to be the disciple referred to as the beloved in John's Gospel. James and John, sons of Zebedee, were, says Ernest Renan (*The Life of Jesus*, IX), 'full of fire and passion' (p. 307 below); and also ambition (*Matthew*, XX. 20–4; *Mark*, III. 17; X. 35–41; *Luke*, IX. 49–55). John was quite young (Renan, IX, referring to the 'authorities collected by Eusebius'). In the Church resurrection plays of the Middle Ages he was always performed as a young man.

His position beside Jesus and somewhat apart from the rest at the Last Supper marks the enjoyment of an intimacy beyond that of Peter. Jesus has just referred to his approaching betrayal by one of the disciples:

> The disciples looked at each other, at a loss to know which of them he meant. As one of his disciples was reclining on his breast – he was the favourite of Jesus – Peter nodded to him, saying 'Tell us who he means'.
>
> The disciple just leant back on the breast of Jesus and said, 'Lord, who is it?'
>
> (*John*, XIII. 23)[1]

---

[1] This is the passage which Christopher Marlowe is said to have adduced when imputing to Jesus a physical relationship (*The Life of Marlowe*, etc., C. F. Tucker Brooke, 1930; Apps. IX, XII; 99, 107). On this issue New Testament morality remains firm (*Romans*, I. 27; *1 Corinthians*, VI. 9; *1 Timotheus*, I. 10). But that ἀνακείμενος . . . ἐν τῷ κόλπῳ suggests more

According to Sir Edwyn Hoskyns and Noel Davey, John was probably the disciple who as a friend of the High Priest entered and returned from within his house and gained entrance for Peter after Jesus' arrest (Sir Edwyn Hoskyns and Noel Davey, *The Riddle of the New Testament*, 1958; App. A, 198–9; also in Hoskyns' *The Fourth Gospel*, 1940, II. 609; and see the listed reasons given by William Webster and W. F. Wilkinson in the note to XVIII. 15 in their *Greek Testament*, 2 vols., 1855–1861. But the likelihood is not strong enough to be used negatively as proof that the Beloved cannot have been a simple Galilean; see Ronald Knox's note in his translation of the New Testament). Peter no sooner entered than he proceeded to deny that he was one of the disciples, though the other seems to have been fearlessly interceding (*John*, XVIII. 15–27). We hear that 'his favourite disciple' is with Jesus' Mother and other women supporters by the cross (*John*, XIX. 26), whereas 'all except the Beloved Disciple had fled' (Hoskyns, *The Fourth Gospel*, II. 660; *Matthew*, XXVI. 57; R.V., 56), thus falsifying Jesus' own expectation of desertion (*John*, XVI. 32). Whilst

than proximity at a recumbent feast is demonstrated by Sir Edwyn Hoskyns in *The Fourth Gospel*, II. 519 (where references to *John*, XX. 20 and I. 15 appear to be misprints for XXI. 20 and I. 18; and see *Luke*, XVI. 22). C. K. Barrett in *The Gospel According to St John*, II. 372, quotes Pliny, *Epist.*, IV. xxii. 4, 'Cenabat Nerua cum paucis; Ueiento proximus atque etiam in sinu recumbebat'. The Revised Version at *John*, I. 18 compares *Deuteronomy*, XIII. 6, translated by Moffatt '. . . your son or your daughter, the wife of your *bosom* or the friend who is your other self' (my italics). The recumbent position may have lent itself naturally to gestures which would seem abnormal at a table-dinner. Even so, the second-century authorities Irenaeus and Polycrates refer to John as the disciple who 'reclined on the bosom of the Lord' (Barrett, I. 84), as though the phrase held an especial importance; and so does Dante (*Paradise*, XXV. 112–13). Besides, it would be rash to deny any physical element at all to these higher types of male love. For Plato and Shakespeare beauty was certainly a constituent; kisses appear to have been regarded as normal by Plato (*Phaedrus*, 255), in the Old Testament (*I Samuel*, XX. 41), and by Renaissance moralists (*The Mutual Flame*, I. iv. 89, and II. iv. 199, notes). We need not suppose that the customs of the ancient world necessarily obeyed twentieth-century conventions.

on the cross Jesus leaves his Mother to the care of the Beloved (*John*, XIX. 26–7). When Peter and 'the favourite of Jesus' hear of the resurrection, they run to the tomb, but the favourite runs the faster and is the first to be 'convinced' (*John*, XX. 2–8): 'The pre-eminence of the faith of the Beloved Disciple is the climax of the narrative' (Hoskyns, *The Fourth Gospel*, II. 644). When the resurrected Jesus appears on the shore while the disciples are fishing, it is Jesus' 'favourite' who first recognizes him and tells Peter who it is (*John*, XXI. 7). Jesus three times asks Peter, with an implied reference to Peter's earlier denials, if he loves him, and finally commands him, as prototype of administrative and pastoral authority, to 'feed my sheep', adding a prophecy of Peter's martyrdom and concluding 'Follow me'. Then:

> Peter turned round and saw that the favourite disciple of Jesus was following (the disciple who had leant on his breast at supper and put the question, 'Lord, who is to betray you?'). So, on catching sight of him, Peter said to Jesus, 'And what about him, Lord?' Jesus replied, 'If I choose that he should survive till I come back, what does that matter to you? Follow me yourself.'
>
> (*John*, XXI. 20)

Lastly, we are told of Jesus' favourite:

> This was the disciple who bears testimony to these facts and who wrote them down; his testimony, we know, is true.
>
> (*John*, XXI. 24)

The description of the crucifixion is accompanied by a similar claim: 'He who saw it has borne witness (his witness is true; God knows he is telling the truth), that you may believe' (*John*, XIX. 35); and John's First Epistle opens with the assertion 'it is . . . of what we heard, of what we saw, of what we witnessed and touched with our own hands . . . that we bring you word' (*John*, Epistle 1; I. 1–3). Renan regards John's Gospel as deriving from a better acquaintance 'with the exterior circumstances' of Jesus' life than he finds in the Synoptics (*The Life of Jesus*, Introduction).[1]

Jesus was perhaps especially attracted by the fire and zeal (*Mark*, IX. 38; *Luke*, IX. 49, 54) of John and his brother James whom he called 'Boanerges', or 'sons of thunder' (*Mark*, III. 17; or perhaps 'Sons of the Wild Ox'; Graves and Podro, as above; Part II, 372–3); the one lovingly humorous phrase recorded in the Gospels. The all-too-human ambition of the young men for a place in glory (*Mark*, X. 37) – in *Matthew* (XX. 20) they are brought to Jesus by their Mother, who makes the claim – may have had something of the immature attraction we sense in the princes of Shakespeare's *Cymbeline*. The Beloved seems to have enjoyed an intimacy and affection of which the other disciples were well aware, which they normally accepted, but of which they could on occasion be jealous (*Matthew*, XX. 24; *Mark*, X. 41). Though Peter and John, forming with James the inner circle of Jesus' disciples, are throughout the New Testament regarded as companions (e.g. *Matthew*, XVII. i, XXVI. 37; *Mark*, V. 37, IX. 2; *Luke*, IX. 28, XXII. 8; *Acts*, III. 1–11, VIII. 14; *Galatians*, II. 9), yet in John's Gospel a rivalry between them is written subtly into the account, which appears to be deliberately emphasizing John's privileged place; not now, it seems, despite his former ambition, out of pride, but rather, since the disciple's name is suppressed, as by an old man humbly wishing to establish this vital love-link in the story and assert its strength beyond the strength of Peter, rather as Dante puts Beatrice beyond

[1] Moffatt's 'favourite' does not quite cover the Greek which always runs 'the disciple whom Jesus loved', denoting a difference in kind rather than degree. But neither does the original cover the whole intention, since Jesus 'loved' others (XI. 5, 36; XIII. 1, 34; XV. 12). The Greek words offer little help, using, for John, ἠγάπα at XIII. 23, XIX. 26, XXI. 7 and 20, and ἐφίλει at XX. 2. Hoskyns notes that here and elsewhere John's Gospel uses the two verbs without any particular discrimination (*The Fourth Gospel*, II. 666–7.).

Virgil. In the *Paradiso*, after Peter and James, representing
Faith and Hope, have been talking with Dante, John himself, called 'he who lay upon the bosom' of Christ, signifying
Love, appears like a young 'virgin', at once 'gay' and 'innocent', and yet with so splendorous a sun-brilliance that
Dante is for a while blinded (*Paradise*, XXV. 103–39;
XXVI. 9–10). The passage may serve as a poetic pointer to
the fires housed in our Gospel. C. K. Barrett gains the impression that the author was not interested in publication and
wrote primarily to satisfy himself: 'His gospel must be
written: it was no concern of his whether it was also read'
(*The Gospel according to St John*, I. 115). A peculiarly neat
statement was made by William Sanday:

> The beloved disciple had a special reason for not wishing to obtrude
> his own personality. He was conscious of a great privilege that
> would single him out for all time among the children of men. He
> could not resist the temptation to speak of this privilege. The
> impulse of affection responding to affection prompted him to
> claim it. But the consciousness that he was doing so and the reac-
> tion of modesty led him at the same moment to suppress what
> a vulgar egotism might have accentuated, the lower plane of his
> own individuality. The son of Zebedee (if it was he) desired to be
> merged and lost in the disciple whom Jesus loved.
>
> (*Criticism of the Fourth Gospel*, 1905, 79–80; –
> quoted by H. P. V. Nunn, p. 303 above; II. iii. 125)

Beside this we may place Charles E. Raven's profound treatment in *Jesus and the Gospel of Love* (1931). John's Gospel
he reads, thereby illuminating many obscurities, as pre-
eminently the work of a lover:

> These are faults, but they are the faults of love. Every lover
> stresses the wonder of his friend even to the point of boredom: every
> lover is quicker to resent criticism of his friend than of himself:
> every lover dwells upon the picture gained in moments of insight
> to the exclusion of all other memories: every lover sees his friend
> not only in relation to the events of their actual contact but to his

own later history. The Gospel is not immune from such tendencies: it is a very human book – not a series of cryptograms, nor an apologetic fiction, nor a mystical romance, but the story of its author's discipleship, love's memory of Love incarnate, with the marks of a great devotion writ plainly upon it. (VIII. 227)

The book has accordingly an authority denied to other, more impersonal, media, letting us see Jesus for once 'through the eyes of one whom he loved'; 'Jesus as he was to his friend'; and, therefore, 'Jesus as he essentially is'. Raven's remains perhaps of all our commentaries the most coherent and convincing.

All questions here of authorship and authority, all relevant hints and suppressions both here and in the Synoptics, must henceforth be studied in strict reference to the diffidence and consequent *silences* existing in every age regarding such love as this which beats as a heart within John's Gospel, infusing alike all Jesus' actions and speeches at the Last Supper: his washing of his disciples' feet, his closeness to the Beloved, and the divine harmonies of his farewell. This is the one key that throws the rest into pattern. We can see why the inauguration of the Eucharist, recorded by the other three evangelists, is not mentioned. The Eucharist represents at best a secondary, provisional and symbolic, union, dependent on food and drink. Here we have something nobler, its place being taken by the embrace of love. Love alone is sovereign.

The Apocryphal New Testament (ed. M. R. James, 1924, 1926) contains some relevant, though not necessarily historical, accounts. In the 'Story of Joseph of Arimathea' John is recorded as saying to Jesus, 'Lord, I know that thou hast loved me from the beginning' (164). In the *Acts of John* John in his later life is strongly against marriage and grateful to Jesus for his celibacy: 'O thou who hast kept me until this hour for thyself and untouched by union with a woman ...' Three times he had wanted to marry, but Jesus had appeared to him, saying with lover-like accents: 'John, if thou hadst not been mine, I would have suffered thee to marry' (269).

Without ceasing to be devotional John's own accent may be that of a lover: 'Receive also the soul of thy John . . .' (269). In so far as we accept the account as true we may assume that the sense of marriage as contamination so strong in this book (266) was motivated less by any abstract principle than by John's vivid sense of his contraction to Jesus. Hugh Ross Williamson notes (V. 86) that the *Acts of John* were not 'specifically rejected' until the second Council of Nicaea in 787, and that until then the faithful could accept them. That such a Platonic relationship was out-of-tune with Hebraic feeling cannot be asserted; not only had Greek culture already saturated the civilized world, but the greatest figure in the Old Testament, Jesus' reputed ancestor David, is recorded as experiencing with Jonathan an emotional and demonstrative love beyond the love of women (*1 Samuel*, XVIII. 1–4; XX. 41; *2 Samuel*, I. 26). It is remarkable how often, whenever a superlative person is being figured for us – Homer's Achilles is an example – this tendency recurs.

John's Gospel, with its marriage feast, Jesus' refusal to condemn the adultress and his raising of the loved Lazarus (II. 1–11; VII. 53–VIII. 11; XI. 1–44), is a gospel of active love. 'Others', writes W. F. Howard, 'had taught that God is Spirit. Contemporary theosophies declared that God is Light. It was for Christianity, and especially St. John, to tell the world a higher truth, without which religion may not rise above metaphysics, or may sink into mythology' (*Christianity according to St John*, 1943, 1947; III. 63). But the message would have had little sap without a personal origin, or centre:

This is my command: you are to love one another as I have loved you. To lay life down for his friends, man has no greater love than that. (*John*, XV. 12)

Notice how the *personal* love of 'friends' is felt as *widening out* into a more *general* love such as that asserted by St Paul. It was the same with Socrates, whose 'relation to his young disciples' was, in the words of G. Lowes Dickinson, 'that of a lover and a friend' (*The Greek View of Life*, 1896, 1907; III. vii). Whatever may be the exact truth regarding the authorship of John's Gospel and the First Epistle of John, it is clear that they relate closely together (Hoskyns and Davey, *The Riddle of the New Testament*, 1958, Additional Note, IX. 169), and it is natural to suppose that their especial concentration on love relates to Jesus' relation to the Beloved (Hugh Ross Williamson, V. 85). Now in the Epistle we have, as nowhere else in the New Testament, a tight, metaphysical and Platonic, statement:

> Beloved, let us love one another, for love belongs to God, and every-one who loves is born of God and knows God; he who does not love, does not know God, for God is love.
>
> (*John*, Epistle 1; IV. 7)

Again:

> God is love, and he who remains in love remains in God, and God remains in him. (*John*, Epistle 1; IV. 16)

These statements occur in contexts asserting a precise theology of God's love in sending to man his Son, but even so we must recognize a human centre, or they become sterile, if not meaningless:

> God no one has ever seen; but if we love one another, then God remains within us, and love for him is complete in us.
>
> (*John*, Epistle 1; IV. 12)

Again:

> . . . he who will not love his brother whom he has seen, cannot pos-sibly love the God whom he has never seen.
>
> (*John*, Epistle 1; IV. 20)

This process, or expansion, from mankind to God depends on that other expansion from love of an individual to mankind, as shadowed by Jesus' raising of *all* his disciples to the status already enjoyed by John (XV. 14–15); and in Plato's *Symposium* (211); and Shakespeare's Sonnets (p. 292). There are two steps, not one.

We must, following our earlier analysis (p. 271), understand the relationship of Jesus and John as a relationship less of opposites than of unities and unity. Above is the one God whose love this unity-experience both reflects and, acting as a conductor, passes to the disciples, and through them to mankind, and thence back, through human experience of love, to God. Each term is a unity, like concentric circles out-rippling in water. At the centre was a personal element, and in response the personal must be preserved, or the widely deployed love counselled by Paul and John becomes impossible. Seeley defines Christian love as love for 'the ideal of man in each individual' and says that, to generate this love, the admiration of *one* individual will suffice (p. 292 above). That 'one individual' may, for some, be Christ himself. Christ may exist for us as the 'essence' of 'human friendships' (Robert Bridges, *The Testament of Beauty*, IV. 1416). Christianity alone among religions exists through experiences of a personal love; that is, through the individual's response, as successor to the Beloved in love and loyalty, to Jesus the Christ, or King.[1]

---

[1] Space is lacking for a discussion of *eros* and *agapé*, but my whole book constitutes an assertion of their interdependence. This interdependence I discussed more exactly in *Atlantic Crossing* (1936; VII. iv. 203–9). Neither should be regarded as more transcendental or more natural than the other. Biologically *agapé* is as surely to be related to the parental and filial instincts as *eros* to the sexual. Often you cannot easily distinguish: the Socratic *paederastia* and similar semi-educational friendships, such as some of Byron's, are as near the parental as the sexual. We may in general call *eros* the flower and *agapé* the fruit; one is a unity, the other diverse; one the golden rocket, the other its coloured lights.

In M. C. D'Arcy's *The Mind and Heart of Love* (1945) *eros* and *agapé* are

The Fourth Gospel is pre-eminently personal; it is interested less in God than in Jesus as God's ambassador; it is
recorded as by a lover using in old age his reminiscences to
endue, like Shakespeare's Cleopatra, his lost hero with a
divine lustre. But, though the narrative is peculiarly rich in
theological thought, it simultaneously guards against misunderstanding with an emphasis not found elsewhere. Jesus
insists, again and again, as though with his own voice breaking through the theologizing of the Beloved or the embellish-
ments of the scribe, that he is nothing compared with God.

He is here simply 'to do the will of him who sent me' (IV.
34; V. 24) and has come from Heaven 'not to carry out my
own will' but God's (VI. 38); believing in Jesus means
believing 'not in me but in him who sent me' (XII. 44). He
insists that he can do 'nothing' of his own 'accord', but is
simply 'taught by God' to function as a medium for the
Father's 'deeds' (V. 19, 30; VIII. 28; XIV. 10). He is
under the Father's 'orders'; 'he it was who ordered me what
to say' (X. 18; XII. 49). What he says 'is not my word but
the word of the Father' (XIV. 24). Since his teaching 'is not
my own', he claims no personal 'authority' or 'credit' (VII.
16–18). 'Were I to glorify myself, my glory would be nothing' (VIII. 54). Like all prophetic genius, he simultaneously
asserts and refuses a personal pre-eminence:

> But I have not come on my own initiative; I am sent; I am sent,
> and sent by Him who is real. You do not know Him, but I know
> Him, because I have come from Him and He sent me.
>
> (VII. 28)

Again:

> Though I do testify to myself, my evidence is valid, because I know
> where I have come from and where I am going to . . . There is
> myself and the Father who sent me.   (VIII. 14)

associated respectively with the male-acquisitive and female-sacrificial principles (IX. 215–18). Father D'Arcy's view of their biological interdependence
is similar to that advanced in *Atlantic Crossing*.

Though the God who 'sent' him is at his 'side' (VIII. 29), he is not himself God:

> The Jews retorted, 'We mean to stone you, not for a good deed, but for blasphemy, because you, a mere man, make yourself God.'
> Jesus answered: 'Is it not written in your Law, "*I said, you are gods*"? If the Law said they were gods, to whom the word of God came – and scripture cannot be broken – do you mean to tell me, whom the Father consecrated and sent into the world, "You are blaspheming", because I said, "I am God's Son"? If I am not doing the deeds of my Father, do not believe me; but if I am, then believe the deeds, though you will not believe me . . .'   (X. 33)

Which means, 'Believe in the power which I am channelling.' He insists not only that 'the Father is greater than I am' (XIV. 28), but that 'he who believes in me will do the very deeds I do, and still greater deeds than these', through the power of his intercession (XIV. 12). After his resurrection he says, 'I am ascending to my Father and yours, to my God and yours' (XX. 17).

There are many phrases loaded with a more strictly theological emphasis, but whereas it is impossible to say what precise allowance is to be made for either metaphor coming from the zeal and passion still active in the aged and once so ambitious (*Mark* X. 35–41) young disciple, or for the exaggeration of his scribe and collaborator, and also, even while we admit that John's Gospel emphasizes a unique sonship, for the widespread use of such terms as 'god' or 'gods' in the ancient world,[1] these emphatic *disclaimers* remain today as uncompromising as when they were written. With them we

---

[1] Seeley regards 'Son of God' as a natural Hebrew equivalent to 'King' (*Ecce Homo*, III). Evidence to this effect, including *2 Samuel* VII. 14 and a list of 'rites', has been adduced by Robert Graves and Joshua Podro (*The Nazarene Gospel Restored*, Part II, 107 and note, 108, 259, 703, 800; Part III, 833, 923, 980). F. C. Grant appears to deny the equivalency (*The Gospels: their Origin and Growth*, 1959, XII. 177). The terms appear together in John's Gospel (I. 49).

may group Jesus' insistence that only God may be called 'good' (*Matthew*, XIX. 17; *Mark*, X. 18) and his favourite title as 'Son of Man'; and whatever its Old Testament and apocalyptic connotations, the title is surely first a human and evolutionary term, or language becomes meaningless. Like Nietzsche's Superman, the 'Son of Man' may be supposed to break from man as lightning from a cloud (*Thus Spake Zarathustra*, Introductory Discourse; following *Matthew*, XXIV. 27); but it is from man that he breaks. The term, in contrast to 'Son of God', is human (Hoskyns and Davey, *The Riddle of the New Testament*, 1958; VII. 112; IX. 159): it may be more than evolutionary, but it is not less. The emblematic use of Mother and Child in the Christian tradition deliberately underlines the evolutionary process.

In both life and teaching Jesus radiates a blend of power and love, like Nietzsche's Zarathustra (*Thus Spake Zarathustra*; 'love' and 'power', 22; 'love', 58, 75). In Jesus we are aware of a God-power and a God-love which are both inextricably entwined with his own personality. We must suppose that within that personality there has been a marriage of male and female principles such as that which we have already discussed, leading to a perfected integration which reveals the God-head.

Of this inward marriage the canonical Gospels say nothing, but such a teaching was recorded in the early Christian period among the sects grouped under the general term of 'Gnosticism', the term indicating a claim to *know* the secret of spiritual attainment.[1] Much that they stood for is fantastic and the Church's rejection of it reasonable, but in places Gnostic thinkers seem to have faced subtleties which the canon ignores. For the New Testament certainly advertises an esoteric attitude to the sexual; it does not deny the rights of normality and the creative process, but its central persons

[1] An authoritative recent account is given in *Gnosticism and Early Christianity*, R. M. Grant, 1959.

stand above them and for centuries the highest ambition of
the devotee has been to do likewise. Such thinking some of
the Gnostic sects drove to an unnecessary extreme, regarding
marriage as a pollution; but in the process they also defined
the kind of integration implied by the New Testament itself.
This integration may be called 'bisexual', or perhaps 'supersexual'.

In *The Apocryphal New Testament* (ed. M. R. James;
1924, 1926) we are given two interesting references to the
lost *Gospel According to the Egyptians*. The first, recorded by
Clement of Alexandria, runs:

> When Salome inquired when the things concerning which she
> asked should be known, the Lord said: 'When ye have trampled on
> the garment of shame, and when the two become one and the male
> with the female is neither male nor female.' In the first place, then,
> we have not this saying in the four Gospels that have been delivered
> to us, but in that according to the Egyptians.   (James, 11)

A different version goes:

> For the Lord himself being asked by someone when his kingdom
> should come, said: 'When the two shall be one, and the outside
> (that which is without) as the inside (that which is within), and the
> male with the female neither male nor female.'   (James, 11)

The union of 'male' and 'female' might be a union of persons
in identity such as that of the fictional beings in Shakespeare's *The Phoenix and the Turtle* and according with the
philosophy of Emanuel Swedenborg's chapter 'Marriages in
Heaven' in his *Heaven and Hell*, where marriage in general
is defined as the mating of male 'understanding' with female
'will'. But, as we shall see, it is best read as a union of elements within the personality. The fusion of 'outside' and
'inside' may be related to Wordsworth's sense of the mind as
unified with objective nature (p. 93) and a Socrates' or a
Shakespeare's finding of his soul-equivalent in a form of

youthful beauty. All poetic imagery represents such a self-objectifying process. As Wilde says in *De Profundis*, 'Truth in art is the unity of a thing with itself: the outward rendered expressive of the inward; the soul made incarnate; the body instinct with spirit' (*Works*, ed. Maine; 864). The Gnostic teaching is here not only sound, but central.

The recently published *Gospel of Thomas* attributes similar statements to Jesus. It has been published in London in two translations: *The Gospel According to Thomas*, translated by A. Guillaumont and others, 1959; and *The Secret Sayings of Jesus*, translated by W. R. Schoedel and edited with commentary by R. M. Grant and D. N. Freedman, 1960. The numerals of the two versions do not exactly tally. My references will apply to Grant and Freedman.

After noting that the Gospel of Thomas 'is the only complete early extra-canonical gospel which has come down to us', a reviewer in *The Times Literary Supplement* writes: 'We can now see what one of these apocryphal gospels, which caused the Church so much concern, looked like.'

As in the canonical gospels (*Matthew* XVIII. 4, 10; XIX. 14; *Mark* X. 14–15), Jesus regards children as truth-bearers:

> The old man in his days will not hesitate to ask an infant of seven days about the place of life, and he will live.   (Saying 3)

Which recalls Wordsworth's address to the Child as 'Mighty prophet! Seer blest!' in his *Immortality* ode. Maturity regains such a state through integration: Nietzsche sees the spirit as passing from Camel through Lion to Child (*Thus Spake Zarathustra*, 1; and see 44). After comparing those who enter the Kingdom to little children, Jesus elucidates his meaning by saying:

> When you make the two one, and make the inside like the outside, and the outside like the inside, and the upper side like the under side,

and (in such a way) that you make the man (with) the woman a
single one, in order that the man is not the man and the woman
is not the woman . . . then you will go into (the kingdom)
(Saying 23)

Instead of 'make the man with the woman a single one'
Guillaumont (saying 22) translates 'make the male and the
female into a single one', which better suits what is here the
obvious intention of describing an inward condition rather
than a relationship of two people. This is clearer in Grant
and Freedman elsewhere:

When you make the two one, you will become sons of man; and if
you say, Mountain, be removed! it will move.   (Saying 103)

A state resembling Wordsworth's sense of reciprocity with
nature is indicated. It is a state simultaneously of self-know-
ing and sonship:

When you know yourselves, then you will be known; and you will
know that you are the sons of the living Father.   (Saying 2)

The aim is to be 'single' (Saying 3). Only one in a thousand
is 'single', but such a one is 'blessed' and belongs to 'the
Kingdom' (Sayings 24 and 50). He is a 'light-man' illuminating the world (Saying 25). Finally, with a welcome repudiation of the unsatisfactory denigration of women in ancient
times, we have:

Simon Peter said to them: 'Let Mariham go away from us. For
women are not worthy of life.'
Jesus said: 'Lo, I will draw her so that I will make her a man
so that she too may become a living spirit which is like you men; for
every woman who makes herself a man will enter into the Kingdom
of Heaven.'   (Saying 112)

Jesus was not content with the conventional attitude; elsewhere, as Grant and Freedman note, he had surprised his disciples by engaging in a lengthy discussion with a woman (*John*, IV. 27), and here he makes it plain that exactly the same integration is open to a woman as to a man. 'The primal man was androgynous' and therefore the Naassenes rejected sexual intercourse; 'all Gnostics become bridegrooms, "having been made male through the virginal Spirit" ' (Grant and Freedman, VIII. 137, quoting Hippolytus).

Nicholas Berdyaev in *The Destiny of Man* (1937) writes:

> According to his Idea, to God's conception of him, man is a complete, masculinely feminine being, solar and tellurgic, logoic and cosmic at the same time. Only in so far as he is complete is he chaste, wise and Sophian in his perfect wholeness. As a sexual, halved, divided being he is not chaste, not wise, and is doomed to disharmony, to passionate longing and dissatisfaction.
>
> (I. iii. 83)

In *Solitude and Society* (1938) we are told that the Ego is by nature 'bisexual', 'male and female', and that this unity is broken by sex. So the ultimate goal is bisexual:

> Thus the ultimate triumph over solitude may be regarded as the realization of the image of a perfect androgyne. But this in its turn implies the transfiguration of nature.   (III. iii. 119–21)

Some such recognition it was that made the aged Tolstoy regard sexual intercourse as, for himself at least, a sin. We are being pointed to a childlike state, such as that of the angels in Heaven who do not marry (*Matthew*, XVIII. 10; XXII. 30; *Mark*, XII. 25; *Luke*, XX. 35–6). In the chapter 'Male and Female' of Vera Stanley Alder's *The Finding of the Third Eye* (1938, 1955) we read:

> This force is called by the Easterns the Kundalini, and is likened to a serpent of fire lying coiled at the base of the spine. If man

steadily purifies his mind and nature through living chastely and moderately, he is able to magnetise the Kundalini serpent upwards through the channel of his spine, until finally it reaches the Masculine-Feminine principles of the brain and fires them into coördination. The man is then filled with inspiration and becomes attuned to the inner world of Wisdom. This can only be accomplished with the help of the 'Kundalini Serpent'. Perhaps Christ gave a hint of this when He said: 'Be ye wise as serpents'.

(VI. 52)

We are also told:

If he once arouses the 'serpent', and then subconsciously repents of his endeavours, the serpent rushes downwards and plunges his owner into the worst of orgies and excesses. Unfortunately this sometimes happens to saintly men who have been just a little too ambitious for spiritual gain.   (VI. 53)

Which reads like a comment on what we have called Wilde's 'lust for the transcendent' (p. 290; and compare pp. 286–294). The Kundalini process is described by W. Y. Evans-Wentz in *The Tibetan Book of the Dead* (3rd edn. 1957; Addenda, 216, 221, 224).

During the process the aspirant towards the supersexual may derive help from the sight and company of some objective equivalent – Berdyaev's 'image' – to the bisexual perfection, corresponding to the command in the Gospel of Thomas: 'Love your brother *as your soul*; keep him like the apple of your eye' (Saying 26; my italics). And this is why so many seers take pleasure in a youthful friend as soul-equivalent and why the Beloved is necessary to the pattern of the New Testament: it is precisely the absence of this personal link which leaves the universal benevolence of Shakespeare's Timon a little pallid. 'An impersonal love', writes Berdyaev, 'which is not concentrated on any individual image, does not deserve to be called love' (*Solitude and Society*, III. iii. 119). That Jesus knew the bisexual integration was recognized by the mystic Jacob Boëhme, who wrote of him: 'This champion or lion is no man or woman, but he is both'; while Venus and Mars, God's 'love' and 'anger', are separated, there is anguish and desire, but when they are unified joy 'burns in one will' and the 'Holy Ghost', or 'life of the Deity' is born (*Signatura Rerum*, Everyman Edn., XI. 43). Seeley observes that Jesus' 'enormous pretensions were advanced by one whose special peculiarity, not only among his contemporaries but among the remarkable men that have appeared before and since, was an almost feminine tenderness and humanity' (*Ecce Homo*, XV). So too Nietzsche's Superman is to show a blend of power with grace and strength with gentleness (*Thus Spake Zarathustra*, 35).

The New Testament presents a hero in close relationship to his Mother and of unusual gifts. He is severely tempted by power but instead through love of youth from children to John, who serve as images of his own perfecting, attains a consummate integration of the male and female principles, of power and love. Denied realization on the biological plane, this supersexual love-wisdom expands and becomes the heart of his acts and teaching. But he encountered a severe opposition. Like Byron (*Lord Byron: Christian Virtues*; V. 256) and Wilde, he was accused of behaving like 'a glutton and a drunkard' in most unprophet-like style in association with the dregs of society (*Matthew*, IX. 11, XI.19; *Mark*, II. 16; *Luke*, VII. 34). Harlots were more sympathetic and received more favour from him in return, than the priests (*Matthew*, XXI. 31–2). His own family circle, in the manner of Byron's wife and relatives in 1816, thought him 'out of his mind' (*Mark*, III. 21). Like Socrates he was accused, according to Ernest Renan, of misleading the innocent. 'Children and women', writes Renan, 'adored him', and 'the reproach of alienating from their families these gentle creatures, always easily misled, was one of the most frequent charges of his enemies[1] . . . The new religion was thus in many respects a movement of women and children . . . The idea of disciples is in his mind almost synonymous with that of children' (Renan, *The Life of Jesus*, XI).

Such integral living is hard. What John Cowper Powys once in *The Pleasures of Literature* called the 'divine narcissism' of Jesus craved external contact and expression. In the words of Robinson Jeffers' *Meditation on Saviours* he had 'turned inward to love the people' with a love which culminated in torment:

> Out of incestuous love power and then ruin. A man forcing the
>   imaginations of men,
> Possessing with love and power the people; a man defiling his
>   own household with impious desire.
>
> King Oedipus reeling blinded from the palace doorway, red
>   tears pouring from the torn pits
> Under the forehead; and the young Jew writhing on the domed
>   hill in the earthquake, against the eclipse
>
> Frightfully uplifted for having turned inward to love the people:
>   – that root was so sweet Oh, dreadful agonist? –
> I saw the same pierced feet, that walked in the same crime to its
>   expiation; I heard the same cry.

Wilde has a parable *The Master* in which a young man is found weeping because, in spite of his having performed many Christ-like wonders, he has *not* been crucified (Pearson, XIII. 218; *Works*, 845). Imaginative genius willed the crucifixion as the means to rivet all men's eyes (*John*, XII. 32–3; also III. 14, VIII. 28); it was as a sublime *alternative* to the wickedness Zarathustra craved in order to 'touch' the 'souls' of men (p. 286 above). So a spectacular self-humilia-

---

[1] Renan here refers to an addition to *Luke*, XXIII. 2 in the *Gospel of Marcion*, stating that Marcion's additions have value when they derive from the manuscripts which he was using.

tion strikes through shame to fame, and thence to glory. Suffering there was, at Gethsemane; but what is conceived in rapture may be accomplished with pain. Nietzsche has a word for it:

> If ever I laughed with the laughter of the creative lightning that is followed by the long thunder of the deed, growling but obedient
> . . .   (*Thus Spake Zarathustra*, 60)

Zarathustra too knows the 'thirst' for self-giving (22; and see *Christ and Nietzsche*, V. 194, 211). Like that of Socrates, Jesus' even more extraordinary impact necessarily aroused a violent opposition. Accusations of impiety and subversion of morals were the surface causes; the deep cause, as John's Gospel, taking the raising of Lazarus whom Jesus loved (XI. 36) as its turning-point (XI. 45–54), makes clear, was the fearful power of love-wisdom and its staggering works; the power of one, like Nietzsche's Superman, 'terrible in his goodness' (*Thus Spake Zarathustra*, 43). This was his fault, his sin before society, and there is an ironic aptitude in his betrayal for arrest with a kiss.

His every moment was an unnatural challenge demanding, in Berdyaev's words, 'the transfiguration of nature'. In Thomas' gospel there are hints of dangerous secrets which if divulged would arouse anger (Saying 13).[1] The living waters distributed by Jesus (Sayings 12, 105; *John*, IV. 14, VII. 37, and see 38) were intoxicating (Saying 12). Water may be replaced by 'fire' (Saying 13): 'I have cast a fire upon the world' (Saying 9) corresponds to Luke's 'I have come to throw fire on earth' (XII. 49). Instead of peace, Jesus (as also at *Matthew*, X. 34–6 and *Luke*, XII. 51–3) prophesies

---

[1] 'No doubt a good deal of illumination of Thomas's secret meaning will be provided by some of the other Nag Hammadi documents, but since most of them have not been published, and are not likely to be published in the immediate future, the non-Gnostic reader must make the best sense he can by trying to treat the sayings in Thomas more or less systematically' (Grant and Freedman, VII. 105).

'fire, sword, war' (Saying 16), not for their own sake, but because his message has the terror of a high, disturbing good:

> He who is near me is near the fire, and he who is far from me is far
> from the kingdom.   (Saying 82)

What does it all mean? One can hardly blame the authorities for accusing the first Christians of turning the world upside down (*Acts*, XVII. 6), nor the later Church for its caution.

Jesus speaks from a perfected and fully conscious self-marriage transparent to the origins of creation; and from that cosmic centre challenges society. This is why, as both Renan and Wilde emphasize, his enemies are not the sinners, who are lively enough, but the 'whited sepulchres' (*Matthew*, XXIII. 27) of theological and academic respectability. In *Ecce Homo* (XXI) Seeley writes:

> The glory of the original man is this, that he does not take his
> virtues and his views of things at second hand, but draws wisdom
> fresh from nature and from the inspiration within him. To the
> majority in every age, that is, to the superficial and the feeble, such
> originality is alarming, perplexing, fatiguing. They unite to crush
> the innovator.

Eventually acceptance is compelled. They are at first frightened:

> And then there occurs to them a thought which brings inexpressible
> relief. Out of the example of the original man they can make a new
> routine. They may imitate him in everything except his originality.
> For one routine is as easy to pace as another. What they dread is
> the necessity of originating, the fatigue of being really alive. And
> thus the second half of the original man's destiny is really worse
> than the first, and his failure is written more legibly in the blind
> veneration of succeeding ages than in the blind hostility of his own.

Such is Seeley's comment on

> those who in clinging to the wisdom of the past suppose they love

wisdom but in fact love only the past, and love the past only because they hate the living present; those, in a word, who set Abraham, Isaac, and Jacob in opposition to Christ, and appeal to the God of the dead against the God of the living.

The process we recognize and we all share in the condemnation; and yet caution seems inevitable. Sanity alone forces it.

We can see why the Cross so blazed in Paul's imagination. As Hermann Keyserling in *From Suffering to Fulfilment* (1938; II. 80–1) once said, the conflict of a great man with society is itself a necessary part of his greatness. Wilde's significance would have been far less without his imprisonment, if only because, as Shaw's *Saint Joan* so excellently drives home, the forces of convention have their rights. The Cross signalizes a necessary disparity. St Paul's insistence that we have been 'bought for a *price*' and his sense of 'Christ the crucified' as 'the power of God and the wisdom of God' (*I Corinthians*, VI. 20; I. 23–4) can today be interpreted as meaning that the great God of Evolution willingly *expends* genius, its supreme creative achievement, or son, in order to point a disparity and lift mankind. And there is a corresponding compulsion on us to respond.

We have been discussing Jesus as harbinger of 'the sons of God to be revealed' and 'the first-born of a great brotherhood' (*Romans*, VIII. 19, 29); as Luke puts it, 'sons of the Most High' (VI. 35). To resent a human comparison with others who have in love's name acted from their deepest convictions against society would be to group ourselves too uncompromisingly with the Pharisees. To compare is not to identify; comparisons hurt no one and accomplish much. Besides, we have orthodoxy on our side: in the Athanasian Creed we are told that the Incarnation came about 'not by the changing of Godhead into man but by the taking up of manhood into God'.

v

The Jesus of the New Testament possesses powers which out-distance the kind of genius at work in Socrates and Shakespeare, and we shall now enquire how far these too may be susceptible of a reasoned approach.

Since writing *The Christian Renaissance* my poetic studies have found many more symbols of the immortal or eternal dimension which can be used to illustrate my chapter on Immortality. Primary among these were Pope's sense of man as a cog touching some greater wheel in the unseen dimension (*An Essay on Man*, I. 57–60); Coleridge's Dome in *Kubla Khan* vertical above the time-stream of biological existence; Browning's sense of a great orb surrounding the thread of man's temporal existence in his *Epistle of Karshish*; and Yeats' Dome in *Byzantium* (*The Starlit Dome*; 1941 and 1959; V; for Browning, the 1959 Appendix). These are picturings of what I had already, in rough fashion, described. In Yeats' poem we have both a dome and a vision of 'earth-begotten spirits' arriving in a dimension beyond death. Yeats was interested in the vast and ever-growing accumulation of evidence given by what is known as 'Spiritualism'.

With this evidence I was not myself seriously engaged until 1950, though my first published piece of poetic commentary 'The Poet and Immortality' in *The Adelphi Magazine* of September, 1926 referred to Spiritualism as a modern support to poetic insight. My more direct association came in 1950 through the agencies of Professor T. J. Haarhoff and my brother, W. F. Jackson Knight.

Spiritualism has always been active, from the ancient world onwards.[1] Socrates had his *daimon* and in *The Symposium* claims to have received his central love-doctrine from the professional (208) medium, Diotima; and Aristophanes

---

[1] See 'The After-Life in Greek and Roman Antiquity' by W. F. Jackson Knight; *Folklore*, Vol. 69; December, 1958.

in *The Birds* (1553-5) associates him directly with spiritual-istic practices. Spiritualism suffered eclipse in the medieval period, under the domination of the Christian Church, but re-arose to notice with Emanuel Swedenborg, and since the last quarter of the nineteenth century has been active throughout the West. Of its main teaching we have varia-tions in many oriental religions, particularly close in the rituals of Tibetan Buddhism, as described in W. Y. Evans-Wentz's *The Tibetan Book of the Dead*.

Its importance to our present enquiry is less a matter of religious devotion than of the masses of mediumistic evi-dence constituting an objective attack on the pseudo-intel-lectualism of the received word-order in our era. It includes clairvoyance and clairaudience; psychometry, or the reading of the past from an inanimate object; 'physical phenomena' of the 'direct voice' and spirit-materializations; and spirit-healing, through the agency of spirit doctors. The presence of a medium is necessary and these mediums may work either in normal consciousness or in trance; and there are various degrees of trance, from light to deep. Acceptance of such phenomena has been widespread and the evidence been accepted by leading scientists. Works of poetic genius such as those of W. B. Yeats and John Masefield are saturated in spiritualism and so is twentieth-century drama (*The Golden Labyrinth*, XIV, XV, XVI). There should be no need to adduce authorities. Anyone today can – as T. S. Eliot once said of Dante – easily find more literature on the subject than anyone can easily read;[1] and what is more important, first-hand evidence is attainable to the studious enquirer throughout Europe, Britain, North and South America and South Africa.

[1] Among the best recent propagandists the following may be named: Maurice Barbanell, Anthony Borgia, Geraldine Cummins, Shaw Desmond, Lord Dowding, Harry Edwards, J. Arthur Findlay, Raynor C. Johnson, C. Drayton Thomas.

In my earlier discussions I repudiated the concept 'spirit' with a corresponding emphasis on 'incarnation'; but we must not be dominated by words. Subsequent experience has drawn me to Spiritualism for the very reason that, properly understood, it is the most concretely convincing of any religious philosophy in existence. The philosophy delivered to us by the communicating personalities makes the needed link between the earth-world and the transcendental; instead of a sharp distinction, there is that interpenetration and graded ascent which Diotima, seeing Eros as the spirit-link, regarded as necessary to prevent the universe from falling into two separate halves (*The Symposium*, 202; p. 284 above). That the New Testament is in some confusion regarding the life-beyond-death is clear enough from Michael C. Perry's attempted elucidation in *The Easter Enigma* (1959). The resurrection of Christ is related to an empty tomb; and yet St Paul, when driven to explain himself, makes it clear that we ourselves shall be raised with a 'spiritual' body (p. 138 above). Spiritualism explains that the 'etheric' or 'astral' body is at death detached from the physical and exists on the etheric level; on, so to speak, a new wavelength. The etheric interpenetrates the earthly and has similar attributes; as good a description as any occurs at the conclusion to Plato's *Phaedo*, with its vivid realization of the new life as an expansion of earth-life within a richer and more-dimensional understanding, like a butterfly from a chrysalis. Beyond the etheric there are higher and yet higher planes, but with these we need not here concern ourselves.

Among the attributes of etheric or astral existence is a new immediacy and totality of sense-perception. At present we rely on separate sense-inlets of sight, hearing, smell and touch, but in the new sphere reality is not so split up, nor is there the same distinction between subject and object, or mind and matter. There music *is* colour; flowers may sing; and mind creates directly, without the laborious technical intermediaries needed on the earth-plane to translate thought into material structure. We are in the world of myth and poetry: in poetic imagery sound and sight are often indistinguishable; in the more romantic statements of Shelley and Keats nature is alive and personal, as it was in the Greek myths; and the mind's union with objective and supposedly inanimate nature is the theme of Wordsworth's, as of Powys', central doctrine. In poetry, music and architecture may be interchangeable: space and time, spirit and matter, interfuse (*Laureate of Peace*, III, 'Symbolic Eternities'; *The Starlit Dome*, 1959 edn.; App., 'Spiritualism and Poetry').

The drive of art is always towards this 'etheric' sphere. It may be felt shining impressionistically through the different cosmologies of Dante, Shakespeare and Goethe. Whenever a great artist such as Wagner aims, successfully or not – and complete success on our plane is scarcely achievable – to create a total art appealing simultaneously to different senses and rendering the massive ethereal, he is tuning in to etheric life. Whenever we feel that a great work of poetry has a *solidity* and *endurability* beyond the material, we are recognizing that the mental *is*, in some strange way, the solid, as Bishop Berkeley insisted: as Wilde puts it, 'it is in the brain that the poppy is red' and 'the skylark sings' (*De Profundis*; *Works*, ed. Maine, 874). To anyone of poetic training and sensitivity the beautiful and coherent metaphysic of Spiritualism carries its own credentials. It is the only metaphysic to make coherent sense of the human enigma. And when we realize also that it has been delivered, and is day by day being redelivered, not by earthly minds but by the Spirit Personalities themselves speaking either through trance-mediumship or the direct voice, we have cause to question the sufficiency of our established sources of learning.

Not only does Spiritualism introduce us to a poetic world, but poetry and drama have always been making incursions into the spiritualistic. Greek and Renaissance drama and the plays of Byron, Beddoes, Ibsen, Yeats and Masefield have found the occult a natural language; all poetry is on the fringe of it. Often these perceptions are darkly toned, but the *Faust* tradition shows a gradual turning from fear to light. Henceforth not only must spirit-power and spirit-knowledge be brought to bear on earthly life but we on earth must strive for spirit-converse, for the 'white-sailed fleet' and 'shining ships' plying between our existence and the etheric for which Ibsen's Julian cries (*Emperor and Galilean*, 'The Emperor Julian', V. i). Among the most lucid literary expositions of the truth we most need to grasp are John Masefield's *King Cole* and *Melloney Holtspur* (and see my general appreciation in *John Masefield*, O.M., ed. Geoffrey Handley-Taylor, 1960).

The great principle of 'incarnation' still, however, holds. In literature a too exact attention to the facts of occult science may be less potent than an entwining of them with earth-plane apprehensions and experiences. Aristophanes' *The Birds* is almost a fantasy of spirit-life; but the birds remain birds. Ibsen's sea in *Little Eyolf* is, pretty nearly, the dimension of death; but it is first, and remains, the sea. Shakespeare's majestic Ghost in *Hamlet*, his artificially manipulated *séance* in *Macbeth* and the fantastic white magic of *The Winter's Tale* and *The Tempest*, all have an imaginative and dramatic cogency beyond the more scientifically exact evidences of occult learning which we find in Chapman's plays and in the dramas of the Restoration. So, too, though mediumistic spiritualism has in all ages existed and is probably the basis of all religions, yet each orthodoxy in turn builds it into its own system, with its own dogmas, additions and restrictions. Why is this? The answer is simple: it is not enough to know; religion, drama and poetry exist to make us experience; and if the truth alone is insufficient for this, it must be doctored, as the historical dramatist doctors his sources, even at the seeming cost of factual falsity. A spirit-message describing the etheric life may be informative, but even when delivered from a spirit on a higher plane, it may still not rise beyond the level of a scientific or journalistic report, if only through difficulties of transmission; and the knowledge dissolves. The imagination, Shelley's 'imperial faculty curtained within the invisible nature of man', must still be regarded as our final test, as when the Church Fathers arbitrarily but imaginatively decided which books of the New Testament were to be regarded as inspired, and which not. Until the etheric becomes as solid, colourful and natural to us as earthly existence we need not simply a reported and passively received knowledge of it, however authentic, but rather a knowledge that appeals to and engages earthly apprehensions, and solicits an active collaboration, like that of an audience in a theatre. To use my earlier distinction (pp. 37, 70, 72), the factual must always be regarded as of a lesser order than the actual. So, though the raising of Lazarus does not easily lend itself to a spiritualistic and historical interpretation,[1] its dramatic power and climactic significance and appeal within John's Gospel is such, as F. Noel Davey appears to be arguing in Hoskyns' *The Fourth Gospel* (I. xxi–xlviii), that questions of historicity become irrelevant. It is, as it were, dramatically justified, if not dramatically essential; and the same may be said of Jesus' empty tomb. In both accounts we are faced by a staggering conquest of death that would be greatly weakened if expressed less dramatically; even, one might say, less crudely; and perhaps for this reason, for purpose of effect, they really happened like that. The raising of Lazarus is clearly conceived as an act of superlative propaganda, and the empty tomb, though it bears little relevance to Jesus'

[1] The Spirit Philosopher who speaks in Miss Dorothy Perkins' circle at Exeter tells me that such resuscitations have been known to the occult sciences of the East, but with no more than a strictly temporary effect.

subsequent appearances, which are in the nature of spirit-materializations (*Luke*, XXIV. 31, 36–43, 51; *John*, XX, 14–29; XXI. 4–14) – the taking on of recent earth-conditions such as the wounds is spiritualistically normal – has an impact which nothing could quite replace. When Jesus after his resurrection is able to appear suddenly in a room with closed doors, the effect is bound to be a little 'ghostly', and lacking in human warmth. It is so fearfully difficult to realize that from the etheric viewpoint it is the doors and not the figure that are ghostly.[1]

These reservations made, we can suggest that the spiritualistic approach to the New Testament may be of importance. Jesus was, in modern terminology, 'clair-voyant', as when he surprised the woman at the well with his knowledge of her past (*John*, IV. 6–29). His miracles of healing were of the kind done today by such famous healers as Harry Edwards. Descriptions of spirit-appearances at Jesus' Transfiguration, his own appearances after death and his ascension, and the wind, flames and 'foreign tongues' at the coming of the Holy Spirit at Pentecost (*Acts*, II. 1–4; p. 123 above) are all susceptible of a spiritualistic analysis. St Paul's use of the term 'spiritual body' we have already noticed (p. 328 above). The Pharisees believed in spirit communications (*Acts*, XXIII. 9) and the early Christian Church was spiritualistically active. While refusing, as the spirit communicators of today themselves refuse, to allow psychic gifts such as 'tongues' (i.e. speaking in a foreign language under spirit-control) and other mediumistic activities more than secondary honours in comparison with love, St Paul clearly valued them (*1 Corinthians*, XII; XIII). He counsels a critical approach: 'Do not quench the Spirit;

---

[1] The contention that Jesus never really died is only tenable on the sup-position of Roman sympathy and collusion. It is strange how many *details* from the arrest to the empty tomb could on such a supposition be shown to cohere. But we should still be left with the spirit-manifestations.

do not despise prophesyings; test everything; hold on to what is fine; abstain from every form of wickedness' (*1 Thessalonians*, V. 19; Moffatt's translation is not followed here). In the First Epistle of John we read: 'Do not believe every spirit, beloved, but test the spirits to see if they come from God' (IV. 1). The test is, whether they acknowledge Christ. St Paul's denigratory reference to the 'cult' or 'worship' of 'angels' (*Colossians*, II. 18; p. 135 above) may be relevant, but his aspersions on 'elemental spirits' in Moffatt's translation (*Galations*, IV. 9–10; *Colossians*, II. 8, 20–3) are not. Not only does the Greek appear to contain no thought of spirits, but the words are associated with external ceremonies and ritual tradition; and these stand in strongest contrast to spirit power. Only gradually did the spiritualistic fires cool and the Church itself come to rely on tradition and dogma. The more spiritualistic elements of the Gospels have been explored by the Rev. G. Maurice Elliott in *The Psychic Life of Jesus* (1938, 1946; and see too his *Bible as Psychic History*, 1959).

I offer two examples of the spiritualistic approach. Throughout the ages women appear to be more spiritualistic than men. There are more women-mediums, like Socrates' Diotima, than men-mediums. Now though throughout the Gospel story men dominate, with women, except for the Mother, assuming comparatively humble positions, women and John alone, as exponents of love, attend the Crucifixion; and it is they, whatever their humble position in matters of earth-life, who appear to have been the first to receive evidence of Jesus' resurrection from the angels and Jesus himself (*Matthew*, XXVIII. 5–9; *Mark*, XVI. 4–9; *Luke*, XXIV. 4–10; *John*, XX. 11–18). When Peter and John race for the tomb, we have a pretty allegory: Peter, the prototype of organized authority, is out-paced by John, representing love. The grouping of persons at this point in the narrative has an imaginative cogency.

John, symbolizing Jesus' especial love, in Socratic or Platonic wise, for a young disciple, may be aligned with what I have called the 'Seraphic intuition'. This too can be placed within our spiritualistic field. We have seen how dangerous it may be to rely alone on spirit-knowledge independent of earthly experience. Plato describes how we are to see into and through earthly beauty to higher realms: 'This is the right way . . . to begin with examples of beauty in this world' (*The Symposium*, 211). What the Platonic lover sees may be equated with the etheric or astral body, the 'diamond' body (p. 289). This, we are told, has after death a youthful form; and conversely a youthful form may best focus our vision to supernal realities. In *Mark* the angel at the tomb was at first mistaken for a young man (XVI. 5), and on his first appearance to her St Joan mistook the angel Michael for a youth or boy (V. Sackville-West, *Saint Joan of Arc*, 1936, IV. 57–60). Grant and Freedman quote a reported, strangely worded, saying from the Gospel of Thomas, not included in the new text:

> He who seeks me will find me in children over seven years old; for there, in the fourteenth age, though hidden I shall be manifest.
> (Grant and Freedman, II. 35)

The angels announcing the Resurrection in medieval plays were performed by boys, and the ritual of the Boy Bishop assumed a central importance (*The Golden Labyrinth*, II.)

Our remarks in this section may be neatly summed up by two quotations from the great spiritualist F. W. H. Myers. At the conclusion to *Human Personality and its Survival of Bodily Death* (Abridged Edition, 1927) he writes:

> I venture now on a bold saying; for I predict that, in consequence of the new evidence, all reasonable men, a century hence, will believe the Resurrection of Christ, whereas, in default of the new evidence, no reasonable men, a century hence, would have believed it. The ground of this forecast is plain enough. Our ever-

growing recognition of the continuity and the uniformity of cosmic law has gradually made of the alleged *uniqueness* of any incident its almost inevitable refutation. Ever more clearly must our age of science realise that any relation between a material and a spiritual world cannot be an ethical or emotional relation alone; that it must needs be a great structural fact of the Universe, involving laws at least as persistent, as identical from age to age, as our known laws of Energy or of Motion. And especially as to that central claim, of the soul's life manifested after the body's death, it is plain that this can less and less be supported by remote tradition alone; that it must more and more be tested by modern experience and enquiry. Suppose, for instance, that we collect many such histories, recorded on first-hand evidence in our critical age; and suppose that all these narratives break down on analysis; that they can all be traced to hallucination, misdescription, and other persistent sources of error; – can we then expect reasonable men to believe that this marvellous phenomenon, always vanishing into nothingness when closely scrutinised in a modern English scene, must yet compel adoring credence when alleged to have occurred in an Oriental country, and in a remote and superstitious age? Had the results (in short) of 'psychical research' been purely negative, would not Christian evidence – I do not say Christian *emotion*, but Christian *evidence* – have received an overwhelming blow?

As a matter of fact – or, if you prefer the phrase, in my own personal opinion – our research has led us to results of a quite different type. They have not been negative only, but largely positive. We have shown that amid much deception and self-deception, fraud and illusion, veritable manifestations do reach us from beyond the grave. The central claim of Christianity is thus confirmed, as never before. If our own friends, men like ourselves, can sometimes return to tell us of love and hope, a mightier Spirit may well have used the eternal laws with a more commanding power.

(X. 297)

Myers was a classical scholar and in communications purporting to come from him through the automatic writing of the famous automatist Geraldine Cummins (*Beyond Human Personality*; 1935, 1952), he explicitly relates the world which he calls 'Eidos', on the plane above the etheric, to the culture of ancient Greece:

> Further, this Greek vision dimly reflects existence in that world beyond death which I have called 'Eidos'. It conveys, shadowily, the spirit of that splendid world, where the subtle body, in glowing perfection, expresses form in its greatest and in its highest intensity, where the mere act of living may be accompanied by an exultation that transcends the lofty ecstasy of the greatest earthly artist.
>
> (I. 21)

Even in the realms beyond Eidos the Greek ideal persists:

> All who share this spirit of high endeavour may cross that thresh-hold and, pausing on the edge of the Immensities to gaze back-wards, perceive the limitations of the crude, dense first disguise, and the perfection of the second and finer disguise. Its perfected form embodies beauty such as the great Greek sculptors dreamed of and by which the great poets, musicians, painters and prophets of all time have been inspired.　　　　　　　　　　　　　(X. 100)

Here we may see a new precision in Diotima's insistence in *The Symposium* that Eros constitutes the link between man and divinity. These quotations from F. W. H. Myers, so similar in style, composed before and after his own earthly 'death', contain together a wisdom which our era may find it hard to assimilate. But the task is worth attempting.

Jesus as perfected man is necessarily also essential man, revealing human destiny. He speaks and acts, to use Cole-ridge's fine phrase, 'from the dread watch-tower of man's absolute self' (*To William Wordsworth*). So his divine birth reflects ours, 'trailing clouds of glory'; for we too have, as in Plato's *Phaedrus*, come from, and may return to, 'the Kingdom' (*Gospel of Thomas*, Grant and Freedman, Saying 50). His miracles may be ours; and our raising from death will be like his. The New Testament unveils our true self-hood, life and destiny. Jesus' divinity is accordingly less a divinity of difference than of summation and completion. Whether as imaginative genius or as spiritualistic adept, he outdistances all recorded rivals. Few men can have been both; to have been both with unquestioned supremacy was the achievement of a man-god such as Shakespeare's Prospero; and he had a superlative, physical courage. Of the two apparent lacks in the New Testament, its silence regarding (i) personal love and (ii) politics, the first we have explained by concentrating on Jesus' love for John in association with the bisexual integration, so giving him his right place among such lesser eminences as King David, Socrates, Shakespeare and Michelangelo.[1] The second is harder to discuss. 'Messiah' and 'Christ' are royalistic terms, and Jesus to his first followers was a royal figure. It is for us to adjust our politics to his challenge and crown him as our sovereign. We have only to turn to Seeley's *Ecce Homo*, now so interestingly supported in *The Nazarene Gospel Restored* (p. 301 above), to realize that, in the true, best and most universal sense of his nation's divinely royalistic traditions and the contemporary world-situation, Jesus the Christ did, during his life on earth, not only win the reputation, but also maintained the bearing and performed the actions, of a King.

In this royal challenge of the Hebraic to imperial Rome, we attend the impact of eastern spirituality on western politics and thought. But this impact is also a marriage; among the first Christians Hebrew and Greek confusingly intermingle; and at this moment of grand-scale racial, east-west integration or bisexuality an opacity is being broken, a channel is cleared, and spirit-power rushes through, sometimes, as with the foreign tongues that St Paul found so baffling (*I Corinthians*, XIV. 2–40), in too wild a manner. Control was needed, but under control the principles inevitably

---

[1] The list can be extended. See the imposing names recorded by Hugh Ross Williamson in his discussion of the 'prevailing Uranian temper' of 'the great ages of European culture' (*The Arrow and the Sword*, V. 80).

Appendix

EVER A FIGHTER: ON SEAN O'CASEY'S
THE DRUMS OF FATHER NED[1]

'I WAS ever a fighter' wrote Browning in *Prospice*, and the Sean O'Casey of the Autobiographies might say the same. So might the dramatist: his dramas cover the Irish fight for freedom; Eire's subsequent civil conflict; the first Great War; Fascism and Communism in armed opposition; the second Great War; strike action in Ireland. He has missed no contemporary opportunity, and where actual fighting is not the issue its place is taken by the many richly developed serio-comic theological, social and scientific arguments that enliven his dramatic world. Nor is it strange that he should also have composed our most comprehensive dramatic document on peace. Peace and conflict are interdependent; a true diagnosis of peace will expose the dominant forces battling beneath its apparent calm; and this is just what O'Casey did in *Within the Gates*, patterning out the life of peace-time London in a series of ritual-conflicts.

In most of the plays written after *Within the Gates* we are aware of a certain weakening. The reiterated attacks on the Irish priesthood lack balance; attempts to build youthful sexuality into a saving force pall; and the author's proclaimed communism is never, not even in *The Star Turns Red* where the communist leader Red Jim is little more than a figure of accepted morality, loaded with human fire. O'Casey is a visionary; his various conflicts are always part of some patterned whole suffused with melody and colour; but technical patterning is not enough and it is far from easy to establish any more exact relation of contemporary energies and ideologies to the harmony. Neither communism nor sex-love can bridge the gap. But he fights on, always striving

[1] First published in *Stand*, IV. iii; Summer, 1960.

for solutions in human and dramatic terms; striving to relate man to his vision.

Of the later dramas *Oak Leaves and Lavender* with its eighteenth-century spirits and its extraordinarily skilful realization of a society on the brink of death during the Battle of Britain comes nearer to success. A new dimension is felt, with the impingement of spirit-beings on man's transitory life. Humanity touches the unseen.

And now we have *The Drums of Father Ned*. At first sight it looks unexciting. There is little action and though much of the dialogue has the usual force and humour, some of it is a trifle laboured; but it registers nevertheless an advance of some importance. O'Casey is here doing rather differently what he did in *Within the Gates*. He is deliberately tidying up his sense of forces and values and this tidying up is his governing concern. The result is the clarification for which we have been waiting.

We find the usual repudiation of spoil-sport old fogeys and a restrictive Irish priest, Father Fillifogue, set against young people standing for youth, love and freedom. Gestures are made towards Communism. Protestantism, which had backing in *Red Roses for Me*, is given a strong exponent in the Ulsterman Skerighan. Religion dominates. Hitherto O'Casey has never been able to find the human powers he wants; his women are brave and efficient, but his men only power-bearers in so far as they are poets or visionaries, like Davouren in *The Shadow of a Gunman*, the Dreamer in *Within the Gates* and Ayamon in *Red Roses for Me*. But dreamers are not enough; what are they to dream about, or for, and with what result? None of our established ideologies or theologies have proved adquate to O'Casey's visionary and human concern. So now he invents, pressing, as he did, though differently, in *Oak Leaves and Lavender*, into the unseen. He creates beings in whom he can believe. It is a private theology.

We have two dominating symbolic persons. One is 'Father Ned', who does not appear but is continually referred to as their leader and authority by those who stand for advance. We hear his drumming. If we ask where he is, we are told:

> Here; but he might be anywhere, though some may think he's nowhere; again he may be everywhere; but he's always with th' drums. (II)

Later we have a semi-comic description of his visionary appearance with 'a body thot wasna there' and 'fierce green eyes' in 'a white face that was careerin' aboot though stayin' stull as an evenin' star, starin' up tae me frum doon in th' valley below' (II). Father Ned is conceived, on the analogy of an Irish parish priest, as an ultimate local authority. Dramatically he exists through oblique reference and the sound of his drums as a summoning, potent and beneficient deity. In close association is the mysterious Echo, heard from time to time, recalling Webster's echo in *The Duchess of Malfi*.

Our second personification is Angus the Young, depicted emblematically as a symbol of youth and enlightenment. He has 'a thin poetic face' and 'long black hair'; a harp with golden strings and 'a gaily-plumaged bird' of 'green breast, black satiny head', and 'wings tipped with crimson and gold' (III). Angus is called 'th' Keltic god of youth an' loveliness' (III); in Greek terms we may regard him as a composite of Eros and Apollo. A near analogy in Irish drama may be found in the Greco-Irish dreams of Edward Martyn's *Maeve* and *An Enchanted Sea*.

Throughout Western drama we find a continual play on those two principles which Nietzsche designated by the terms 'Dionysian' and 'Apollonian'; the one aural and mysterious, the other visual and seraphic. Here we have them.

But, it may be asked, of what use are such purely symbolic persons? How do they help us? And can they, anyway, be called 'dramatic'? Well, Father Ned is certainly 'dramatic', since nothing is more powerful on the stage than a properly prepared-for background power defined through sound. Of their more exact meanings there is much to say.

Drama exists by showing the conflict of recognizable yet not wholly satisfying powers, with the expectation that it may generate in us some further sense of a new development beyond what we at present understand, either in this sphere or some other. In so far as the new power is defined at all, it *must* be defined symbolically. If it could be defined by pointing to an existent ideology or person, there would be no need for a drama; we should want a pamphlet, a sermon or a biography.

The symbolic persons here house rich meanings. Father Ned constitutes an obvious admission that the aim of O'Casey's dramatic world cannot be defined in social terms. O'Casey's communism has never been dramatically established. For the most part, despite the attempt in *The Star Turns Red*, it is simultaneously saluted and side-stepped. In our new play, when some timber from Soviet Russia arouses opposition, we are given an interesting symbolic statement in the manner of Ibsen:

> It is the very wood we need to make fine sturdy window-frames an' fine doors for our homes; to put a sturdy an' sensible roof over our heads, and a safe an' pleasant floor undher our feet. What's more, Father Ned has said: Take it, and be thankful.   (III)

The 'red wood', though excellent, is limited to material utility, and everything depends on Father Ned's approval. The ultimate authority is religious.

Nor, despite his advanced counsels, can we call Father Ned unorthodox. The title he goes by is Catholic or Anglo-Catholic and his authority is recognized just as an Irish community today recognizes the authority of its local priest. O'Casey's attacks have always been against particular examples of the priesthood falsifying, as he sees it, their great office, not against Christianity itself, nor against the Church. That Skerighan the Protestant from Ulster should radiate some peculiarly strong lines of force recalling *Red Roses for Me* is interesting. It is still more interesting that his Protestant marching-song with its *imitation* drumming should blend into the *actual* drumming of Father Ned, who must accordingly be regarded as covering the best of both Catholicism and Protestantism, the traditional authority of the one and the critical impetus of the other. Father Ned is a fighter; his drumming is militant; he is 'on the march' (III).

That Father Ned does not appear constitutes an admission that he cannot as yet be defined in visual terms, and for those we must turn to our second symbolic person, Angus the Young.

Angus might at first be supposed to add little to O'Casey's prepossession with youthful life-joy, but he is far more than a symbol of this alone. That young people in love are wonderful and experience wonders we know; but we also know that there are many attendant difficulties; that love passes, that free-love does not solve our psychological problems, and that there are high loves of many kinds, homosexual as well as heterosexual, and other sexual divagations, some of them dangerous. The sexual problem is not solved, and still less does it solve *us*, by showing two young people in love. The emblematical Angus, however, does not incur such criticisms. He is the Platonic Eros, with all its multi-directional potentialities; he is also Apollo, god of art, with his harp; and a bird, for aspiration to higher spheres. He includes O'Casey's poet-dreamers as well as his youthful lovers. What the emblem asserts is what O'Casey has always been meaning: that is, that within the *essence* of youth-beauty there is a pointer of appalling importance. It is the inward and universal essence that is being honoured, independent of particular forms; and since it has this especial independence, this essence must be posited as an external myth-person, in his own right. The young lovers recognize all this:

NORA: The sky of Doonavale is a casket of stars. Look, Michael, that glittering glow there to the west — is it the west? I wonder what stars stay there?

MICHAEL: I don't know. Maybe the Pleiades. What's this I read about them once? — Many a night, I saw the Pleiades — Oh, I've forgotten the poem, and the poet too.

NORA: Tennyson, I think, dear:

> Many a night I saw the Pleiads, rising thro' the mellow shade,
> Glitter like a swarm of fire-flies tangled in a silver braid.

MICHAEL: My God, an' we're tangled, too, in life's great glittering braid! To know the stars only through the song of a poet; then to forget the poet and the song he sang! All the stars of heaven are close to me when you are near. Angus the Young is by our side; we hear his harp-music, and his brilliant birds are perching on our shoulders.

NORA: For a brief while, my Michael. The purple tint of love must fade, and its passion becomes a whisper from a night that's gone. May our love pass quietly into companionship, for that is the one consummation of united life.

MICHAEL: Yes, the Bard and his harp, with his birds, must go one day, leaving us to live in our own light, and make our own music. So we shall; then take a kiss for what it's worth, and let the dream go by. (III)

Angus, or Eros-Apollo, is a deity known transiently, but it is that knowing which is to be built into us, as a permanency of 'companionship' and a new 'music', irrespective of the vision's passing. Though we cannot be always on the level where the splendour exists, it is enough to have known that there is such a level and such a splendour.

And if we know this, we shall know too that Eros may

encompass the whole of life. Angus' Bird has the colours of the various *aspirations* handled in O'Casey's dramas: black for the priesthood; red for Communism; green for Eire; gold, perhaps for Ulster, but for more too, since gold is O'Casey's highest colour. Elsewhere in the play colours are used purposefully, though without any exact consistency, and this purpose, and it is a purpose driven home by speech on speech, is generously inclusive, with the will to a harmony of all the forces contained.

And yet why do we need two symbolic persons? Because, as the central opposition of *Within the Gates* showed, there are still two positive rival powers in our western culture: Christ and Eros, Hebraic and Hellenic. Until we recognize and establish their identity, both are needed.

One last point. We seem to be travelling far from O'Casey the 'fighter'. But even here, when the obstructive priest Father Fillifogue begins to wilt under Father Ned's drumming, the Ulsterman Skerighan shakes him: 'Are ye no' gangin' tae ootface yon Feyther Nud?' (III). Despite his succession of attacks O'Casey's ingrained respect for the priesthood is such that he half wants Father Fillifogue to assert himself. If the Priest of the old order is vanquished, it is not because he is wrong, but because in the last resort the will to fight is not in him.

INDEX

References to footnotes are listed without distinction under the pages on which they occur.